DIG HERE!

Lost Mines &
Buried Treasure of the Southwest

LEGEND

The eighty-one locations spotted on the end sheet maps are numbered in sequence to correspond with the chapter headings in DIG HERE!, showing approximate locations. That is, No. 1 on the map refers to the first chapter heading in the book.

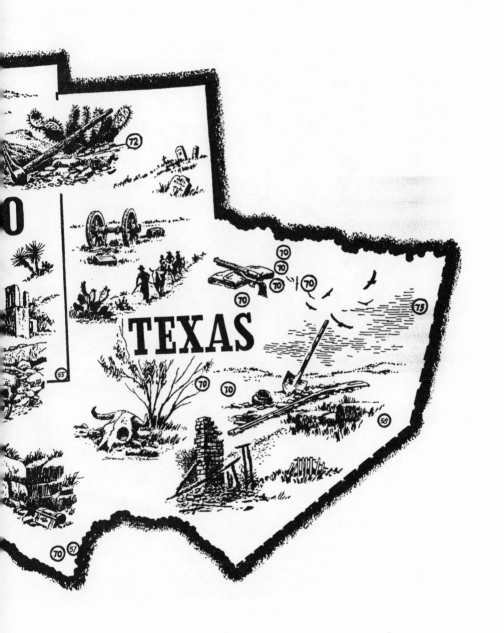

LEGEND

The eighty-one locations spotted on the end sheet maps are numbered in sequence to correspond with the chapter headings in DIG HERE!, showing approximate locations. That is, No. 1 on the map refers to the first chapter heading in the book.

DIG HERE!

Lost Mines &
Buried Treasure of the Southwest

By Thomas Penfield
Introduction by David Hatcher Childress

DIG HERE!
Lost Mines & Buried Treasure of the Southwest

ISBN: 1-931882-35-5

Printed in the United States of America

Published by
Adventures Unlimited Press
One Adventure Place
Kempton, Illinois 60946

www.adventuresunlimitedpress.com

TABLE OF CONTENTS

Introduction
by David Hatcher Childress

Thomas Penfield's classic book on ancient mines and lost treasure is one of the more enjoyable reads on this fascinating subject.

As I began researching the lost treasure of Montezuma I came head-on into a little-known controversy surrounding Mexico and surrounding areas: allegedly they did not know how to work metals until about the time of the Aztecs and their empire. Incredibly, sophisticated metalworking techniques were developed in South America as far back as 1200 BC, but such metalwork was not supposedly apparent in Mexico until thousands of years later.

Mexico in 1519, as the archeologist C. A. Burland said, "was where Sumer and Egypt stood in 3500 BC." In other words, mainstream archeologists say that the cultures of Central America were lagging by thousands of years the progress made by the civilizations in Asia, Europe and Africa. South American cultures such as Tiwanaku and the later Incas did have sophisticated mining and metalworking endeavors over a thousand years before those of Mexico, but still lacked, supposedly, knowledge of the wheel and writing.

Von Hagen and other mainstream archeologists claim that none of the early Mexican cultures worked metal, and that this ability came up from South America by slow stages through indirect trade. Says von Hagen in his 1958 work *The Aztec: Man and Tribe*, "It does not appear at Teotihuacán, which was already a memory when the technique of gold and copper working reached Mexico. It was unknown to the early Mayas, and the Olmec craftsman contented himself with making diadems of jade. It was not practiced in Mexico much before the eleventh century."

This assumption that metalworking was non-existent in Mexico until 400 years before the conquest seems rather curious. It seems likely that metalworking in Mexico, as in the old world and South America, would have been going on for thousands of years. In fact, as we shall see, many of the Toltec and Aztec mines were in parts of Mexico now known as the American states of Arizona, New Mexico, Colorado, Utah, California and Nevada.

In a 1995 article in the *Boston Globe* by journalist David L. Chandler entitled "Ancient Mariners: Strong Evidence of Andean-Mexican Seagoing Trade as Early as 600 AD," the author echoes mainstream thought on the lack of metals in Mexico and says, "Sophisticated and unique metalworking techniques, developed in South America as far as 1200 BC, suddenly appeared in Western Mexico in about 600 AD—without ever being seen anywhere in between. The only reasonable explanation, according to archeologist Dorothy Hosler, is seaborne trade."

Discussing Hosler's work, Chandler says, "Centuries after their development in South America, metal objects appeared suddenly on Mexico's west coast. But the absence of any metal artifacts from that period in all of Central America in between, or in the interior and east coast of Mexico, indicates that these casting methods, alloys and designs could not have been exported via overland trade... Unlike the use of metals elsewhere in the ancient world, where the focus was usually on weapons and agricultural tools, much of the emphasis of both the Mexican and Andean metallurgists was on decorative and ceremonial objects such as bells and jewelry, and small tools such as needles and tweezers."

Chandler goes on to mention how the lost wax process was used in both Colombia and Mexico. Hosler's detailed analysis of the metals from both North and South America showed that, rather than Mexican metals having been transported up from the south, that virtually all the objects found in Mexico were made from native Mexican ores, so what must have come up from the south was metalworking *technology*. In order to have imparted such knowledge, Hosler concluded, the visits must have been much longer and more extensive than would have been needed simply to trade finished goods.

At the end of the article, Chandler quotes Hosler, "One of the aspects that's very interesting for archeologists is that we tend to think these two great civilizations [Mexican and Andean] grew without much influence from one another... This is fairly unambiguous evidence that there was more extensive interaction than was thought."

So, already there are major cracks in the mainstream archeological dogma that metalworking came late to Mexico. While in 1958 it was thought that metals were not found in Mexico until the 11th century, they are now thought to have occurred by the 7th century AD, still a relatively late date in my opinion. One problem with most metal artifacts is that if they are left exposed to the elements they will corrode and deteriorate. In the steamy jungle environment that covers much of the area in question, this would happen very quickly. Gold, on the other hand is indestructible, but is often reused and turned into gold bars or hammered into different objects. Cortez was given gold bars by emissaries of Montezuma when he landed at Veracruz from Cuba in 1519.

But is it true that the Mayans and Olmecs did not know metals? Mormon archeologists, seeking proof that the Book of Mormon gives an accurate account of Mesoamerican history—including early metalworking—have pointed out that language studies help confirm that metallurgy was indeed used in very ancient Mexico. Mayan and Olmec scholars who were reconstructing parts of several Mesoamerican languages were puzzled to find that a word for "metal" existed as early as 1000 BC, while the language of the Olmecs had a word for metal as early as 1500 BC. (John L. Sorenson, *An Ancient American Setting for the Book of Mormon,* 1985, Deseret Book Company, Salt Lake City)

More importantly, metals that predate 600 AD have been found in Mesoamerica. A pottery vessel dating to around 300 AD (mentioned by Sorenson) might have been used for smelting. A metallic mass within this vessel contained copper and iron. The archeologist who made this find has also found a refined piece of iron in an ancient Mesoamerican tomb.

Much older are the tons of iron that the Olmecs apparently mined. In 1996, a non-Mormon archeologist named Dr. Anne Cyphers asserted that "a total of 10 tons of iron has been found at San Lorenzo, in several massive hoards, the largest of which was four tons. Before the discovery of these hoards, only a few pieces of iron were known. They were discovered by using metal detectors." (William J. Hamblin, "Talk on the Olmecs by Cypher," posted 9/26/96 SAMU-L)

So, the origin and practice of metalworking in Mexico, as we see, is controversial. Like many things in archeology, the use of metals in Mexico is being continually pushed further and further back in time, to a point where metallurgy in Mexico is contemporary with metallurgy in South America. What concerns us here, though, is that the Aztecs did indeed have gold, silver, copper and other metals, as well as, presumably, mines.

Von Hagen says that mining was rudimentary. "Gold was panned or collected in nuggets; silver, which seldom occurs pure in nature, was more of a problem and was less used. Gold is a metal of great ductility, for a single grain can be drawn into a wire five hundred feet long. It was worked by the Aztecs with the simplest of techniques. It was melted in a furnace, heated by charcoal, draft being supplied by a man blowing through a tube into the charcoal embers. There are few implements extant but we have been left illustrations of goldsmithery. They worked the gold by means of hammering, embossing, plating, gilding, sheathing."

The marketplaces in Mexico typically contained goose quills filled with gold dust. The Conquistador Bernal Diaz saw gold being freely traded in marketplaces: "placed in thin quills of geese, so that the gold could be seen through it." Goldsmiths had a guild. Those attached to Montezuma's many-roomed household were nontaxpayers; they were supplied with placer gold and busied themselves making pieces for Montezuma and other officials. Bernal Diaz speaks of the "workers in gold and silver ... and of these there were a great number in a town named Atzcapotzalco, a league from Mexico [City]." Since the gold was sold in the market, presumably any craftsman who had enough to barter for goose quills of gold dust could work it up into jewelry for himself or else for trade.

Most of the gold extracted by the conquistadors from Montezuma, some 600,000 pesos weight of it, was melted down into ingots; some of it they thought too beautiful to destroy, like the pieces they received at Veracruz at the beginning of the adventure. According to Diaz's account, these included: "a wheel like a sun, as big as a cartwheel with many sorts of pictures on it, the whole of fine gold; and a wonderful thing to behold... Then another wheel was presented of greater size made of silver of great brilliancy in imitation of the moon... Then were brought twenty golden ducks, beautifully worked and very natural looking, and some [ornaments] like dogs, and many articles of gold worked in the shape of tigers and lions and monkeys... Twelve arrows and a bow with its string... all in beautiful hollow work of fine gold."

All this was sent intact to Charles VI of Spain. He being then in Flanders, Cortez's ship was sent after him. He was at last found In Brussels, and, on July 12, 1520, Cortez's ambassadors presented the Aztec goldwork to him. His comment, whatever it was, has not been recorded. That gold, like all the rest that came from the Americas, went into his crucibles to be made into ingots to pay the soldiery to maintain him on the tenuous throne of the Holy Roman Empire. Fortunately the great artist Albrecht Dürer was there at the time, and he left his impressions of it in his diary. A descendant of a line of Hungarian goldsmiths settled in Nuremberg, Dürer knew what he was seeing. He wrote:

I saw the things which were brought to the King [Charles VI from the New Golden Land [Mexico]; a sun entirely of gold, a whole fathom broad; likewise a moon entirely of silver, just as big; likewise sundry curiosities from their weapons, arms and missiles... of all which is fairer to see than marvels...

These things were all so precious that they were valued at 100,000 gulden. But I have never seen in all my days what so rejoiced my heart as these things. For I saw among them amazing artistic objects and I marveled over the subtle ingenuity of the men in these distant lands. Indeed I cannot say enough about the things which were there before me.

That was the only commentary on these things by anyone whose opinion meant anything. Charles V ordered that henceforth all gold and silver coming from the Indies be smelted down on arrival. Little survived—except the wonderful descriptions of the early conquistadors. So little gold was later to be found or seen, historians of the 18th century began to believe that the treasures of the Aztecs had been greatly exaggerated by the conquistadors. While there might have been some gold bars and some nicely-worked ornaments, it was nothing like what was earlier claimed—the Aztecs simply not having had much gold or other metals for the conquistadors to loot.

This was proved wrong in 1931 when the Mexican archeologist Dr. Alfonso Caso found the undisturbed tomb of a Mexican chieftain at Monte Albán, south of Mexico City, containing superbly beautiful necklaces, earplugs, and rings. Historians realized that the simple, honest Bernal Diaz was making a magnificent understatement and that Montezuma must have had, indeed, a vast store of metallurgical treasures.

So here begins the mystery of Montezuma's lost gold—the conquistadors had managed to acquire a fortune in gold and jewels from the Aztecs, but shortly afterward, no gold or jewels were to be found in the Aztec lands. So where did all the Aztec gold come from—and where did it go?

Aztec Work in Jade, Turquoise, Obsidian and Emeralds

The Aztecs and other Mesoamericans used gold and silver to inlay precious stones. Lapidaries, workers in precious stones, were many, and "skilled workmen Montezuma employed." Foremost of the stones was jade. This was found in southern Mexico (now Guatemala) and valued more than gold itself, which Bernal Diaz found to his satisfaction, for he took four jades during the first Spanish retreat from Tenochtitlán and they "served me well in healing my wounds and gathering me food."

Jade was an article of tribute and the glyph for it is found in the *Aztec Book of Tributes,* a rare codex. It is utterly amazing how the Aztec craftsman achieved the delicate handling of so hard a stone; it required great patience. Everything of jade was saved, even the smallest pieces of the "precious green," to be put in the mouths of the dead to take the place of the stifled heart.

Jade was the most valuable of all stones to the ancient Chinese, Mayans, Olmecs, Mixtecs, Toltecs and Aztecs. A mystery surrounds the wide use of jade in Mesoamerica, as it was apparently abundant, yet only one source of jade in the Americas has ever been recognized: the jade mines near Quirigua in Guatemala. Von Hagen says that there is a difference, mineralogically, between the jade of America and that of the Orient, which should put to rest the idea that the American Indian got his jade from China; it is "American." Yet, we are not sure where it all came from. Some jade may have come from southern Nevada, where jade mines also exist, but historians fail to accept this.

Masks were often made of jade, or, when it was not available, of less valued greenstone. Masks, with their expressionless slit eyes and swollen lips, were a feature among all of these cultures. Some are exquisite, others are repetitious and "vulgar." The skill among the lapidaries was broad; the large objects doubtlessly were done by the "professionals," yet much was done by the ordinary craftsman. Crystal, a very hard stone, is not easily worked, yet the Aztecs shaped art forms out of it from the smallest of pieces to the life-size crystal skull. This latter symbiosis of beauty and death currently sits before black velvet curtains in the British Museum. The postcard of this crystal skull is the most popular postcard bought at the museum, I was told by the administrator of the gift shop when I visited it last year.

It is known that turquoise came by trade from the north. It was much in demand and traveled almost as far as the Yucatan. The Aztec exacted turquoise as a form of tribute according to records from eleven towns on the tribute rolls; it was used with other materials for the making of mosaics on masks, knives, and even walls.

And so the mystery of Montezuma's lost treasure unfolds. Is some of it in the American Southwest?

Preface

The fascination of buried treasure and lost mines caught my attention many years ago when I was engaged in researching a nationally-syndicated newspaper feature. Being a collector of various things, I started an accumulation of lost treasure and mine stories that has now grown into a hundred thousand or so items.

At first when I read these stories of buried treasure and lost mines, I was inclined to believe almost everything that met my eyes. Soon I discovered that different writers handling the same story, more often than not, gave different and contradicting "facts." Which was I to believe? What were the facts? Being trained and engaged in documentary research, it was natural that I tried digging into the background of these stories in an attempt to uncover some solid facts. This book and the others I am working on are the result of some thirty years of painstaking research — slow, often fruitless, but always exciting.

Every legend, it has been said, has a basis of fact, and a few "legendary" treasures have actually been found. One can never tell. In the rare instances when a treasure story is known to be based upon documentary facts, the original facts are clouded beyond recognition by writers who color the story with their own vivid apocryphal creations.

The locations given herein are those generally accepted. In presenting them, no pretense is made that they are waybills to the treasure. If the writer had knowledge of any *precise* treasure or lost mine locations, he obviously would be out digging. Most treasure "locations" are far too generalized to be of any practical value. Except in a few rare instances, the finding of treasure is quite by accident.

In my library of treasure-trove I can turn to only a few books wherein the authors have shared their sources of information with their readers. Most writers on the subject seem to wish to give the impression that they are guarding sources known only to them. Actually, there are very few who have any sources that are not available to anyone. I strongly suspect that most writers on the subject of treasure-trove and lost mines simply do a re-write job on the material from the work of another, label it as "true" or "authentic" and let it go at that. Some attempt to conceal this literary indiscretion is often made by changing place names, common names, dates, directions, or by resorting to other deceptions. This, of course, creates a great deal of confusion and further adds to the great storehouse of misinformation we have pertaining to lost mines and buried treasures. It is hoped that the reading sources given in this work will supply clues to further reading for those who enjoy treasure hunts.

Most of our southwestern lost mine stories have a background in Spanish mining activities; yet historians do not agree among themselves as to the extent of mining operations carried on by the early Spanish colonists. Peplow writes, "There is a considerable more substance to validate the stories of the rich mining operations conducted by the Spaniards of the 16th, 17th and early 18th centuries. During the Pima uprising of 1751 the Indians did actually fill in a great many Spanish mining tunnels and quite effectively obliterated most of the Spanish mines in Pimeria." Pimeria comprised northern Sonora and what is today southern Arizona.

On the other hand, Twitchell says, "All the traditions concerning lost Spanish mines, buried treasures of the Franciscan friars, and kindred tales are only myths." This is quite a positive statement, but one in which the writer does not wholly concur. It is a known fact that the Spanish did carry on extensive mining operations in northern Sonora. It is almost a certain fact that they engaged in gold and silver recovery operations in Southern Arizona, but probably not to the same extent. The "mines" of Arizona were probably surface operations or shallow tunnels.

vi

The padres knew of this search for gold and had a saying which went something like this, "ALL MEN WILL DARE DEATH FOR GOLD — FEW THERE ARE WHO WILL DARE IT FOR GOD!" Is this why the desert floor and the mountain canyons are literally covered with the bones of men who went in search of treasure — treasure that often did not exist?

Illustrations

DIG HERE!

(1) Treasure of La Esmerelda

VALUE: Gold and silver ore of unknown quantity and value; gold and silver bullion; church ornaments and decorations.

LOCATION: In the southern ranges of the Santa Catalina Mountains, southeast of Tucson, Pima County, Arizona.

AUTHENTICATION: Questionable, although substantiated somewhat by a mass of conflicting stories and claims. It all boils down to whether or not the padres conducted any mining activities in Arizona. There is some physical evidence that they may have mined in a limited manner, but no documentary proof of this has yet been presented.

The beautiful mission of San Xavier del Bac still stands on a slight eminence a few miles south of Tucson and a couple of miles to the west of U. S. 89, overlooking the broad and historic Santa Cruz Valley. Founded by Padre Kino in

1

1700, it was one of a chain of missions extending from Sonora to the Colorado River, such as was established in California a century later.

Kino died in 1711 and the mission system was caught in a web of circumstances that spelled its doom. But San Xavier stands today, drenched in the brilliant desert sun, a monument to the man who brought kindness and Christianity to the Southwest Indians.

All the Arizona missions have their stories of buried treasure and lost mines. San Xavier is no exception. In fact, San Xavier was supposed to be exceedingly rich in ornaments made from the ores of its mines, and miners who saw the interior of the church in 1860 estimated the altar ornaments to be worth at least $60,000. There is no treasure here today. What, then, became of it if it ever existed?

On April 28, 1700, Father Kino carefully noted in his diary that the foundation of San Xavier had been completed with the big stones dragged in by the Indians from the nearby hills. From that day on the good padre watched with swelling pride as the structure (not the present one) emerged above the desert.

Construction was well advanced when an old Papago approached Kino one day and asked for his attention. The padre consented. In the mountains to the east, related the Indian, there was a rich outcropping of silver. If the padre was interested, the Indian would lead him there. And so it was done. Several days later the priest and the Indian set out across the valley to the distant hills.

The outcropping of silver was fabulously rich, and Father Kino lost no time in opening the mine which was to become known as *La Esmerelda* (The Emerald), after the greenish color of the ore. Later on gold was found in the area and other mines were developed.

Through the blistering sun the Indian workers carried the ore in sacks on their backs to the *arrastres* constructed at the mission. Here they smelted the ore into bars and stamped them with the mine code number and the mission symbol. From these bars were later made the rich ornaments which American miners claim to have seen.

Father Kino died in 1711 and the mission passed through

2

many years of hardships during Indian revolts and the constant raids of the Apache. In 1723, when the Papago and Pima jointly revolted and attacked San Xavier, faithful neophytes carried the stored bullion and all the church ornaments to the Esmerelda and buried them deep underground.

Before the revolt of 1723 was over, the missions of San Xavier, Tumacacori and Guevavi were all partially destroyed and completely abandoned by the padres. Eight years later the priests returned and remained in more or less peaceful possession of their missions, now rebuilt, until the second uprising of the Pimas in 1751, when all the buildings were again burned and damaged.

Three years later the priests once more returned to the troubled land and this time the great treasure was brought down from its hiding place in the Santa Catalina Mountains and stored at San Xavier. For a number of years only the occasional raids of the Apache broke the peace and contentment of Santa Cruz Valley, and the missions prospered in their agricultural, cattle raising and mining ventures.

Then, in 1767, came the order from the King expelling all the members of the Society of Jesus from the New World. The vast treasure, now increased many times through the accumulated product of the mines, was once again packed on carts and hauled across the valley to the Esmerelda, where it was safely stored and the entrance to the mine concealed.

A year after the departure of the Jesuits, the Franciscan padres arrived to take up the work of their expelled brothers, and once again the treasures of La Esmerelda were returned to San Xavier.

In 1783 the foundation for the present structure was laid, and the building, still noted for its striking and symmetrical beauty, was started. In 1822 Mexico threw off the chains of Spanish domination and five years later drove from its soil all the priests who were not natives of Mexico. This act of secularization meant that all the padres in what is now Arizona had to depart. Before leaving, not being able to take their fabulous riches with them, they once more hauled the

3

treasure back to the depths of La Esmerelda, where it was deposited, and there, supposedly, it still remains.

Now, after all this transporting of the treasure back and forth, it would seem that a well-worn trail would lead right to the Esmerelda. No, say the supporters of the story, the desert obliterates its surface history rapidly. The Treasure of La Esmerelda is still there.

(2) Treasure of Tumacacori

VALUE: Unknown.

LOCATION: Tumacacori National Monument, 48 miles south of Tucson and 18 miles north of Nogales on U.S. 89, Santa Cruz County.

AUTHENTICATION: The whole Tumacacori treasure story is submerged in a hopeless tangle of contradictions, semi-facts, reckless statements and legend. There are visible traces of many treasure searches at the old mission, but this proves only that vandals have always been with us. There will be no more digging there, however, for the National Park Service looks with disfavor upon treasure hunters.

It would require an entire book to relate the treasure tales that have been told about Tumacacori Mission and the surrounding hills where the mission padres are said to have carried on extensive mining operations with the help of their Indian neophytes. Many people have believed, and still believe, that the mission priests spent a large part of their time in mining great quantities of gold and silver from the mountain ranges to the east and west. Some of these stories hold that a vast quantity of gold was gathered at Tumacacori, and that the padres, forced to leave suddenly, buried it and never had the opportunity to recover it. This could hardly

4

be more removed from the truth. Perhaps the padres at Tumacacori had a little gold, a little silver — it is quite likely that they did — but a vast quantity! No.

The hiding place of the treasure frequently takes the form of a secret tunnel which supposedly ran from the mission to the bank of the Santa Cruz River, about a half-mile to the east. (The original mission was located on the west bank of the Santa Cruz; the present mission is on the east bank.) The story has it that the tunnel was used as a means of escape from raiding Apaches, and that part of its interior walls are lined with sacks of gold! No trace of any tunnel has ever been found and the Park Service made an extensive search.

Another story has it that a young American adventurer fell in love with a beautiful Spanish *senorita*, Dolores del Saenz, at Tumacacori and there wooed her. When he was stabbed to death by a jealous Spaniard, the good padres buried the leather pouch full of gold nuggets which he carried with him. The heirs they expected never came and the gold remains where it was concealed. There is absolutely no basis of fact in this romantic tale.

Then, there is the story of the golden chalice. It seems that about 1920 an excited Mexican approached the Monument officials and told them of a golden chalice that had been buried under the sanctuary wall when Apaches raided the mission in 1821. The story goes on in detail, ending with the statement that skeptical Monument officials finally dug in the indicated spot. Sure enough, they removed a box from under the center of the wall, and in it was the golden chalice! In proof of this story, it is usually pointed out that the chalice can be seen today at San Xavier del Bac, where it was dispatched by Church authorities for safekeeping.

Now, there is no golden chalice at San Xavier del Bac, for the simple reason that none was ever found at Tumacacori. Under the date of November 19, 1953, Ray B. Ringenbach, then Superintendent of Tumacacori National Monument, wrote the following denial:

Your inquiry regarding a golden chalice supposedly removed from Tumacacori's church ruins by Park Rangers

5

and now, supposedly, at San Xavier Mission, is one that we receive on occasions. Our records indicate no such occurrence took place, and we consider it legend with no basis in fact. The origin of the story is unknown to us.

The possibility of treasure being buried at Tumacacori, or of lost mines once worked by the mission Indians still to be found, depends in most part upon whether or not the Jesuit fathers, who founded the mission in the very heart of the Apache country, actively worked mines in the area. Upon this subject there is a great deal of controversy. In the mining exhibit at Tumacacori Mission typed material prepared by Sally Brewer reads:

We have no real evidence of mining in this region during the Mission Period; the story on this frontier, in the 18th century and first two decades of the 19th century, is rather that of the occasional prospector and explorer, who knew that the only sure way to capture attention and support for his particular project was to report every possibility of mineral wealth to the King of Spain.

Yet, Patrick Hamilton, in his *The Resources of Arizona* (Bancroft & Co., San Francisco, 1884), states:

The Jesuit fathers were the pioneer miners of Arizona, and the first Europeans to attempt the extraction and reduction of its first silver' ores. . . . That it was prosecuted on an extreme scale, there is reason to believe from the old shafts and tunnels which are found in the mountains surrounding these old missions, and from the piles of slag which are yet seen in the vicinity of the ruins.

Here is another opinion from a great historian, Hubert Howe Bancroft:

The current traditions of Spanish mining are greatly exaggerated. The Jesuits worked no mines; and in their period, down to 1767, nothing was practically accomplished beyond irregular prospecting in connection with military expeditions and the occasional working of a few veins or placers

6

for brief periods, near the presidios. It is doubtful that any traces of such workings have been visible in modern times. Later, however, in about 1790-1815, while the Apaches were comparatively at peace and all industries flourished accordingly, mines were worked on a small scale in several parts of what is now Pima County, and the old shafts and tunnels of this period have sometimes been found, though the extent of such operations have been greatly exaggerated.

Frank C. Lockwood, the eminent Arizona historian, has this to say of Jesuit mining:

Fabulous stories of lost mines have always hung mirage-like upon the horizon of Arizona history. These traditions are such stuff as dreams are made of. They are based on fiction, not on fact. Nor is there any evidence that the Pueblo Indians ever engaged in any mining. The oft-repeated stories that the Jesuit fathers engaged in mining is largely unsubstantiated. They may have done a little prospecting, and may have mined a little ore in the vicinity of Tubac (only a few miles from Tumacacori); but there is no historic ground for the belief that they drew great riches from the mountains of Arizona.

In direct contradiction to this, Richard Hinton, in his authoritative *Handbook of Arizona*, makes this statement:

The Jesuit fathers who built the Tumacacori Mission . . . amassed great wealth. When the Apaches descended upon them, not one padre escaped to tell the story of its hiding place. The love of God and Church was shared with that of silver and gold.
The wealth of this region can be seen in a Spanish report of 1803 which said that there were 150 silver mines in operation within a 15-mile circuit of Tubac.

Nor does Hinton rest with this. He goes on to say:

Traces are not wanting of the Papagoes working mines in the vicinity of present Pima County, even *before* the arrival of the Spanish. (At the time this was written, Pima County embraced all the area and adjacent mountain ranges then

7

occupied by the Spanish in Arizona.) There is evidence, too, that mining was carried on by the Jesuits and others in the 17th century. . . . Most of the Pima County mines were closed about 1780 by continuous attacks from the Apaches.

During the 1934-1935 period, the National Park Service made scientific excavations at Tumacacori Mission to better interpret the area to visitors. They found indications that slag materials were scattered over the grounds, and the ruins of several small *adobe* structures were found that might have served as smelters of some type. It was the impression of the scientist in charge of the excavation that the smelting operations, if any, were of post-mission period. No gold bullion, or any other type of bullion, was found.

There can be little doubt but that the mission padres were aware to some extent of the rich ores in Arizona, even if they did not actively engage in mining. Antonio de Espejo, a wealthy Mexican with a high spirit of adventure, had found silver in 1582 on Bill Williams Fork west of Prescott. The silver ore was so close to the surface that it could be dug with the hands. This is the earliest record of prospecting in what is now Arizona. No mining apparently resulted from this discovery, but word of it certainly must have reached the padres.

And so the argument goes, back and forth, pro and con. Whether or not there is treasure buried at Tumacacori is for you to decide. Of equal controversial nature is the theory that treasure has already been found at Tumacacori. The following story appeared in an 1891 issue of the Phoenix *Republican* (later absorbed by the Arizona *Republican,* now the Arizona *Republic,* leading newspaper in the state).

In the later years of the 1880's, around 1887, it is thought, a stranger in robes came to Tucson in search of help. He had a map which he claimed to have located in Spain while studying there. This map purported to show where gold and silver bullion was buried at Tumacacori. Furthermore, it showed where the mine was located that this ore was taken from.

The priest interested a number of influential persons and they went in search of the treasure. At the mission they followed instructions and dug under the altar. Under the floor they uncovered a number of metallic boxes which contained the treasure, just as the map had described. After the treasure had been taken to Tucson, the party made an attempt to locate the mine, but either they failed to follow directions, or the chart was faulty, for it was never found. The priest returned to Spain with the treasure and gave the chart to Judge Barnes of Tucson.

Years later a man named Crussinbury, who was one of the original searchers, stated that he felt certain that the party had reached the exact spot from which the gold and silver ore had been taken, but that they had not at the time recognized it as the right spot. They had followed a blind trail down a gulch and had come upon an abandoned mine shaft which appeared to have been worked for a long time. The men supposed, however, that it had been worked out and did not bother to investigate further. Later they realized their mistake, but exasperatingly failed to relate why they did not return to the mine!

Where was the mine located? About 80 miles southwest of Tucson, which would place it in Mexico. The mine was supposed to be that from which the Montezumas got the greater portion of their gold, and which was later worked by the Jesuits. Hinton says that the Ostrich Mine, 80 miles southwest of Tucson, is claimed by some to be the old Tumacacori Mine "where the Jesuit operators were totally extinguished by the Apaches." This claim, of course, has been made for other mines. One historian states that skeletons were found in the old mine, as well as sacks of silver ore worth $7000 per ton.

It may only be a coincidence, but when the National Park Service took over abandoned Tumacacori in 1908, officials found many evidences of extensive treasure hunting, including a large hole dug under the altar.

Other treasure stories pertaining to Tumacacori hold that ore-bearing caravans used to stop at the mission on their way to Sonora, and that some of the wealth they carried was buried here. Other stories follow the line that ore, not valuable church treasures, was hidden here by the padres when they departed. Any such valuables concealed at Tumacacori

9

must have been on a purely temporary basis, for it is a well established fact that priests continued to transgress the area even after the mission was abandoned.

There is yet another story that the missionary fathers cleverly concealed gold dust by mixing it with the soil from which the *adobe* bricks in the church were made. This is so ridiculous that it is mentioned here only to show what an incredulous thing the human imagination is.

Here is still another claim, and a very positive one, that treasure was found at Tumacacori — treasure from the mines worked by the padres. In his popular, but highly-colored *Thunder Gods Gold*, Barry Storm states:

> . . . the buried Spanish smelters in the mission yard of Tumacacori were actually found stuffed with gold, silver and copper ingots!
> In the winter of 1934-35 a complete excavation with a view to renewing the buildings was made by the National Park Service under the direction of Paul Beaubein upon the present Tumacacori site, *but no report of buried treasure they found ever reached the public,* though John D. Mitchell who had used a Fisher radionic locator there, wrote June 14, 1935 to Herbert Sutherland of Mesa, Arizona: 'Some weeks ago while making a trip to the southern part of the state, I happened at the Tumacacori Mission and there saw a number of men excavating on the east side of the building where your treasure finding machine indicated to us some months ago that something was buried there. Directly under the spot where we marked a cross and placed a rock on it, they found a large adobe smelter and a large amount of gold, silver and copper bullion. By the side of the smelter was found some large pieces of silver bullion, too large for us to lift. These pieces are now in the storeroom at the mission. Several smaller smelters were found a short distance east of the large one and under places marked by us when going over the ground with your radio machine.'

When I confronted the National Park Service with this statement, I received a categorical denial that any treasure had been uncovered at Tumacacori at the time of the 1934-1935 excavations, or at any other time during the Park Service's occupation of the property. Also denied was the statement that silver bullion was kept in the storeroom of the mission. Either Storm misquoted the facts as related by Mitchell, or Mitchell is guilty of careless and reckless reporting, or the National Park Service is covering up the finding of some buried treasure at Tumacacori!

Barry Storm is a self-professed treasure *expert*. He states so in his book which he also illustrates generously with photos of himself. Mitchell is a prolific writer on lost mines and treasures of the Southwest. While his stories are highly romanticized, he, at least in most instances, labels fiction as such. The personnel of the National Park Service stands high in my opinion. It is your privilege to believe whom you wish in this contradiction.

Is treasure buried at Tumacacori? This is unimportant for no search will be made for it now. Was treasure found at Tumacacori? The answer to this question would throw a lot of light on the mining activities of the mission padres and give new birth to the many lost Southwest mission mines stories, the existence of which hinges upon this controversial point.

(3) Lost Mine of the Tonto Apaches

VALUE: Unknown quantity of white quartz liberally sprinkled with gold.

LOCATION: On the north slope of Mount Ord in the Mazatzal Range, northeast of Phoenix, Maricopa or Gila County.

AUTHENTICATION: There are many stories in Arizona of soldiers finding rich locations which they were never able to return to. No doubt it actually happened on occasion, but these stories are almost impossible to trace to any reliable historical source. This is no different.

The Tonto Apaches were a renegade band under the leadership of Chief Del Shay, or Del Che, meaning "red ant." (He is sometimes regarded as the worst enemy the white man had in that section of Arizona.) They more or less made their permanent home in Tonto Basin (a triangle of wild, striking beauty, 3000 feet below, and formed by, the Mogollon Rim, the Mazatzal Range and the Sierra Anchas) and in the surrounding mountains. They were long believed to be in possession of gold deposits because they frequently came in from the hills with rich pieces of ore to exchange for merchandise in the military posts and frontier settlements. One old Indian is said to have described the gold as coming from a vein of white quartz taken from an eight-foot hole covered by a packrat nest.

The Apaches were fanatically secret about their sources of gold, and the foolhardy prospector who wandered alone into their country usually paid with his life. They knew the white man would dare anything to locate their sources, and they were determined that they would not be found.

Camp Reno, an outpost of Fort McDowell, was established at the foot of Reno Pass to help contain the Tonto Apaches. Soldiers stationed here and at Fort McDowell frequently suffered from gold fever due to the many stories they heard of Apache gold existing almost under their very noses. However, they were generally kept too busy chasing Apaches to do any serious prospecting. Upon being discharged, many turned to prospecting the dangerous Apache country.

Camp Reno was abandoned in 1870 and the troops stationed there were moved to the garrison at Fort McDowell. On their march out of the mountains, they met two recently discharged soldiers still in their army uniforms. They carried rifles and an ample supply of provisions, and they said they were headed for the Mount Ord country to search for the rumored gold source of the Tonto Apaches. They were warned of the danger ahead of them and urged to turn back. Determined, however, they proceeded on their way and were never heard of again.

About five years later two sheepherders came upon five male skeletons scattered over the rocky northern slopes of Mount Ord. Two of the dead men were judged to be white,

12

the remainder were thought to be Indians. On the bodies of the white men were remnants of army uniforms. Empty cartridge shells from army rifles were found nearby. Adding to the evidence that these were the remains of the two soldiers seeking the Tonto Apache gold, was a piece of white quartz found in the pack of one of the dead men. It was liberally sprinkled with gold.

It is believed that the two soldiers found the Apache gold and were on their way out of the mountains when they were attacked by the Indians. This is a natural conclusion, but it proves nothing.

(4) La Purisima Concepcion Mine

VALUE: Unknown, but said to be one of the richest of the several gold and silver mines supposedly discovered and worked by the Arizona mission Indians.

LOCATION: In a narrow pass in the western end of the El Pajarito Mountains, near Cerro Ruido Mountain, about 13 miles southwest of Tumacacori Mission, Santa Cruz County. This distance places the mine very close to the Mexican border. As the Pajarito Range extends into Mexico, it could be located in Mexico.

AUTHENTICATION: Supported by fragments of documentary evidence, but almost hopelessly engulfed in the accumulated legends of years.

Members of the Opata Indians are said to have discovered a rich silver float (fragments of mineral broken away from its original source and found on the surface) and its outcrop (the exposed vein on the surface of the ground) in 1508. This, of course, they kept a tribal secret, but when the Spanish arrived, the newcomers weren't very long in getting the location from the Indians. After all, that was their chief reason for being there.

13

The Spanish lost no time in opening the mine which they named *La Purisima Concepcion*. This mine is supposed to have been in operation as late as 1750, when the Pima Indians revolted the second time and drove all the soldiers and priests from the region and burned and plundered the missions. Four years later the mine was reopened.

So rich was the ore taken from La Purisima Concepcion that 12 *arrastres* were required to crush it and its yield was one-half silver and one-half gold. *Planchas de plata* (planks of silver) lay scattered about in 25 to 50-pound slabs and all the workers had to do was to pick them up.

Gil Proctor, owner of the old Pete Kitchen Ranch south of Tumacacori, in searching for information on the Lost Guadalupe Mine, uncovered and copied this information at Tumacacori Mission.

About three leagues from the mine of Nuestra Senora de Guadalupe, in a southerly direction, there is a pass called "Pass of Janos." From this pass emerges a rivulet which emties into the Santa Cruz River. The mine is to the left of the pass. Below the pass there are two *patios* (open spaces) and 12 *arrastres*.

The mine was a tunnel 300 *varas* (a vara was 33 inches) in length. This tunnel had the name of "LA PURISIMA CONCEPCION" carved out with a chisel. The tunnel runs in a northerly direction, 100 *varas* in length.

The ore is yellow and runs half silver and 1/5th gold. In a northerly direction, 50 *varas* from the mouth of the mine, there are some ash pits. Here virgin silver was found that ranged in weight from one pound to five *arrobas* (an *arroba* was 25 pounds, hence: 125 pounds).

The mine was closed with a copper door which had enormous hinges and a hasp.

The first mission of Tumacacori was located about three miles to the south and a little west of the present mission, and on the opposite side of the Santa Cruz River. The location of the Guadalupe Mine was given as one league south of the original church, and La Purisima Concepcion about three leagues south of Guadalupe. If the Spanish used the 2.5 mile league at the time, this places La Purisima Con-

14

cepcion mine about 13 miles south of the present Tumaca-cori Mission, and about five miles north of the International Boundary and a few miles west of Nogales. But we have no assurance that the 2.5 mile league was in use and, therefore, the distance could vary considerably.

It is said that a Nogales saloonkeeper once grubstaked an old prospector to work the area between the west end of the Pajarito Mountains and Cerro Ruido. After an absence of some weeks, the prospector returned to Nogales with two burros loaded with large chunks of native silver which he said he had found scattered over the surface of the ground in the pass between the Pajaritos and Cerro Ruido. Pass of Janos?

One night the old man celebrated his good fortune too well, and the next morning he was found dead. Neither the saloon-keeper nor others were ever able to locate the spot where the *planchas de plata* had been found. Some believe that he may have deliberately lied about its location in order to keep the ore for himself.

La Purisima Concepcion was eventually closed and abandoned during one of the several Indian uprisings in the region. Apparently the mine is "lost," but there are stories (unconfirmed as far as is known) that prospectors upon several occasions have found large chunks of native silver on the surface of a narrow pass that separates the western end of El Pajarito (little bird) Mountains from Cerro Ruido (mountain of noise). If La Purisima Concepcion ever existed — and, indeed, it may have, it must be guarded by the spirits which Mexicans believe hover over Cerro Ruido and create the strange sounds coming from the mountain.

(5) Pancho's Lost Mine

VALUE: Unknown.

LOCATION: Probably in the vicinity of the northern slopes of the Little Horn Mountains, Yuma County.

AUTHENTICATION: This is a story told by the Indians. Like many of their tales, it seems to have been fabricated for the amusement of white men.

Pancho was a Tonto Apache who lived on the San Carlos Indian Reservation of northeastern Arizona. Among his Mexican friends he numbered a certain Jose Alvarado. When Pancho's small son became ill, the Alvarado family cared for him. When he was well again, Pancho, of course, wanted to reward his good friend Jose for his kindness. But before he got around to it, the Alvarado family moved to Yuma County.

But Pancho's sense of gratitude was strong. He went to Yuma County and located Jose at a little place called Palomas. Pancho knew where there was much gold and he offered to take Jose to it. Jose wanted to take along some friends. Reluctantly, Pancho finally agreed. Trouble started at once when some of the friends refused to eat with the Apache. Jose and the other Mexicans decided to return to Palomas. Pancho said that he would stay in the area and do some hunting, but secretly he had made arrangements to meet Jose later at a certain waterhole.

On the appointed day, Jose appeared at the rendezvous, but his Mexican friends were still with him. In their absence, Pancho had recovered a large piece of gold-bearing ore from his secret mine. He showed this to Jose and told him where the gold could be found. That night he slipped out of the camp and was never seen again.

Jose did not then search for the gold, nor did he tell his Mexican friends that he knew where it was located. It seems that Jose never did find the time to look for the mine, but when he was seriously ill in Yuma, he called his son and told him the long-kept secret. He urged his son to go to the place where they had camped with the Indian. Near there he was to locate a dry wash where a pair of deer antlers would be found. The gold was there. The son diligently followed his father's instructions, but never found the gold or the antlers.

(6) Treasure of Guadalupe Mine

VALUE: Approximately $25,000,000, consisting of 2050 mule loads of virgin silver and 205 loads of gold bullion! (The estimate is not mine!)

LOCATION: About three miles (again, depending upon the length of the *league* at the time) southwest of Tumacacori Mission, Santa Cruz County.

AUTHENTICATION: None. The so-called documentation of the existence of this mine is pretty questionable. As to the value of the treasure, well, whoever dreamed that up should load his pipe again.

According to an old legend of the Papago Indians — and many of the tribe still living can repeat the story with a straight face — the gold and silver treasure accumulated by the padres of Tumacacori Mission through their years of mining activities in the surrounding mountains, was hidden in the tunnel of the old Guadalupe Mine, located, we are told, about one league southwest of Tumacacori. Most researchers agree that a league in Mexican history represented 5000 *pasos* (steps) of a Spanish soldier, each step approximately 32 inches long, or about 2.52 miles. Bolton estimated the Spanish league to be 2.5 miles.

This treasure was said to consist of the incredible sum of 2050 mule loads of virgin silver and 205 loads of gold bullion. McAllister reports it as 905 mule loads of gold and silver bullion "from the mines of Tumacacori and Tascasa (sic) Mountains."

"Guadalupe" mines exist all over the map of the southwestern part of the United States and northwestern Mexico, but this one was said to be one league southwest of Tumacacori. What was a league to the Indians? To the padres? To their Spanish masters? Does "southwest" mean southwest by the compass or by a general point of the finger? The site of the first mission of Tumacacori (San Cayetano de Tumaca-

18

cori) has never definitely been located, so where do we start measuring from?

Considering the crude mining methods of the day, the constant fear of Apache raids, the many Indian uprisings and the general lazy character of the mission Indians, it seems highly improbable that all the mission mines of Arizona, during all the years of Spanish history there, ever produced a fraction of the value placed on this treasure.

However, that's what the old Indians say and will go on saying, and men will continue to believe them and pack off into the hills in search of the fabulous treasure of the Guadalupe mine. Gil Proctor, the ex-Army officer who has converted the old Pete Kitchen Ranch, located south of Tumacacori, into one of the most historic and interesting museums in the Southwest, tells this story about the Guadalupe mine.

Proctor had befriended an old Indian who, out of gratitude, told him that his father had left him a description of the mine, and that he had actually been taken there when a small boy. The old Spanish document called the mine "La Virgen de Guadalupe," and said that it was the Tumacacori mine. It was situated, according to the document, one league from the entrance of the church to the south, and from the water of San Roman toward the left in a northerly direction, 1800 *varas*.

Upon approaching the mine there was a rock marker on which was chiseled the symbol CC B/TD, the meaning of which is uncertain. South of this rock about 20 *varas* was a small monument. Two peaks were blasted over the mine to hide it. The treasure — white silver, gold and coined silver — was left partly inside the mine and partly outside. Part of the silver was stamped MMDCL and the white silver was stamped DCCCV x 40.

And, of course, to further confuse the story, the Guadalupe Mine has been reported found at least a half-dozen times. It seems, however, that the $25,000,000 treasure never makes an appearance.

19

(7) Treasure of Carreta Canyon

VALUE: Eight mule loads of treasure from the mines of Sonora; one *carreta* of gold and silver bullion from the mission mines of Arizona; mission fixtures and ornaments and a copper box which contains a map showing the location of eight mission mines.

LOCATION: In the foothills of the Tascosa Mountains, near the village of Arivaca, Pima County.

AUTHENTICATION: None.

The first wheeled transportation in the Southwest consisted of a long pole to which was attached two log wheels. It was pulled by half-wild oxen. These were the Mexican *carretas* which bumped and creaked along the desert trails of early Arizona, and the remains of one of these crude vehicles is the clue to the lost treasure of Carreta Canyon.

One of the many trails laid out by Padre Kino as he labored diligently to bring Christianity to the Indians, was one leading from the mission of Tumacacori, south of Tucson, to Sonoyta in Sonora, Mexico. Here it connected with the most famous road in the Southwest, *El Camino del Diablo* — Devil's Highway — which stretched on across the desert to the mouth of the Gila where Yuma now stands. Many later day pioneers came to know this road, strewn with sun-dried skeletons and discarded equipment, as "the Road of Death."

The Tumacacori-Sonoyta trail skirted the north end of the Tumacacori mountains, wound through the rugged, mesquite-covered foothills of the Tascosas to the pueblo of Arivaca, now a mining and cattle town of a hundred or so population; zig-zagged through the northern approaches to the Oro Blanco Mountains and then twisted crazily back and forth across what is now the boundary between the United States and Mexico, and eventually arrived at the dry little outpost of Sonoyta.

In 1750, when word was received at Tumacacori that the Pima Indians were rising in arms against the Spanish

20

colonists, preparations were hurriedly made to conceal the entrances to the mission mines and to transport the accumulated treasure to a place of safekeeping. This latter task was delegated as the responsibility of a small band of Indians who could be trusted. The name of the padre in charge of the treasure party is lost in history.

All through the night the Indians carried bars of gold and silver and stacked them on the *carreta* drawn up before the mission patio. Then followed such church fixtures and ornaments that could be carried away. At last the faithful padre hurried out with a copper box containing a map showing the detailed locations of Tumacacori's eight gold and silver mines and the *carreta* bumped off across the valley floor to the distant mountains in the west.

On the second day of the journey the *carreta* was jolting and bouncing through a little canyon in the foothills of the Tascosa Mountains, about to approach *el pueblo Arivaca,* when the clomp of hooves against rock was heard in the distance. The little party pulled up in anxiety and waited, for they did not know whether they were about to meet friends or enemies. Presently the figure of a robed man appeared around the bend ahead, followed by a small band of Indians and eight heavily-loaded pack mules. It was a moment of great relief and the two padres fell into a lengthy discussion of their experiences.

The pack train was from the Mission Altar, in Sonora, and was loaded with the treasure from that mission's mines. It was fleeing north to escape the uprising which had begun there several days earlier. Several Spaniards and padres had already been killed and the treasure train had barely escaped without detection. They were headed for the safety of the missions of Arizona, unaware that the uprising had also engulfed that area.

As the two padres stood in deep contemplation of their plight, a runner appeared with word that a Pima war party was approaching. The padres agreed to bury their combined treasures in the tunnel of an abandoned silver mine nearby. They would then leave the trail and attempt to make their way by mule across the desert to the Gulf of California, where a ship could take them to safety.

21

After completing the transfer of the huge treasure to the mine tunnel, the entrance was sealed with rocks and earth. The *carreta* was abandoned and the Indians were instructed to shift for themselves as best they could. Mounting their mules, the two padres turned their faces to the west and headed into the unknown.

In the early 1880's a Mexican cowboy, rounding up stray cattle in the Tascosa foothills, came upon the remains of an ancient *carreta* in one of the many small canyons which gash into the slopes of the Tascosas. Nearby he picked up a few rocks from what appeared to be an old mine dump. They showed traces of silver and he put them in his pocket. A few days later the Mexican related the incident to his boss and showed him the silver ore. There was little interest and the incident was forgotten.

A few years later a group of U. S. soldiers pursued a band of renegade Apaches across the Tascosa foothills and saw them disappear into the mouth of a small canyon. The troops followed, but lost the trail and had to give up. On threading their way out of the canyon, they noted the remains of an old *carreta* and the canyon became known as Carreta Canyon.

The *carreta* has not been seen for many years, and it is possible that it has been washed away in a flash flood, or covered up with falling rocks from the canyon wall. If you can locate that old *carreta*, you are near the closed entrance to the old mine tunnel which holds a treasure fit for a rajah — that is, if the treasure was ever placed there.

(8) Treasure of San Jose Del Tucson Mission

VALUE: Unknown.

LOCATION: On or near the old mission grounds about one and a half miles southwest of downtown Tucson, Pima County.

AUTHENTICATION: Some writers have tried to establish an aura of mystery around the ruins of the old mission at Tucson, where there seems to be no mystery at all, nor any buried treasure. The Arizona missions were notably poor in worldly things and this was probably the poorest of the lot. In spite of these known facts, a great lot of treasure digging was done at one time.

In 1768 Padre Francisco Tomas Garces was placed in charge of the mission San Xavier del Bac on the outskirts of Tucson. Although Apache raids were a constant threat, he proceeded with his dedicated work of converting the local Indians to Christianity. When Captain Juan Bautista de Anza passed through the region and noted the violence of the Apaches, he ordered the garrison stationed at Tubac, a few miles to the south, removed to Tucson to afford the settlers, the padres and their converts a measure of protection. After the military forces had made its transfer, Padre Garces built a new mission nearby and named it San Jose del Tucson.

It is not known how long this mission was in use because its history has always been overshadowed by that of San Xavier which is still in active use. At any rate, San Jose del Tucson was abandoned and all that remains of it today are some shapeless forms of crumbled adobe that give little idea of its original shape. Much of the original material was used in the making of firebricks for Tucson's modern homes.

A. S. Reynolds, a pioneer who knew the mission and gardens in its early days, was among those who told tales of treasure hunters digging into the old ruins in search of treasure that was never defined. It was an old mission, and it should have buried treasure! All that was ever found, so far as is known, were the skeletons of a man and a dog, and a single old Spanish coin. In the late 1880's J. D. Burges found a bronze box or casket that has been described as a "treasure box" but it may or may not have been.

If there is any treasure at Mission San Jose del Tucson, the mystery is where it came from, for it is almost a fact beyond question that the early Arizona missions were indeed as poor as church mice. But a hundred years from now the legend will still be alive, and the treasure will have grown to a vast sum.

(9) Lost Dutchman Mine

VALUE: You name it. Any figure you will come up with will be topped sooner or later.

LOCATION: Generally agreed to be in the Superstition Mountains near Phoenix, but other widely scattered locations are given. The legend becomes a larger part of the lore of the Superstitions every year. In fact, the name "Lost Dutchman" has become almost synonymous with the Superstitions. The storied mountains are a huge uplift about 40 miles east of Phoenix, and were originally called *Sierra de la Espuma* (Mountain of the Foam) by the Spanish after hearing the Pima flood legend and seeing the white limestone stripe around the crest near the top which marked the foam at the crest of the flood.

AUTHENTICATION: "Authentic" stories of the Lost Dutchman Mine are a dime a dozen. And so are Lost Dutchman "experts." You can even buy "genuine" Lost Dutchman Mine maps! Outside of the indisputable fact that there was a Dutchman (every character in the old West with a slight German accent was called "The Dutchman"), known as Walz, Walzer, Waltz, or by some other variation of the name, and that he did frequently turn up with gold after mysterious trips, presumably into the Superstition Mountains, there is absolutely no documentary evidence that has yet been brought to light to give the slightest basis in fact to the story that he had a secret mine. But it is, nevertheless, a good story, an intriguing story, a story dripping with mystery, romance and murder. Barnes says: "It is one of those legendary

24

affairs for which nothing historical exists." This writer agrees.

Of all the lost mine legends of the West, that of the Lost Dutchman is perhaps the most widely told, the most written about, the most controversial, and the most confusing. Hundreds of theories have been presented by serious students of the legend and by self-styled treasure experts. The tragedy of it is that these legends, told and retold, exaggerated and compounded, have led, and still lead, men to their death in search of an El Dorado that almost certainly does not exist. As late as June, 1959, Stanley Fernandez, who had come all the way from Hawaii to search for the Lost Dutchman Mine, was murdered in the Superstitions by his partner, Benjamin Ferreira, because he wouldn't dig! And almost every year someone reports finding the Lost Dutchman. I have seen at least two dozen newspaper accounts of this!

The Lost Dutchman legend begins with the story of a young Mexican lover fleeing the wrath of his sweetheart's irate father. He left his country forever, as frustrated young lovers do, and fled north into the Superstition Mountains where he found rich gold ore. Armed with the good news that he was wealthy, he dared to go back to his people and face his sweetheart and her angry father. This he did, and he was received with open arms. Ah, what a difference it makes when a man owns a gold mine!

Led by Don Miguel Peralta, father of the young lover, the whole Peralta clan made preparations to travel north and work the mine. When they were ready to depart, everybody else in the community got the urge and they marched away 400 strong, headed for the Superstitions!

The journey north seems to have been uneventful. They found the mine and took out as much of the gold as the entire party could pack back to Mexico. When all of the mules were loaded to the last ounce they could carry, these 400 people started out jubilantly for home, intending to return later for more gold, and more, and more. The supply was simply inexhaustible.

Winding their way down the rugged canyons, they were hardly out of sight of the mine when Apaches struck with

25

such sudden fury that the party was annihilated — all excepting two young boys who managed to hide in the bushes and escape unseen. Then the Indians hid all the gold from the pack train and obliterated all traces of the mine so that it would never be found again.

In what manner of a miracle the two young boys could survive and eventually find their way back to Sonora is not revealed in the legend, but this they did. When they grew up they took in a third party and again returned to the Superstitions, where they apparently found the mine without too much difficulty. They had hardly begun to take out the gold when the Dutchman appeared.

The Dutchman was a white-bearded German prospector named Walz (or Walzer, or Waltz, etc., etc., depending upon which version you are reading) who was known to friendly Indians as "Snowbeard." He was picking his way through the Superstitions one day when very unfriendly Apaches chased him into a section of the mountains he had never visited before, and he stumbled straight into the camp of the three Mexican gold miners. They were more than glad to have his company and before long they were all friends, but they signed their death warrants when they told him of their rich mine. Walz turned on the three and killed them. This was in the 1870's. From that time on until his death in 1891, the fabulous mine was his alone.

Walz had been attracted to Arizona by the news of the discovery of the sensational Vulture Mine by Henry Wickenburg. For a brief time he was employed at the Vulture but was fired for "high grading" — stealing ore from the mine. Somewhere in his travels he met and took up with another German prospector named Jacob Wiser. They became partners. Some say that Wiser was with the Dutchman when the three Mexicans were slain, and that he, too, was later killed by Walz. And some contend that the ore Walz supposedly took from the mine in the Superstitions, actually was that which he had stolen from the Vulture.

When the news of the Dutchman's find became common knowledge around Florence and Phoenix, prospectors tried to trail him into the mountains, but he either outwitted or killed them. For years Walz played this game of hide and

26

seek with his followers, seeming content to bring out only enough ore at a time to finance a prolonged drunken spree.

By 1877 the years were catching up with the old prospector and he decided to retire. He bought or rented a plot of ground and an adobe hut, along the Salt River on the outskirts of Phoenix, and passed away the time by raising a few chickens and some grapes, but mostly by hitting the bottle. Nevertheless, there was spark enough of manhood in him to court Julia Thomas, a Negress who supposedly operated a small run-down ice cream parlor. There are many stories told of this romance; of how he took her gifts of wine, purchased a new fountain for her, and of how she cared for him when he was ill. Gossip said the two were more than good friends.

When the Dutchman died in '1891, Julia Thomas showed up with a map and directions to the mine, which she said were given to her by Walz. Apparently he also shared his secret with a German baker named Reinhart Petrash. These two were about the only friends he is accused of having.

According to Thomas and Petrash, this is what the Dutchman told them about his mine: it was composed of an 18-inch vein of rose quartz heavily impregnated with gold nuggets. A second vein of hematite quartz was one-third pure gold. He had worked both veins for years, he said, and was not even near the end. He estimated that there was at least $100,000,000 to be taken out!

And where was the mine? In a secluded spot in the Superstitions there was a cave which he used as a hideout when eluding pursuers. About a mile from the cave there was a rock with a natural face looking east. To the south was Weaver's Needle (long a popular landmark associated with the mine). Follow the right of two canyons, he directed, but not far. The mine faces west and at certain times of the year the sinking sun shines through a pass between two high ridges and then the gold can actually be seen to glitter.

Julia Thomas and Reinhart Petrash never found the Dutchman's mine although they searched for three months. Were the directions faulty due to the failing memory of a dying man? Was it a diabolical trick designed purposely to mislead his friends? Was the mine covered by the earthquake which rocked most of Arizona in 1877? Was there a mine at all? These are the questions treasure hunters ask themselves.

Literally thousands of prospectors, professional and amateur, have searched for the Lost Dutchman Mine, and their luck has been uniformly bad. Many have never returned from the Superstitions. The tragedy and violence connected with the mine have added to the strong convictions of many that the Superstitions are cursed. We know, of course, that the only curse is the legend.

This briefly is the general story of the Lost Dutchman Mine. There are many, many versions, theories, contradictions, clues. Visitors to the Superstitions tell of being impressed with the awesomeness of the region; with a feeling of impending violence and disaster. Some of those who get carried away say that pygmies guard the mine; some think it possible that a few wild Apaches lurk in its rugged canyons, and still others believe that some lucky prospector has found the mine and shoots to kill all those who approach his bonanza. So you can believe what you wish and not be called crazy in Arizona, unless, of course, you don't believe in the Lost Dutchman.

(10) Wagoner's Lost Ledge

VALUE: Unknown.

LOCATION: Generally believed to be La Barge Canyon, in the Superstition Mountains, Maricopa County.

AUTHENTICATION: No more, no less than any of the other lost mine stories with a Superstition Mountain setting. No historical record of a man named Wagoner, the principal in this story, has been located. There is a record of an Ed Waggoner (sic), an early settler, after whom the town of Wagoner (sic) in Yavapai County was named. We do not know that this was the same man.

A prospector known only as Wagoner frequently rode the Pinal-Mesa stage from Pinal to the western edge of the Superstitions where he would take off afoot in the direction of Apache Gap. On his return trip he always caught the stage in the same lonely spot. Usually the two sacks in which he carried provisions were empty on the homeward trip. When he was broke, which was most of the time, the stage driver obligingly carried him without pay.

One day Wagoner changed his stage loading and unloading place to a spot near Whitlow's Ranch, and the two provision sacks were replaced with two expensive looking leather suitcases. When he returned from the mountains, the driver noticed, the suitcases appeared to be full and heavy. About a week would pass between the time Wagoner left the stage and made his return. The stage driver guessed, therefore, that his strange passenger had found something in the mountains. It was not his place to ask questions, nor was it the custom of the day.

Sometimes a party would try to trail Wagoner, but the lone prospector was apparently too wise to be followed. There were rumors that he was selling quantities of free gold. He paid the stage driver for the free trips that he had been given and thereafter he always seemed to have plenty of money.

One day he showed up as usual at Whitlow's Ranch to catch the stage. The driver noticed that he appeared to be weak and ill. In fact, Wagoner asked the driver to load his bags for him, something that he had never done before. When the driver remarked about their great weight, Wagoner replied that it was his last trip, and that it would be all right if he cared to take a look at their contents. Opening one of the bags, the stage driver found it to be full of extremely rich gold ore.

"You may as well have the mine," Wagoner said. And then he gave the driver instructions for finding the outcropping of rose quartz from which the ore had been taken. It was covered with brush, Wagoner said, and lay within a circle of trees he had planted for a landmark. Wagoner reckoned that he had enough gold to last a lifetime. He was going east to retire.

The stage driver never located the ledge, nor did the man who turned up twenty years or so later with a detailed map purportedly drawn by Wagoner as he lay ill in a Tucson hospital where he later died. This map supposedly described the mine as being in La Barge Canyon, and this is a strange coincidence. La Barge, after whom the canyon and creek were named, was a French prospector who kept a camp near a spring at the base of Weaver's Needle. He was a friend and one-time companion of Jacob Walz, the Dutchman. After Walz's death, La Barge spent all his time and money searching for the Lost Dutchman Mine.

(11) Gonzales' Lost Mine

VALUE: Unknown.

LOCATION: Near Sombrero Peak, in the Superstition Mountains, Maricopa County.

AUTHENTICATION: Anything connected with the Superstition Mountains and the Lost Dutchman Mine are subject to suspicions of legendary origin. Year after year these stories grow in number and in complexity. Yes, the lure of the Superstitions sweep all men before it — treasure hunters and treasure trove writers alike.

In the year 1874 a Mexican who called himself Ramon Peralta Gonzales rode into Maricopa, Arizona, and made his way to the store kept by Charles Clark. He was tired and hungry and broke. He traded his good horse to Clark for food and two Indian ponies. He had just come from California he said, and he wanted to rest. After a stay of a few weeks, he received word of his father's death in Sonora and left for his home.

Several months later Gonzales was back in Maricopa and he looked up his friend Clark. He needed a grubstake, he

30

said, to locate a mine which was indicated on a map he had brought back from Sonora. Clark was reluctant to make a deal with Gonzales until he was shown the map and told the story behind it. This is the story Ramon Peralta Gonzales told.

Before his father had died in Sonora he told of taking much gold out of the Superstition Mountains near Sombrero Peak. He drew a map and left instructions for his son — and this was the map. His father's name, Gonzales continued, was Manuel Peralta, one of three sons — Manuel, Ramon and Pedro — of the original founder of the famed Peralta Mine.

Now, even then the Lost Dutchman Mine was famous throughout Arizona, and Clark was fascinated with the thought that this might be an authentic map to the old Peralta Mine, possibly even the Lost Dutchman. But he had not yet seen the map and he refused to deal with Gonzales until he produced it. Finally the Mexican gave in and brought out the map showing the location of old *arrastres*, breast-works, ruins and other landmarks.

Gonzales made the trip in search of the mine alone. He found it with little trouble. There were rotted sacks of gold and several human skeletons. Much sooner than Clark had anticipated, Gonzales was back in Maricopa, but he only partially reported what he had actually found. With his share of the proceeds from a large can full of gold dust and nuggets which he brought back, he bought a good horse from Clark and left immediately, saying that he was going to California to visit relatives.

When Clark never saw the Mexican again, he figured that he had been taken in, but he could not explain the can of gold. With a copy made from the original map, Clark searched the Superstitions but found nothing.

In 1930, it is said, Gonzales again turned up in the Superstitions and came upon a prospector named Bradford who was searching for the Lost Dutchman Mine. Believing that the Mexican was also looking for clues to the Lost Dutchman, Bradford deliberately misdirected him and the Mexican was never seen nor heard from again.

Now many Mexicans have strange ideas about lost mines

and buried treasures. They believe that they belong to their original owners and anyone who disturbs them will meet with disaster. Yet, Gonzales returned to Maricopa with a can of gold. Why did he wait 56 years before coming back for more? Could it have been, as some suspect, that he stole the gold from an unfortunate prospector? If so, why did he return to split it with Clark?

(12) Lost Mine of Squaw Hollow

VALUE: A gold ore ledge of rich but unknown value.

LOCATION: In Squaw Hollow, northeast of Phoenix, Maricopa County.

AUTHENTICATION: This story appears to be well authenticated from records left by men of repute who were there when the find was made. It is located in one of the most thickly overgrown brush areas in central Arizona where an effective search would almost have to be made on hands and knees. Almost all treasure finds are made by accident, and that certainly will be the case if the Lost Mine of Squaw Hollow is ever found.

A bridge on U. S. Highway 60-70, on the western outskirts of Miami, Arizona, approximately marks the site of Bloody Tanks, scene of an 1864 engagement between a band of white men and their Maricopa Indian allies under the command of King S. Woolsey, a veteran Indian fighter, and a party of Apaches. The fighting began at a peace parley in which both sides appear to have fired in violation of their agreement. Nineteen Apaches died; no Maricopas or whites. The blood of the Apache dead colored the mountain stream a deep crimson and the place and battle became known as Bloody Tanks.

Familiar with the ways of the red man, Woolsey was

32

more than a match for their cunning, courage and strength, and he played a conspicuous part in the struggle between the Arizona pioneers and the dreaded Apaches. The section of Arizona Highway 69 north of Phoenix was once known as the Woolsey Trail. About 30 miles east of New River, on Arizona 69, in what was known then, as now, as the Camp Creek country, Woolsey and a party of Indian hunters made their camp at a place known locally as Squaw Hollow after an engagement with another band of Apaches near the vicinity. On the following night, after things had quieted down, someone reported that this was good country in which to prospect. Accordingly on the next day members of the party fanned out through the mesquite-covered hills. According to Judge John T. Alsap ("Father of Maricopa County"), a well-known and reputable Arizona pioneer, it was not long before some of the men brought in a hat-full of the richest gold ore he had ever seen. It had been broken from a rich ledge, and the men finding it reported that there was a great quantity of the ore exposed. Judge Alsap did not know the exact location of the ore as he was not with the party that brought it in, and did not later visit the spot.

While the excitement over the discovery was at a fever pitch in the camp, and before anyone could return to the ledge, the Apaches returned with reinforcements and resumed the fight. Outnumbered now, Woolsey and his party had to break camp hurriedly and leave the area. Later the members of the party became separated and it was many years before the Apaches were driven from the area and a search for the gold ledge could be undertaken. Meantime, all of the men sharing in the secret remained quiet about the find, each probably planning to return at a later date and mine the ledge legally. Judge Alsap, however, was one of the few who ever made a real search for the ore. Headquartering at Camp Creek, he spent many weeks prospecting the region. He found no indication that any of his companions had been there, nor did he find the rich ledge of gold. Camp Creek can be located on a quad map. It rises at Maverick Butte, near Ashdale Ranger Station, and flows southeast into the Verde River at Needle Rock, a popular recreational area for Phoenix citizens.

Years later a sheepherder passing through the region reported to have come across a man who had built a cabin in the Camp Creek region and was working a rich gold mine nearby. The sheepherder said that the miner was bringing gold ore out on burros, grinding it in a large iron mortar and washing the gold out in the creek. The miner said that he was shipping the gold east. When the sheepherder returned to the area years later, he found the cabin in ruins and beside it was a small pile of tailings. His search for the mine was futile.

The area around Squaw Hollow is highly mineralized. The word of Judge Alsap can be taken as the gospel truth. He was there and he saw the gold. The story told by the sheepherder is open to question — it can neither be proved nor disproved. Here, then, is a lost ledge that, if it has not been found and worked out, has definite promise. It should not be too difficult to locate the old Woolsey camp in Squaw Hollow. From here a detailed search would have to be made, "on hands and knees" if the nature of the country has not changed.

(13) Treasure of the Cursed Cerro Colorado

VALUE: $70,000 in silver bullion.

LOCATION: Somewhere on the slopes between Cerro Colorado and Cerro Chiquito, northeast of Arivaca, Pima County. This is a region rather easy to reach on a dirt road off U. S. Highway 89 at Arivaca Junction.

AUTHENTICATION: Although this story can be substantially verified in general, the actual burying of the treasure cannot be proved. It could have happened; it may have happened, but it lacks proof.

Samuel P. Heintzelman, a name well known in Arizona mining history, became interested in mining while serving as a soldier in Fort Yuma, where he arrived in 1850 as a captain with the 2nd U. S. Infantry from San Diego. Like most men of the time, he found himself filled with gold fever, a common ailment that swept the country after the Gadsen Purchase. One day Heintzelman happened to notice a piece of gray ore in Warner's Store in Phoenix. Trained as a mineralogist in Germany, he immediately recognized the ore as being rich in silver. From Solomon Warner he learned that a Mexican had brought the ore in for trading.

Heintzelman persisted in his search for the Mexican and finally located him in Tucson. Slyly he approached the subject of the gray ore, but when he asked where it came from, the Mexican froze up. It was only after Heintzelman offered a $500 bribe that the Mexican found his tongue and agreed to take Heintzelman to the place where he had found the ore. They left Tucson together and headed south, but in the Serritas the Mexican refused to go a step further until he was paid his $500. Heintzelman just as stubbornly refused to hand over the money until he saw the ore. In a huff the Mexican returned to Tucson.

Finally Heintzelman agreed to deposit the money with Solomon Warner, to be turned over to the Mexican when definite proof of the existence of the ore was produced. The Mexican sulked, but eventually agreed to the new terms and the two men again left Tucson and traveled south. They passed Cerro Colorado (Red Mountain) at night and made camp at the foot of another small red mountain, Cerro Chiquito. At sunrise the next morning they climbed a rocky slope to a crude, shrub-covered shaft. The Mexican pulled away the cover and pried off a piece of the gray ore with his knife. One look at the ore proved to Heintzelman that this was the same ore that he had seen at Warner's store. It was almost pure silver. He filled his saddle bags and returned jubilantly to Tucson, followed closely by the Mexican who demanded his $500. Heintzelman produced a fifty-cent piece and said: "Here, this is enough for a Mexican!"

After cheating the Mexican in this brazen manner (apparently Solomon Warner was in on the fraud), Heintzelman lost no time in developing his mine, sinking a 50-foot shaft into the rich ore. But eventually the bilked Mexican arrived with countrymen who claimed to be the legal owners of the property and they drove Heintzelman away. The property was then sold to the Sonora Exploring & Mining Co., of which Charles D. Poston, a prominent Arizona pioneer, was one of the organizers. Heintzelman later turned up as president of this firm, so he got his hand in the mine after all.

John Poston, brother of Charles, was placed in charge at the mine. It immediately became a rich producer, yielding $100,000 in its first year of operation. In 1857, twelve wagons, each pulled by twelve mules, hauled the ore from the mine to Kansas City at a cost of 12½ cents per pound. But soon disaster struck the mine, now known as the Cerro Colorado, and it never lived down its bad reputation. The Mexicans said it was cursed.

Deep in the dimly-lit depths of the Cerro Colorado, fifteen Mexican and Indian workers were entombed under tons of fallen rock. Their bones are still there. With the coming of the Civil War, troops were removed from the area and the Apaches started to make good their threats to wipe out the white men. And there were other troubles.

With the mine guards reduced in number, Mexican workers started stealing ore right and left. Matters were brought to a head when John Poston caught his mine foreman, Juanito, heading south with a heavy load of stolen silver. Determined to make an example of the Sonoran, Poston grabbed his rifle and killed the foreman in cold blood. This act brought an abrupt halt to all work at the mine, and the enraged miners carried away everything that could be put on a mule.

Learning of the helpless condition of the mine from fleeing miners, a band of outlaws swooped down on the Cerro Colorado, killed John Poston and two other white men, and all but tore the place apart in a search for the silver supposedly stored there. But the silver, according to most accounts, had already been stolen by the fleeing miners, and the story persists to this day that $70,000 in silver bullion from the Cerro Colorado Mine was buried on the slope between the Cerro Colorado and the red hill called Cerro Chi-

36

quito to the north. Whether this is true or not, we do not know. Hinton, in his *The Handbook of Arizona* says: "It was a well known fact that the town of Saric (Sonora) has been built upon the proceeds of ore stolen from the Heintzelman (Cerro Colorado) Mine."

(14) Lost Mine of the Orphans

VALUE: Gold nuggets of unknown value.

LOCATION: Near Tule Tank in the Cabeza Prieta Mountains, western Pima County. This is no area to play around in. If you are not familiar with conditions in this section of Arizona, stay out unless you are accompanied by an experienced, reliable party. All warnings you have ever read or heard about the southwestern deserts apply here.

AUTHENTICATION: There is no reason to doubt this story. It was related in a letter by Thomas Childs, Jr., son of the man whose mining claims were developed into the enormous Ajo copper mine holdings, in 1946, and is now in possession of the Pioneers' Historical Society in Tucson. Childs, a most reliable authority, knew the principals in the story and there is every reason to accept his words as the truth.

Many years ago an epidemic of cholera struck Caborca, Sonora, Mexico, leaving homeless a young Mexican girl and a Papago Indian boy. Neither having any relatives to care for them, the boy suggested to the girl that she go with him to Gila City, Arizona (now only a site on the Gila River about 24 miles west of Yuma) where he had some distant relatives they could live with. She agreed to accompany him and they traveled across the waterless stretches of the Camino del Diablo, that awesome stretch of desert country that has

38

claimed so many lives. Along the way the girl suffered so many hardships that she came to the point where she could no longer go on. The young Papago found a shady spot for her and instructed her to remain there until he returned with water.

In the nearby Cabeza Prieta Mountains the boy found a tank (a natural depression in rock where rain water is held until it evaporates) and he managed somehow to take some of it to the suffering girl. When she was able to travel again, they made their way to the tank which is now known as Tule Tank, not to be confused with Tule Well which is to the east in the same general area. Here the couple rested until the girl had regained her strength. When they were ready to leave the Papago boy led the girl up an arroyo and on to the top of a granite mesa looking down into a draw on the opposite side. He told her to look down. In the clear water of a small stream she could see a layer of gold nuggets, much as if the stream bed had been paved with them.

Picking their way down to the water's edge, the girl gathered some of the nuggets and tied them in her *rebozo*. Then they proceeded on their journey, eventually arriving in Gila City where both were taken in by the boy's people. One day the girl happened to show the nuggets to a man named George Whistler. Of course, he wanted to know where they had come from, but the girl declined to tell. They became friendly and later on they were married, but still she kept the secret to herself.

Eventually the Whistler family had two or three boys, and they moved to Burks Station where Whistler was killed by a Mexican named Nunes or Nunez. A party of Mexicans sent out to capture Nunes, who had fled after the slaying, overtook him in the Cabeza Prieta Mountains. He was taken to Agua Caliente and hanged.

After the death of her husband, Whistler's wife revealed that she had never told him where the stream bed of gold was because she thought he had married her only to secure the secret. Now, however, she told Thomas Childs where the gold could be found, asking only that he go and find it and share a portion of it with her sons. Childs made a search in due time, but found nothing. He, and others, presumed

39

that the stream had been covered with debris shaken down by an earthquake, or that a sudden cloudburst had changed the course of the stream.

(15) Treasure of Rancho De Los Yumas

VALUE: Unknown.

LOCATION: On or near the old Rancho de los Yumas, on the east bank of the Colorado River about 40 miles north of Yuma, Yuma County. The ruins of the old ranch buildings can still be located.

AUTHENTICATION: Although there is no actual documentation of this story, there is strong reason to believe that this treasure really exists, unless, of course, it has been found and not reported. Several reliable firsthand accounts have come down through the years to give credence to the story.

When the wagons of the Illinois "Jayhawkers" pulled out of Galesburg on April 1, 1849, for the golden land of California, the village church bells tolled for the adventuresome travelers, for it was commonly thought that they faced almost certain death. They became the famed Death Valley Forty-niners, and some, not all, did meet death on that fateful journey.

One who survived the fatal trip and lived to become a California and Arizona pioneer, was William B. Rood (the name is found variously: Roode, Roods, Rude, Rhodes, Rode, Roade and Rhoade). And it was Rood who left behind this tale of buried treasure.

Reaching Salt Lake City in mid-August, the Mormon settlers warned the Jayhawkers that a trip across the Sierras might lead to another tragedy similar to that suffered by the Donner Party when they were trapped in the Sierra's early

40

winter snows. The Jayhawkers decided to take the old Mexican pack trail southwest to San Bernardino. Although no wagons had ever made the journey, they were hopeful of success and started out in high spirits.

During the course of the journey the Jayhawkers passed a pack outfit which told them of a direct short-cut to California. There was disagreement and the emigrant train split up, almost all of the Illinois Jayhawkers, including William B. Rood, taking the short-cut. It was this party, trapped in the great desert sink, that made Death Valley a famous and terrifying name.

William Rood seems to have taken the desert hardships in stride. He reached California and eventually settled in San Jose. Later he went to Sacramento and tried his fortunes at various enterprises. From California he traveled to that part of northern Sonora that was to become Arizona. While not fighting Indians, he seems to have prospered at ranching around Tucson.

When Pauline Weaver (that was his real name, and it was after him that Weaver's Needle, famed Lost Dutchman Mine landmark, was named) made his sensational discovery of gold near the Colorado River above Yuma, in 1862, Rood followed the rush to the booming town of La Paz, now a ghost, but once the largest town in Arizona. Here he prospected and ranched, finally selecting a site on the east bank of the Colorado about midway between La Paz and Yuma. To this ranch he gave the name of Rancho de los Yumas.

Running a herd of some 4000 cattle, Rood supplied beef for the several government posts in the region. He operated a meat market in La Paz and his Indians cut wood for the river steamers that stopped for refueling at Rood's Landing. He married a Mexican girl and he was known up and down the river as "Don Guillermo," a substantial and reputable citizen.

But Rood was an adventurer at heart and in 1869 he could not resist the temptation to join a party conducting a search in Death Valley for the famous Lost Gunsight Mine, a silver lode found and lost by members of the Jayhawkers party while making their historic and tragic trip across the desert sink. Nothing of value was found and Rood later returned to his ranch on the Colorado.

In April, 1870, Rood and his foreman, Alex Poindexter, crossed the river to its west bank to pay his Indian woodchoppers. From this trip, made in a small boat, Poindexter returned alone and reported that Rood had been drowned when the vessel had struck a snag and capsized. He had saved his own life, he said, by clinging desperately to the overturned boat. There were those who were skeptical of Poindexter's story, and it is now fairly well established that the foreman killed Rood, presumably in the hope that he could find the wealth Rood was thought to have buried or hidden around the ranch.

On his death bed, Poindexter is said to have confessed the murder to Adaline Godfrey, one of Rood's daughters. In 1957 Arthur Godfrey told this story to television associates of the writer's while shooting a television episode of the Rood treasure story.

When William Rood's estate was settled, Godfrey related, the Public Administrator could find no money except several hundred dollars on deposit with merchants in Yuma. There were no banking facilities in Yuma at that time and this was a custom followed by many people. But from all of Rood's many, and apparently profitable, enterprises, it was generally believed that he had accumulated a sizeable fortune. He was known to have kept gold at the ranch and, following the common practice in a bankless country, it was assumed that he hid his wealth in the ground.

It is stated upon good authority that both Poindexter and his wife searched the Rancho de los Yumas after Rood's death. Was Poindexter, as Rood's trusted foreman, in a position to know where the dead man's wealth was secreted on the estate?

At the time of Rood's death, he had two daughters in a convent in Los Angeles. They, too, are said to have made many searches for the treasure. Did they have definite knowledge that their father had buried or hidden his gold at Rancho de los Yumas?

After the death of the *ranchero*, Rancho de los Yumas rapidly fell into ruins, used by travelers as an overnight

42

stopping place, and searched over by the many people who passed that way. In 1897 Alfredo Pina, a Mexican woodcutter, dug an old baking powder tin from its crumbling walls and recovered about $1000 in gold coins. He found papers, too, he said, but unable to read them, tore them up and threw them away! Did they record the secret burial place of the main treasure — the "big cache" Rood once told a laborer, Leonardo Romo, he had buried?

Under the assault of many treasure seekers, and compounded by the ravages of time and the elements, the last of the adobe walls of Rancho de los Yumas are fast disappearing into the desert landscape. There is treasure there, this writer believes, unless someone has stumbled upon it. The truth of this we probably never will know, for finders of treasure have their reasons for not talking.

(16) John D. Lee Lost Mine

VALUE: Unknown. Rich placer gold ore and seven cans of mined gold dust.

LOCATION: Generally believed to be in Grand Canyon near the mouth of the Little Colorado River, or in a side gulch above Vulcan's Throne, Coconino County.

AUTHENTICATION: John D. Lee, a prominent pioneer figure in Utah and Arizona, almost certainly did have a source of gold, and we have his own written word for it that he had a "mine." It must be concluded that this mine and treasure actually exist, unless, of course, one or both have been found.

The story of the Lost Lee Mine begins with the Mountain Meadows Massacre in 1857, a black page in Western history, in which Lee was a leading figure. During the period of Mormon emigration to Utah, a party of 140 men, women and children, known as Francher's Company, came to Salt Lake City. The section of Arkansas from which they had come had been the scene of the slaying of a Mormon apostle. The Francher party found itself unwelcome in Salt Lake City and pushed southward, headed for California. In September they halted to rest at the pleasant little village of Mountain Meadows, about 30 miles south of Cedar City.

Isaac C. Haight, Mormon leader in those parts, decided that the members of the Francher Company were heretics, and gave orders to John Doyle Lee, one of his subordinates, to kill them.

Lee assigned the task to a band of Paiute Indians, who attacked the camp and killed seven men before the return fire drove them off. After this defeat, Lee recruited about 100 Indians and 75 Mormons and renewed the attack. While Lee and the Mormons waited at the rear, the Indians maneuvered and poured a deadly fire into the camp. Again the massed fire of the party drove them off. Haight railed at the bungling and ordered Lee to get on with the matter of disposing of the "heretics."

A few days later Lee and a companion visited the emigrants under a flag of truce. They assured the emigrants that if they would abandon their wagons and arms they would be guaranteed safe conduct through the Mormon settlements. After a parley Francher's Company agreed to disarm themselves. Almost immediately they marched into an ambush of Paiutes and Mormons, many of the latter disguised as Indians. Of the 140 people all excepting 17 children were slain in cold blood, and it was twenty years before anyone paid for the murders.

In 1872 the United States Government finally got around to gathering evidence, and Lee was advised to flee Utah Territory before he was arrested. He selected an isolated spot where Paria Creek empties into the Colorado River, just above Marble Canyon. To this ideally located hideout, which he called Lonely Dell, he moved two of his wives, Rachel and Emma, leaving 17 more behind in Utah. Here Lee built a house, a fort and eventually established a ferry across the Colorado, over which he aided many of his companions in the massacre to escape into the wilds of northern Arizona.

Lee explored Grand Canyon systematically for mineral deposits. Although his movements during this period of hiding out are understandably vague, it was persistently rumored that he was the first white man to visit the Havasupai Indians, being taken captive and living with them for two years. During his captivity he is believed to have found rich deposits of ore.

Robert B. Hildebrand, who went to live with Lee when he was a boy of 15, always insisted that Lee had a rich mine somewhere in Grand Canyon, but he did not know its exact location. Lee kept a journal in which he entered accounts of many of his activities, but these were either destroyed or lost. In a letter written to one of his daughters while he was imprisoned in Salt Lake City, he mentioned his gold ledges.

In November, 1874, while visiting some of his scattered wives in Panguitch, Utah, Lee was arrested by United States officers and later brought to trial in Beaver. In this trial the jury disagreed, and Lee was freed on bail, returning to his ferry on the Colorado. At the second trial he was found guilty and sentenced to death. In March, 1877, John D. Lee was executed for his part in the Mountain Meadows Massacre — the only person to be punished for that crime.

Even before Lee's death the search for the Lost Lee Mine was under way, spurred on by the finding of some rich ore on his property at Lee's Ferry. In facing death, Lee refused to deny or admit that he had a mine, or mines. About this time there appeared a man named Brown who claimed to have certain knowledge that Lee's mine was located in Grand Canyon near the mouth of the Little Colorado River. The site is often said to be within view of Vulcan's Throne, on the north side of the Colorado about six miles southeast of Mt. Emma.

Brown claimed, too, that Lee had also buried seven cans of gold dust near the mine. Did Brown know what he was talking about? Perhaps so, for it turned out that "Brown" was really Isaac C. Haight, Lee's former superior and the man who had ordered the Mountain Meadows Massacre. The information he had may have been given to him by Lee himself, but it is not believed that he ever found the mine or the seven tins of gold.

After the execution of John D. Lee, Emma Lee continued to live at Lee's Ferry, but eventually moved to Holbrook, Arizona, where she married Franklin French, a pioneer miner and stockman. For several years they lived at Hardy Station, west of Holbrook, where French ran a section house. Relying on information supplied him by Emma, French made many trips into Grand Canyon searching for the Lost Lee Mine. Most of his later years were spent in prospecting Grand Canyon, but with no apparent success.

(17) Nigger Ben's Lost Mine

VALUE: Unknown.

LOCATION: Generally believed to be in the vicinity of Antelope Peak, east of Congress Junction, Yavapai County, Arizona.

AUTHENTICATION: Extensive searches for this mine were definitely made by reputable pioneers including Major Peeples and Ed Schieffelin, who had first-hand information from Nigger Ben. Such people were not in the habit of chasing rainbows. It must be concluded that Nigger Ben did have a source of rich gold ore. The question is: has it been found?

"Nigger Ben" in those days was a hand on the Major Peeples Ranch in Peeples Valley. So far as is known he had no other name — simply Nigger Ben. It was a region where rich strikes were common, and Nigger Ben frequently made his own little prospecting trips into the surrounding hills, much to the annoyance of his employer, who had other things for Ben to do.

After the great strike at Rich Hill, local Indians laughed

at the white man's greed for gold and taunted him with statements that they knew where there was a much greater field of gold on *Big Antelope*, a name then familiar only to the Indians.

Traditionally the Indians held the black man in some kind of special awe, and it has been said that a Negro could often pass unharmed through the most hostile Indian country. There was perhaps some truth to this, and so it was not strange that Nigger Ben made friends with several Yavapai chiefs, and in particular with an old Apache who loafed around the Peeples Ranch. From this Indian, Nigger Ben heard the Indian version of the Big Antelope gold.

After some slight persuasion, Nigger Ben induced the old Apache to take him to Big Antelope. They started out secretly together, but at Sycamore Springs the Apache stopped and refused to go another step. "It is near," he said, and that is all Nigger Ben could get out of him.

Nigger Ben searched the area for three days before he returned to the ranch in disgust. Gold fever had him, however, and before long he deserted his job and disappeared into the hills. The next time Major Peeples saw him he was hanging around Wickenburg, apparently in possession of enough gold to remain in a constant state of intoxication. When he went broke, he simply slipped away in the night and returned in a few days with his burro heavily loaded with rich ore that he washed out at the river. With the proceeds of this, he financed another prolonged spree.

Although he was closely watched, Nigger Ben was too cunning to be followed. His usual trip took him west toward the Harquahalas, and he always returned from the same direction, but it was presumed that this was only a ruse to confuse his pursuers. Major Peeples did not believe that his short absence from Wickenburg allowed him sufficient time to make a round trip to the Harquahalas, and figured that he headed north after shaking off any followers. (Peeples told McClintock, in 1891, that the old Apache took Nigger Ben to some waterholes about 65 miles northwest of Antelope Peak, toward McCracken in Mojave County.)

One time Nigger Ben did not return from his periodic trip in the usual period of time. When he was overdue sev-

47

eral days there was considerable concern for his safety. Finally a search party was organized and in due time his body was found. The location of the body should be a clue as to the whereabouts of the mine, but unfortunately accounts do not agree. The Florence (Ariz.) *Tribune* in a 1901 issue stated that the Negro's body was found four miles west of Wickenburg, and that he had undoubtedly been slain by Apaches *because they had been suspicious of his color!* This hardly seems possible. More likely the Apaches knew that sooner or later a white man would succeed in following Nigger Ben, and then would come others to disturb the peace of Big Antelope, which they held in some kind of reverence.

The theory was presented that Nigger Ben's mine was in the vicinity of Oro Grande, north of Wickenburg. The Phoenix *Republican* said, in a story in 1890, that the mine was in the vicinity of McCrackin (McCracken), which was in agreement with Peeples' statement. But the popular location for Nigger Ben's rich mine is near Antelope Peak at the southern end of Peeples Valley, northeast of Wickenburg. The peak was named by Major Peeples who wrote in his diary: "I killed three antelope and we gave the peak this name, Antelope." It should not be confused with Antelope Peak in the Table Top Mountains in Pinal County.

Both Ed Schieffelin and Major Peeples made extensive searches for Nigger Ben's gold, and in the years that followed, many others sought to find the sources of the riches that kept the Negro in whiskey.

"He was a good man," said Peeples, and he had Nigger Ben's body taken to the ranch for burial.

(18) Black Princess Lost Mine

VALUE: Unknown.

LOCATION: In the Cerro Colorado Mountains, northeast of the old mining town of Arivaca, Pima County.

48

AUTHENTICATION: Entirely legendary so far as is known.

The Black Princess is a natural rock formation on the crest of the Cerro Colorado Mountains. The Indians have long held it in a combination of fear and reverence. Resembling the outstretched body of a woman, there are many Opata and Papago legends pertaining to it. This natural figure should not be confused with the Sleeping Beauty formation which is visible on the western skyline from United States Highway 70 just south of Globe.

About the time the United States withdrew troops from Arizona Territory at the start of the Civil War, two Mayo Indian brothers came to the Arivaca country from southern Sonora. Their names were Juan and Fermin Morales. Juan was a blond (a frequent occurrence among the Mayos, and the subject of many Indian stories), and his people knew him as "El Guero Mayo."

Juan and Fermin made a living by panning the placers along Arivaca Creek and in the surrounding mountains which were once thought to be rich in gold. As time went by, Juan — the blond Mayo — spent more and more time in making long excursions into the mountains, while Fermin stayed behind to tend their camp.

One day Juan returned from the mountains with his six burros loaded down with rich gold quartz. The brothers crushed the ore in an *arrastre* which they built along Arivaca Creek a few miles north of the present town of Arivaca.

Each week for many months at a time Juan made the trip into the mountains in the direction of the Black Princess; and each time he returned with his burros — all six — loaded with all the gold ore they could carry. Years went by and the endless stream of ore poured in to the *arrastre* along Arivaca Creek. The brothers grew rich and they began to spend more leisure time in Arivaca, where they were very free with their gold. They engaged in ranching, establishing themselves below the Black Princess where they presumably could keep an eye on their mine.

There are many who believe that the Morales brothers were looking for a particular mine when they came north

49

to Arizona, and that they found it. There are those, too, who believe that the brothers found the Lost Sopori Mine, believed to have first been worked by the Jesuit padres and to have been located in the Black Princess region. The Sopori, according to stories, could have produced the kind of wealth Juan and Fermin Morales possessed.

Juan Morales died in Sonora while on a visit. Fermin lived until the 1900's and still resided in Arivaca when he died. So far as is known they told no one the secret location of their mine, and supposedly it is still there waiting to be found again.

(19) Lost Sopori Mine and Treasure

VALUE: An unknown quantity of gold and silver ore in the mine and a quantity of mined ore buried on the old Sopori Ranch.

LOCATION: There is no general agreement on the location of the Sopori Mine. Wyllys says it is located "near Arivaca." Another historian places it near Black Princess Peak at the northern extremity of the Cerro Colorado Mountains. Still another account places the mine on the old Sopori Ranch, although this seems unlikely. All these locations are in Pima County.

AUTHENTICATION: Several early histories by Americans mention this lost mine, but whether or not these statements were based on documentary evidence is not known. Some of the early historians simply reported what they saw or heard repeated by old-timers and let it go at that. The region around the old Sopori Ranch was highly mineralized and it seems reasonable to believe that the *ranchero* or his workers may have found and worked a mine.

Of this we are certain: the Sopori Mine was known all

over Arizona for its richness in both gold and silver. Supposedly it was discovered by the Spaniards, following in the wake of Coronado, worked by the Jesuit padres for a time, and either it fell into the hands of the owners of the Sopori Ranch, or it was "lost" and later found. Popularly its location is placed somewhere on the 21,000 acre Sopori Ranch in southern Pima County.

Early Spanish and American maps show the location of the Sopori Mine to be in the northern end of the Cerro Colorado Mountains, where the ruins of an adobe smelter and a crude *arrastre* were once found. On a hill projecting into Altar Valley, east of the Baboquivari Mountains, were found the ruins of an old wall believed to have been an old mission, or *visita,* the name of which has been lost for centuries. It is thought that the people who lived at this mission worked the Sopori Mine, but there is no evidence to prove it.

The Sopori Ranch was located along the Altar Road, a well-traveled highway from Sonora to San Xavier del Bac, south of Tucson. Astride the most important road in southern Arizona, the location of the ranch was strategic in those days. It was an area noted for its Apache raids, and according to old Spanish stories, the ranch was frequently attacked by Indians and many of its people killed from time to time. Just before one of these raids occurred, a large amount of silver and gold from the mine is said to have been buried in one corner of an old adobe house that stood on the ranch. This treasure, according to most accounts, has never been found.

Tradition has it, also, that the mine was so poorly operated that the rich vein was lost. Interest then waned in the mine. As Apache raids increased in number and severity, work was stopped at the mine and eventually all trace of it was lost. It should not be too difficult to locate the ruins of the old ranch buildings, nor to establish the exact Sopori holdings. But to locate the old mine — well, that will take some searching.

51

(20) Black Jack Ketchum's Treasure

VALUE: Unknown.

LOCATION: In a cave in Wild Cat Canyon in the Chiricahua Mountains, about 40 miles north of Bisbee, Cochise County.

AUTHENTICATION: The evidence is pretty thin. The manner in which this gang lived it up left little loot to be buried, and most of the known robberies and hold-ups pulled by the Black Jack Gang produced little more than enough for one rip-roaring blow-off.

Tom and Sam Ketchum (the name will also be found: Ketchem and Ketcham) came from Texas to New Mexico when they were both very young. In the mining camp of Kingston nobody was shocked, nor cared much, when they cut adrift and joined the loosely-woven Wild Bunch, a gang that operated from Montana to the Mexican border and produced some of the most notorious outlaws in the West.

Tom and Sam seem not to have hit it off with the Wild Bunch, and they eventually drifted down to Cochise County, Arizona, where they worked for a number of cattle outfits. Tom bore a striking resemblance to a petty badman known as Black Jack Christian, who had just been killed. One day Tom rode into Bisbee and was mistaken for the dead man. Even though the sheriff knew that Christian was dead, he held Tom just to make sure that he was not seeing things. This turn of events so enraged Tom he swore that henceforth he would be known as Black Jack, and that is how he got his name. He organized a small gang, each member of which had to wear, as a kind of a badge of trade, a plain gold ring on the third finger of the left hand.

After a series of post office and stage holdups in southern Arizona and New Mexico, the gang finally became bold enough to tackle a train. From a Southern Pacific train near Willcox, Arizona, they secured several thousand dollars and fled to a small town across the border in Sonora. When they were picked up there for being drunk, they had $9000 among them.

Sam finally broke away from Tom (Black Jack) and organized his own little gang in New Mexico. In a gun battle that followed the holdup of a Colorado & Southern train, Sam was wounded and captured. He refused medical attention on the grounds that it was ridiculous to be healed just so they could have the pleasure of hanging him. The authorities obliged him and he died.

On the day brother Sam died, Black Jack was making plans to holdup another train at exactly the same spot, Twin Mountain Curve near Des Moines, New Mexico. This spot also proved to be the downfall of Black Jack. He received a blast in the right arm and took off into the timber afoot. He was caught a few days later and taken to Trinidad, Colorado, where the injured limb was amputated. Brought to trial at Clayton, New Mexico, he was convicted and sentenced to hang. With fifteen murders to his credit, he climbed the steps to the gallows on April 26, 1901. As the hangman adjusted the noose, Black Jack asked the time of day. Upon being told, he replied: "Hurry it up, or I'll be late in Hell for dinner." The trap sprung, Black Jack's head was jerked from his body, but he made his dinner date.

All bandits are supposed to have buried a lot of treasure — a lot of exaggerated treasure. Sam and Tom were no sooner dead than the stories started about the vast loot they cached, the favorite site being a cave in a lonely section of Wild Cat Canyon in the Chiricahua Mountains. Tom called the cave "Room Forty-Four."

While Leonard Alvorsen, a member of the gang, was serving time in the Territorial Prison at Yuma, he claimed that the gang had buried treasure in the Chiricahuas, and he is supposed to have passed this information on to friends in Tombstone. These confidants, Bert and Harry Macia, are believed to have searched "Room Forty-Four" without any success.

When Black Jack was captured after the Twin Mountain Curve job, he claimed that he was not Black Jack, but a cowboy named Stevens. There was some confusion and then someone recalled that Sheriff Cicero Stewart of Eddy County had once punched cows with Tom and could make a positive identification. He was sent for and nailed the lid to Tom's coffin by positively identifying him. Black Jack asked Stewart to return ten days later when he would have some important information to pass on to him. Stewart kept the date as agreed.

"I've got something very important to tell you," said Black Jack. Noting that Bill Hall, his cellmate, was cupping an ear to hear what was said, Stewart had him removed to another cell.

"Go to Bisbee," Black Jack continued in privacy, "and then go forty miles north to the Turkey Track horse camp in the Chiricahuas. About a quarter of a mile below the ranch house there's a big canyon that runs into a creek. Go up that canyon until it boxes. There you will find a big pile of ashes. Due south of the ashes about fifty feet, at the foot of a juniper tree, you'll find the gang's money buried — money from Old Mexico."

Sheriff Stewart, accompanied by Deputy Sheriff Steve Roup of Bisbee, made a special trip to the canyon. They found the pile of ashes and the juniper tree, but when they dug they found no treasure.

Meantime Bill Hall had been given a life sentence at Lincoln, New Mexico, and by strange coincidence, Sheriff Stewart was assigned as one of the guards to escort him to prison. On the trip Hall said:

"Stewart, do you remember the day you had me removed from the cell so you could talk to Black Jack in private?"

"Yes," replied Stewart. "What about it?"

"Well, after you left, I was put back in the cell. Black Jack was dancing a jig. I asked him what the hell was so funny and he said, 'I'll teach Stewart to come to Trinidad to identify me! If he goes to that canyon after the treasure and the gang happens to be there, they'll fill his damned old hide full of lead!' "

Tom Ketchum had invented the whole story, hoping he could send the sheriff into a dead'y ambush. The doctors had told Black Jack that if he could live ten days, he would be in no danger of dying from the amputation. So he told

Stewart to wait ten days so he would have the pleasure of reading about his slaughter!

(21) Lost Mine of Sierra Azul

VALUE: Unknown. Stories do not even agree on the nature of the treasure, whether it is silver, gold or quicksilver.

LOCATION: Originally the location was centered in the Hopi country south of the Colorado River and north of the Little Colorado, which could place it in Coconino, Navajo or Apache County. In some manner the legend became twisted and the favorite location today is in the San Francisco Peaks region north of Flagstaff, Coconino County.

AUTHENTICATION: The legend dates back to 1662, almost 300 years ago. References to the mine are actually found in old Spanish documents (and in this instance they are authentic), and the mine is shown on at least one early Spanish map of Pimeria Alta. Yet, this story must be considered pure legend.

Various versions of this tale have persisted in the Southwest for as long as white men can remember, handed down, apparently by the Indians from generation to generation. They all concern the rumors of a rich mine located near a red hill *(cerro colorado)* at the foot of a blue mountain *(sierra azul)*. For many years this description was popularly believed to be in the Hopi country in the northeastern section of Arizona.

After the Pueblo Indian uprising of 1680, in which the Spanish were either driven out of New Mexico or killed, the Spanish Viceroy at Mexico City appointed, in 1690, Diego de Vargas (his full name was Don Diego de Vargas Zapata

Lujan Ponce de Leon) as Governor of New Mexico. His job, of course, was to reconquer New Mexico and bring the Indians again under Spanish domination. Vargas established his headquarters at Paseo del Norte (now El Paso, Texas), where he was installed in 1691. While here he received a letter from the Viceroy, the Count of Galva, instructing him to investigate the rumors of rich quicksilver mines to the north. In later accounts the quicksilver magically changed to silver and even gold.

Vargas did not have the slightest idea where these mines were located, so he called an assembly of all the people who might have some knowledge of the deposits and compelled them to swear under oath to reveal anything they knew. No one, it seems, had any definite knowledge, but several, perhaps to save their skins or to ingratiate themselves with the new Governor, professed to have distant friends who knew the location of the mines. They decided that the area to be searched was a part of what is now the State of Arizona.

As a result of the meager information gathered, Vargas was authorized to make his famous *entrada* into New Mexico, later extending it into eastern Arizona. The only accomplishment was an exploration of a lot of new country. No mines were ever found, but Vargas concluded from the journey that the blue mountain (*sierra azul*) was the San Francisco Peaks (which actually appear blue under certain conditions) and that the red hill *(cerro colorado)* was one of the red cinder cones northeast of Flagstaff. There is a great deal of country in between these points, but Vargas did not pause to search further.

This whole region is rich in legends of mines lost and found by the padres, but legends, like the Sierra Azul, they most certainly are . . . and nothing else.

(22) Antlers Gold of Daniel's Canyon

VALUE: "Fabulously Rich" gold ore of unknown value.

LOCATION: In Daniel's Canyon, probably Mojave or Yavapai County. This could be a localized name of a

56

canyon, but research has failed to reveal a canyon of this name in western Arizona in standard geographical reference works.

AUTHENTICATION: Dobie, the source of this story, is a grand story teller and a diligent student of Southwestern folklore.

About 1905 a cowboy, known only as Harper, was working in the Milk Weed Flat section of western Arizona when he became so ill with what he diagnosed as bronchitis that he decided to ride to Prescott and consult a doctor. After passing through Peach Springs (a tank on the Santa Fe railroad in northwestern Mojave County) he became so weak that he could ride no further. He was in Daniel's Canyon, so named, it is said, for the number of mountain lions that frequented the region. Here he dismounted.

While reclining in the shade of a large boulder, Harper observed a buck deer emerge from a clump of bushes. He managed to raise his rifle and shot it. The animal fell nearby. Making a fire under a juniper tree, he cooked some of the venison, and after eating, found himself revived. As he contemplated the continuation of his journey he sat, idly digging the sharp heels of his boots in the ground. They kicked up a rock which he inspected out of curiosity and found in it traces of gold. He dug further and uncovered a pocket of rich ore.

After digging out all the ore he could carry, Harper carefully concealed the spot with earth and brush. He looked about thoughtfully, took note of all the natural landmarks, but was not satisfied. Cutting off the head of the dead buck, he hung the head and antlers in the low branches of the juniper tree. This done, he mounted and rode away.

In Prescott a doctor told Harper that he was suffering from advanced stages of tuberculosis. He was sent immediately to a hospital. As the cowboy's condition became gradually worse, the doctor persuaded him to send for a brother located in Texas. The brother arrived just in time to see Harper alive. Before he died, Harper produced the rocks and gave his brother directions for finding the ore in

Daniel's Canyon, stressing the antlers that would be found in a juniper tree.

After the funeral the brother had the rocks assayed and the gold content turned out to be fabulously rich. The ore the cowboy had packed into Prescott produced enough gold, in fact, to pay the doctor, the hospital, the funeral expenses and the shipment of the body back to Texas.

When all this was taken care of, the brother went to Daniel's Canyon and made a minute search for the tree with the antlers. He found neither it nor the gold, nor did many other searchers who later combed the canyon. It was thought that predatory animals had dragged the head away and the search was finally abandoned.

(23) Lost Treasure of Montezuma's Head

VALUE: A lost mine containing ore of unknown value, and a nearby cave containing 50 gold bars and 30 bags of gold nuggets. Weighing a total of 3000 pounds.

LOCATION: Near Montezuma Head in the Estrella Mountains, south of Phoenix, Pinal County.

AUTHENTICATION: None that can be located. There are almost two identical stories with only a different set of names for the main characters. This, of course, leads to the suspicion that something is fishy, and this is just how the writer views this story.

Montezuma is a popular place name throughout the Southwest, and Arizona has its share of them. There are no less than three different Montezuma Heads in Arizona, one in Pinal County, another in Pima County and the third in Maricopa County. This story concerns the Montezuma Head in the southeastern extremities of the Sierra Estrella Mountains (Star Mountains). If your imagination is working and you know what the real Montezuma's head looked like, you can say that there is a striking similarity.

There are two versions of this story, but essentially they are the same. In the first, a Mexican named Campoy, from Guadalajara, had a rich mine in the Estrellas, where he engaged several Indians and Mexicans to work for him. One day word reached Campoy that American soldiers were riding down from the north. Fearful that his mine and its treasures would be confiscated, he dismissed all his laborers except one old Maricopa Indian. Together they loaded the mined gold — 3000 pounds in 50 bars and 30 bags of nuggets — on mules and started up the trail toward Butterfly Peak and past Montezuma Head. Presently they came to a cave, packed in the gold, dug a hole and buried it. Then Campoy killed the old Maricopa with a blow on the head and hid his body. Next day Campoy was found dead in his blankets. Only the dead man knew the secret of his mine and his buried gold.

In the second version of the story, the mine owner is named Ortega, but he is from the same place — Guadalajara. His rich mine was also located in the Estrellas, and he, too, became frightened when word came that American soldiers were approaching. He sent all his workers away excepting one Pima boy. Together they loaded the gold — the same 50 bars and 30 bags of nuggets — on mules and started up the trail toward Butterfly Peak. Past Montezuma Head they entered a canyon and came to a cave. The gold was hidden and the Pima boy was killed so that its secret hiding place would remain only with Ortega. That night Ortega died in his sleep!

Campoy and Ortega one and the same? Somebody is taking a great deal of liberty with historical accuracy. Or is there any historical background to this story at all?

(24) Aztec Montezuma's Treasure

VALUE: "Millions of dollars!"

LOCATION: In a cave near Montezuma Head, in the Estrella Mountains, Maricopa County.

59

AUTHENTICATION: Purely legendary. This is perhaps one of the very few treasure stories without a single writer to claim its authenticity.

The legendary treasure of the New Mexico Indian god, Montezuma, is buried in at least a dozen places in the Southwest. To further complicate the matter, there are almost as many legends of the Aztec Montezuma's treasure buried in the same area of the United States.

The Papago Indians have a legend that their ancestors helped bury a great treasure belonging to the Aztec Montezuma and brought up from Mexico and hidden in the Estrella Mountains near Montezuma Head. It was gold from the mines of Mexico and valued at untold millions of dollars. According to the legend the gold is secreted in a cave in the mountains beneath or near the well-known landmark known as Montezuma Head. After the treasure was well concealed, according to the story, Montezuma climbed to the top of the mountain and turned to stone, presumably so that he could guard his treasure. We know, of course, that the Aztec Montezuma was never in what is now Arizona.

The great treasure stored in the cave can be released only by Montezuma, and the legend states that someday the spirit of Montezuma will approach from the east. When this happens, the stone Montezuma will climb down from the mountain top, open the secret cave and distribute the vast wealth to its rightful owners who, of course, are the Indians.

Well, this is as it should be.

According to the Papago legend, when the treasure was being buried near Montezuma Head, they were so close to the village of Ajo (a word that means "garlic" in Spanish, and so named because of the abundance of wild garlic in the mountains in certain seasons), that on a still night the workers could hear the dogs barking. This statement is made of several lost mines in the Southwest.

(25) Treasure of Montezuma Well

VALUE: Unknown.

LOCATION: In Montezuma Castle National Monument, 65 miles east of Prescott, Yavapai County.

AUTHENTICATION: Legendary. Montezuma played no part in Arizona, although his name is associated with many legends.

Montezuma legends are common all over Mexico and the southwestern United States. They usually follow a common pattern, and in the case of the Mexican Montezuma, involve the removal of all or part of the Aztec ruler's vast treasure to the north to prevent it falling into the hands of the invading Spanish.

Montezuma Well is a detached portion of Montezuma Castle National Monument within which are the ruins of several prehistoric Indian house clusters, including a large, almost intact structure known as Montezuma Castle. The story is told that a cowboy once swapped a horse for the castle, then traded the castle for two horses. Montezuma, of course, never saw the place.

Montezuma Well is a large limestone sink, 470 feet in diameter and sounded to a depth of 800 feet without touching bottom. It is partially filled with water which flows at the rate of 1,500,000 gallons daily. The people who lived here about 1200 to 1300 A.D. utilized the water for irrigation purposes and ruins of their canals are still visible, due to an incrustation of calcium.

The well was probably discovered by Cortez, since it was shown on a deerskin map that belonged to him. Early white settlers erroneously associated it as well as the castle, with Montezuma, and they repeated the legend that part of the vast treasure of Montezuma was brought here from Mexico and cast into the well to prevent it from being seized by the Spanish.

If all the supposed treasure of Montezuma could be traced down and recovered, we could retire the national debt.

(26) Montezuma Treasure in the Ajo Mountains

VALUE: Unknown.

LOCATION: In the Ajo Mountains of western Pima County.

AUTHENTICATION: Purely legendary.

Not only are the legendary Montezuma treasures all over the map from Utah to Mexico, but to make matters more confusing, there are two Montezumas! One was the legendary Indian god of New Mexico, and the other the real Aztec ruler who was overthrown by Cortez. This story concerns the latter.

When word was brought to the great Montezuma at his capital city in Mexico of the arrival of strange men at Vera Cruz, he did not know that they were Spaniards bent on the Spanish national pastime of treasure hunting. Montezuma thought they might be representatives of the Aztec's great god Quetzalcoatl, and if they were, they must be royally welcomed. If, on the other hand, they were not, his vast treasure might be in danger. He was in a quandary.

Just to be on the safe side, Montezuma made a half-decision. He ordered one-half of his great wealth, the proceeds of the rich mines of Mexico, packed on mules and carried far to the north and hidden where no strange visitors would ever find it. This task he delegated to a court favorite, Tlahuicole, and his explicit instructions were to find a place so remote that the treasure would never be found.

The long treasure train left the Sacred Valley of Anahuac and traveled for weeks across the mountain ranges and desert wastes until it came to the Ajo Mountains in southwestern Arizona. It was a remote place, all right, as anyone will agree who knows the region. Here the treasure was secreted in a cave of vast proportions. One of such size was required to accommodate the huge cache of silver and gold.

It is a matter of history that the strange men were Spaniards, and that they did seize that portion of Montezuma's treasure that remained in Mexico City. There is little doubt but that it was, for those days, a vast treasure. But of the half brought to Arizona and hidden in a cave in the Ajo Mountains? It is not there. It never was there. All of the Montezuma treasure legends are fantastically unrealistic. This, about the least realistic of all.

(27) Lost Padre Mine

VALUE: Unknown.

LOCATION: In the extreme southwestern corner of Coconino County, about 20 miles southwest of Flagstaff. This places the mine in the same general area as the Lost Mine of Coconino and it is possible that the two mines are one and the same.

AUTHENTICATION: There are no known facts to substantiate the story.

There are several "Lost Padre" mines scattered throughout the Southwest. The popular association of the padres with mining activities is a puzzling one. There is very, very little evidence that these early men of the robe had any but a casual interest in mining. And with the crude mining methods of their time, it is doubtful that any great accumulation of wealth was possible. Yet, from time to time, a new "Lost Padre" mine story pops up.

In 1853, so this tale goes, a man named Clifford Haines, fleeing from pursuing Indians in the Coconino country, safely reached Tucson and told a story of having stumbled upon an abandoned village and the remains of an old mine. He had not had time to stop and investigate, but guessed that it may have been the fabled Lost Padre Mine. Determined to secure all the information he could about the mine, he

63

went to Sonora and finally located an aged Opata Indian who claimed that his ancestors had actually worked in the mine. Haines presumably acquired an old map which showed the mine's location. Sometime later this crude map mysteriously turned up in the possession of John Squires. Details of this transaction are hazy, but Haines faded out of the story.

Armed with the Haines map, Squires led a party of prospectors from Santa Fe into the Coconino country and they are said to have located the abandoned village and the mine. In a nearby cave they found two small trunks, rusted Spanish weapons, leather sacks filled with ore, cooking utensils and many other items clearly identified as being of Spanish origin.

The industrious Squires party reopened the mine, repaired one of the largest *arrastres* and established permanent living quarters. After smelting two bars of gold with which to meet current expenses, Squires and a companion left for Santa Fe to secure provisions and to hire additional Indians to work the mine. Upon their return to the mining camp, work was continued with a renewed zeal, the smelted bars being packed to Santa Fe for sale.

Most of the Indians in the area of the mine were friendly enough, or not openly hostile, but a band of Apaches working their way up from the south discovered the little community and decided that the hated white men and their Indian workers must go. They struck at dawn in a furious surprise attack.

Many of the mining party were killed before they even knew what was happening. Others were slain as they fled afoot down the canyon. Squires happened to be away from the camp at the time, but heard the yells and screams and cautiously picked his way back through the brush to see the buildings going up in flames. Remaining concealed in the cover of rocks and brush until nightfall, he managed to escape only to be killed in a saloon brawl in Taos a short time later.

Maps drawn by survivors of the massacre are said to be available in the Southwest, but "lost mine" maps in this region have always been a dime a dozen.

After the Apaches withdrew from the area about 1886, members of the original Squires party tried to find the mine and burned out camp, but failing, concluded that the Indian attackers had erased all traces of it.

In 1896 a Flagstaff character known as "Bearhunter Howard" (William O. Howard), a game hunter for construction gangs working on the Santa Fe railroad, accidentally stumbled onto the mine while riding up the canyon in search of a new game country. He located the cave and brought out the books and papers left there by the original Spanish miners.

Strangely enough, Howard did not attempt to return to the mine until a year or so later, and then he could locate no sign of it. Accompanied by others, he made a thorough search of the region. When the others quit in disgust, Howard never gave up and continued the search. One day he appeared with the news that he had at last found the mine, but he had nothing to prove his statement and many people doubted him. He seems never to have returned to the mine and died a few years later.

The search still goes on for the Lost Padre Mine, and it is said that every now and then that a clue turns up. It has been reported found many times, and as late as the present decade, but for some reason no one ever profits by the find nor produces concrete evidence of it.

Despite its many "discoveries" the Lost Padre Mine is still mysteriously lost, and this writer doubts that it will ever be found for the simple reason that it never existed.

(28) Treasure of Hacienda de San Ysidro

VALUE: Unknown.

LOCATION: In the Gila Valley about 15 miles north of Yuma, Yuma County.

AUTHENTICATION: There is no evidence that treasure was left buried here, and no reason why a family would move away peacefully and leave treasure behind, but the story persists that there is buried treasure at the old Hacienda de San Ysidro and the search still goes on.

When Don Jose Maria Redondo rode across the Gila Valley north of Yuma in 1860, he saw the great potential richness of the area when watered by canals leading from the river. Others saw only visions of gold and silver taken from the surrounding hills. Redondo envisioned a great hacienda, self-sufficient and independent like those he had known in Old Mexico. With a fortune made from various gold strikes, in ferrying and in other enterprises, Redondo realized the dream that was to prove the wealth of the Yuma country.

From Sonora he brought a hundred Yaqui Indians, and with the Mexican laborers he could hire around Yuma, he cleared mesquite, dug irrigation canals, broke ground and laid out a vast estate, most of which he simply appropriated from public domain. His workers, sometimes numbering 300 or more, were paid with script redeemable at Redondo's stores. His irrigation system totaled 27 miles, cost $25,000 and fed 2000 acres of crops, orchards and vineyards.

Mountains of adobe bricks were hand-made to build the massive walls of the two-story hacienda headquarters and the many out-buildings. There was a mill for grinding his grain; a winery to handle the produce of his vineyards; there were offices, warehouses, a blacksmith shop, a cookhouse, and harness shops, stables and corrals. Hacienda de San Ysidro was a grand place where life was lived to the fullest.

The year 1871 found the fortunes of Don Jose Redondo at their peak. In Yuma he operated, with his brother, Jesus, many stores to handle the hacienda's produce. He carried on a profitable contract business with the Army and the mining camps. There can be little doubt but that he profited handsomely.

In 1874 Government land surveyors came to the Gila Valley and divided the vast bacienda fields into sections and townships. Redondo's title to the lands was almost impos-

67

sible to defend. By 1883 the great estate was reduced to a single section of land (640 acres) on which the hacienda buildings stood.

Don Jose served in the Territorial Legislature, the Yuma Council, and in 1878 he became mayor of Yuma. He was only 48 years of age. In June of that year he died, and his passing was the beginning of the end for the hacienda. The Redondos moved away and San Ysidro fell victim to the ravages of neighbors and the destruction of treasure hunters.

Visitors to the extensive ruins as late as 1913 recall having seen a large hole in the floor of the main building. Rusty stains around its edges indicated that a large iron vault had been removed, and it was presumed that this had held the Redondo family wealth, taken away when the family left.

No one has been able to offer any reasonable explanation why any treasure would be left behind by a family moving calmly and peacefully away, but treasure hunters continued to probe through the old ruins and rumors of buried treasure there still persist.

The real treasure at San Ysidro is not the wealth that Don Jose might have left behind, but the remains of his dreams and the accomplishments of a far-seeing man. What a pity that the City of Yuma, the County of Yuma or the State of Arizona has not seen fit before this almost-too-late date to restore and preserve Hacienda de San Ysidro in order that all could view and marvel at the great handiwork of Don Jose Maria Redondo and the hacienda system.

(29) Montezuma's Treasure at Casa Grande

VALUE: If it exists, the value would be tremendous, but why speculate on something that most certainly does not exist?

LOCATION: In the ruins of Casa Grande National Monument, nine miles west of Florence, Pinal County.

AUTHENTICATION: There is not the slimmest thread of reality in this story which is common throughout Mexico and the southwestern United States. There are some puzzling aspects but the story, nevertheless, adds up to pure legend.

Legends of Montezuma, both the ruler and the god, are known to most of the older Pima and Papago Indians, and to some of the older Mexicans. Usually the stories are complex and difficult to follow.

In 1520 when the Spanish in Mexico imprisoned Montezuma and demanded gold, swift runners were sent out from the capital city to all parts of the country telling the people to bury their treasures until the Spanish conquerors departed. According to tradition this was done, and many treasures were accumulated and hidden together. It is said that one of these treasures was found at Monte Alban in modern times and its value had been estimated at from $25,000,000 to $55,000,000.

Several legends relate that a vast quantity of Montezuma's treasure was brought north and hidden in a remote section of the southwestern United States. A labyrinth found in the walls of Casa Grande ruins, the remains of an ancient city, is used to support the theory that Casa Grande was a treasure vault for some of the Montezuma treasure. It is pointed out that the Aztec ruler's so-called "castles" in Mexico had similar vaults used for treasure storage.

The Pima Indians who occupied this section of Arizona before the arrival of the Spaniards, professed little knowledge of the original builders of the pueblos of Casa Grande, but alluded to its former occupants as Hohokam or "the ancient ones; those who have departed." Little else is known of these ancient people, or of their association with Montezuma, if any. But it is puzzling that the Pima and Papago who lived here during the time of Montezuma called their pueblos Casa Montezuma.

In the several extensive excavations at Casa Grande, no

69

treasure in the form of gold or silver was ever found, nor is any likely to be, unless it is uncovered by National Park officials, for Casa Grande is a national monument under the direction of the National Park Service. These people are, as they should be, notably uncooperative with private treasure seekers.

(30) Lost Adams Diggings

VALUE: Unknown.

LOCATION: One night's ride by horse from old Fort Defiance, just north of Window Rock, Apache County. Because of the short distance of Fort Defiance to the Arizona-New Mexico border, the locale is sometimes placed in New Mexico near the Arizona line.

AUTHENTICATION: There was a lot of excitement in the late 1800's over this lost mine, and several accounts of it appeared in early Arizona newspapers. When the facts are analyzed, it boils down to this: Adams was the sole source of the story. How reliable was he? In as much as Adams appears to have invested his personal fortune in a search for the location, it seems obvious that he was telling the truth — or what he thought to be the truth.

There are two well-known lost Adams Mine stories, one placed in Arizona, the other in New Mexico, and the name Adams features in several other lost mine stories, some doubtless inspired by the sensationalism of the original stories. Because the Lost Adams Mine story based in New Mexico had its beginning in Arizona, the two are often confused. The Arizona story is sometimes referred to as the "Lost Adams Cave."

Shortly after the Navajo Indians had been confined to

their reservation along the northern Arizona-New Mexico line, and soldiers were stationed to keep them there, a man named Henry Adams (sometimes given as Jim Adams) came out from the east and established a small trading post at Fort Defiance, Arizona. This post was located about 10 miles west of the New Mexico border, northwest of Gallup.

Adams catered to the Indians, and few white men ever patronized his store. The Indians learned to respect Adams and they were as friendly as their injured pride would permit them to be. Adams minded his own business, got along with the military and didn't force himself on the Indians. If they wanted to be friendly, fine; if not, he left them alone.

One afternoon three young Indians came to the store and made extensive selections of merchandise, helping themselves from the shelves as was their custom. When they were ready to go, one of the Indians dumped the contents of a buckskin bag on the counter. Chattering among themselves, they picked up their merchandise and stalked out. The contents of the bag was gold nuggets — far more than enough to pay for their purchases. Indians were that way with gold. Adams judged that the gold came from the hills on the reservation and determined to find out just where the source was located.

Slowly, discreetly, Adams set out to make friends of the three Indian bucks. They could not be pushed and he had to be extremely careful about showing any interest in their gold lest they become suspicious. After many more visits to the trading post, the three Indians gradually loosened up and talked. Always they paid for their purchases with dust or nuggets. When Adams first mentioned the subject of gold, the bucks froze up immediately. Still Adams did not give up and he did little things for the Indians that eventually won their complete confidence. In time they discussed the gold with him and many visits later they finally agreed to take Adams to see their gold.

Leaving the post at night, the four men rode until early daybreak when they stopped at the mouth of a canyon. Here Adams was asked to submit to a blindfold. The horses were tethered and the Indians led the white man up a rough trail along the canyon wall to the mouth of a cave. As he

71

entered the cave Adams felt the cool rush of air that led him to believe that there was a second entrance. They traveled through a narrow passage to a large room. Here they halted and the bandage was removed from Adams' eyes. What he saw struck him dumb with amazement. The floor of the cavernous room was literally covered with gold nuggets and ingots!

Adams was given no more than a quick look and the blindfold was again applied. He requested permission to carry away some of the wealth, but the Indians politely refused. On the journey down the canyon wall Adams managed to slip the blindfold down and caught a fleeting glimpse of three peaks, alike in shape and standing in the form of a triangle. One of the Indians caught him in the act and he was allowed to see no more. The remainder of the journey to Fort Defiance was made in silence as the Indians felt that Adams had betrayed them.

Adams could not forget the sight of gold he had seen in the cave. As soon as he could make arrangements he sold his stock of merchandise and thereafter devoted his entire time and fortune in searching for the Navajo treasure cave. Every effort failed. Every trail led laboriously to nothing. When he was finally broken in spirits and his funds were exhausted, he found his health failing. He went to Tucson where he told his story to Judge Griscom and the knowledge of the fantastic treasure cave reached the public. Financed by Griscom, Adams returned to the Navajo country and renewed the search for the cave. When his presence was discovered by the Indians, he was wounded and driven out. Judge Griscom advanced more money and the search was carried on for three more years.

When Griscom refused to put up more money, Adams secured help from other parties and led several expeditions into the Navajo country. All ended in dejected failures. Unable to raise any more funds in Tucson, Adams decided to appeal to an old friend in Phoenix, but just before he boarded the stage he learned of the man's death. Nevertheless, Adams left on the Phoenix stage. Just outside Tucson the driver heard a gun report, and looking down, saw the form of a man topple from the open door. Henry Adams, failing to find the Navajo treasure cave, had placed the gun to his own head and pulled the trigger.

(31) Lost Cowboy Mine

VALUE: An unknown quantity of black hematite pebbles filled with free gold.

LOCATION: On the desert along the Colorado River north of Yuma, Yuma County.

AUTHENTICATION: Pure legend.

In the early 1860's there was an adobe corral on the edge of the desert north of Yuma. Its history is unknown and it seems to have been placed there just to make a setting for this story. It was located at the foot of a small hill that was covered with gravel and small black pebbles smoothly rounded through some ancient erosive action. Cowboys in the area found the rounded pebbles ideal for throwing at the cattle when they were being corralled.

There seems to be no record of who owned the ranch nor when the corral was built. It is stated, though, that Apache raids were frequent; yet this was not real Apache country. After one of these raids, in which a number of the ranch employees were killed and all the cattle driven away, the ranch was abandoned.

One of the unemployed cowboys picked up a few of the black pebbles before he left the property, and for some reason he took these with him when he drifted back east. One day he happened to show the rocks to a mining man who recognized them as hematite. Breaking one open, he found it to be filled with free gold.

Now it is said that ever since the cowboy made this discovery, people have been searching for the old adobe corral and the nugget-covered hill nearby. Some old prospectors have told tales of camping at an old abandoned adobe corral, but none could ever return to it when he learned that it was sitting right at the foot of a gold-covered hill.

(32) Outlaw Brothers' Treasure

VALUE: Two heavy bags of gold of unknown value.

LOCATION: About thirty miles northwest of Douglas, Cochise County.

AUTHENTICATION: None.

A young man named only as Simmons hired out to two brothers whom he thought were ranchers. His job was to cook and wrangle horses. It was not long before he suspected that the brothers were not all they pretended to be. At first he did not try to overhear the whispered conversations in his presence, but once his curiosity was aroused, he kept his ears sharply attuned, and he learned that his employers were really outlaws and that they were planning to rob a large gold shipment.

With the knowledge of their activities out in the open, Simmons asked for permission to participate in the robbery. After a long consultation between the two brothers, his request was granted. During the robbery he was accidentally injured and lost the sight of one eye. One of the brothers, angered over Simmons' amateurish performance, threatened to kill him on the spot. His life was spared only when the other brother intervened.

Back at their camp after the robbery, Simmons was ordered to prepare the evening meal in spite of his painful injury. While he was busy at this chore, the brothers took the two heavy bags of gold secured in the holdup and disappeared in the direction of a dike to the north of the camp. About half an hour later they returned to the camp empty-handed. Simmons, of course, presumed that they had hidden the treasure.

After a short rest the three rode south into Mexico where Simmons was informed that his services were no longer required. He had received no share of the robbery loot; his life was again threatened. At this point Simmons left and he never saw the brothers again. Later he learned that the outlaw brothers had been caught and jailed.

Afraid to return to the United States, Simmons drifted around Mexico, his health failing and the sight gradually leaving his remaining eye. He met two Americans with whom he became friendly and eventually he told them of the robbery and the treasure buried north of the old camp. The three went there and thoroughly searched the area, but found nothing.

The creator of this unbelievable story fails to mention whether or not the outlaw brothers eventually got out of jail. If they did, you can be sure that they recovered the two bags of gold.

(33) Lost Shepherd Girl Mine

VALUE: Unknown.

LOCATION: Very vaguely "in the desert sands of Arizona," and this could mean anyplace in the southern or western half of the state — quite an area, indeed.

AUTHENTICATION: Its origin is as vague as the location.

Late one day in a period of time left to the reader's imagination, a Mexican shepherd girl was herding her goats in a desert section of Arizona not defined and was caught in a sudden desert sandstorm. Before she could gather her flock and start them home, the swirling, stinging sands closed in on her and she became completely lost.

Stumbling into a slight depression, she sat with her back to the wind to close out the sand. The wind blew in gusts around her feet until the sand was scooped out and the rock floor exposed, revealing some loose rocks. The girl saw that the rocks glittered. She examined one and found it to be filled with gold. She was sitting on a basin filled with gold nuggets!

During a lull in the storm she arose and looked about. She failed to recognize a single landmark. While pondering her desperate situation, and trying to decide in which direction to strike out, she heard the faint whistle of a train in the distance. Following the horizon with her eyes, she finally picked out the trail of smoke from a locomotive. Here was hope.

Across the desert she picked her way until she finally came to the railroad tracks. But, of course, the train had long since passed by. She settled down to wait for another. Hours passed, but eventually one came and stopped in response to her signal.

Safely aboard the train, she told her story to members of the crew and showed some of the nuggets she had brought with her. She agreed to lead them across the desert to the gold-filled basin, but sometime later, when the search was made, she had to admit finally that she was just as lost as on that day when she had been caught in the storm.

It is said that a cowboy found that same basin later. He was out of water, however, and his horse was about to drop from exhaustion. He had to leave the gold and was never again able to find his way back to the spot.

(34) Lost Treasure of Redrock

VALUE: A great mass of gold and silver accumulated over a period of many years.

LOCATION: In the region between Redrock and the ghost

town of Silver Bell, northwest of Tucson, possibly in the Silver Bell Mountains, Pinal County.

AUTHENTICATION: Strictly legendary with no basis in fact.

From prehistoric times the Papago Indians have inhabited the desert lands of northern Sonora and southern Arizona as far north as the Gila River. This land was known to the Spanish as *Papagueria*. It was a region rich in mineral ores. The Papago, a name meaning "bean people" from their agricultural pursuits, were generally faithful friends to the white man, and were the guardians of the mission system established by the Spanish. To many an American pioneer, a Papago shelter was his haven in time of danger.

For a period of time longer than the oldest Papago could remember, there was a legend of a group of white men who came to live among them. The whites were friendly and kind. They did many favors for the Indians and their stay was welcomed. When the Indians learned of the white man's interest in gold and silver, they showed their appreciation by leading the white men to places where it could be found. So these strange white visitors wandered through the mountains and gathered all the gold and silver they could carry. And many of the Indians collected the precious metal and brought it to them. In time they had accumulated a great mass of gold and silver.

The headquarters of this particular band of Papago Indians was northwest of Tucson near a prominent red butte from which the town of Redrock later took its name. All of the gathered wealth was taken to a spot somewhere between this butte and the Silver Bell Mountains to the east where it was buried or hidden in a cave. This was to serve as a storehouse until the white men were ready and able to take the gold out.

One day a band of enemy Indians swooped down on the *rancheria* at Redrock and killed every white man there. The village was leveled to the ground and in time it completely disappeared. The gold and silver were lost.

77

In the Arizona State Museum at Tucson there are a number of artifacts, including some ancient spears and swords, uncovered in the vicinity of Redrock several years ago. There has been considerable controversy over the authenticity of these relics. Some claim that they are genuine and prove that this region was visited by a band of white men at a very early date. Does it prove, however, that the white men accumulated a great fortune in gold and silver which they hid as the legend states?

The theory has also been presented that these visitors were Norsemen who came to North America long before Columbus made his first voyage. If they buried treasure, the desert has kept the secret.

(35) Bandit Treasure of Stoneman Lake

VALUE: "Several thousand dollars."

LOCATION: In the vicinity of Stoneman Lake, about 35 miles south of Flagstaff, Coconino County.

AUTHENTICATION: The statement that treasure was buried here was made by a captured holdup man in modern times. It was never substantiated and it is well known that bandits frequently use this ruse in an attempt to bargain for freedom. You'll have to decide for yourself whether or not you want to accept the word of this frustrated bank robber.

Earl Nelson and Willard F. Forrester, two small-time crooks, teamed up in Kansas, and went to Clarkdale, Arizona, a small mining town on the sloping desert mesa, where, on the morning of June 21, 1928, they tried to holdup the Bank of Arizona. The fact is easily established.

In spite of the elaborate preparations made for a smooth and successful job, the bandits overlooked old Jim Roberts,

78

a rough, tough, old-time western peace officer whose 72 years hadn't slowed his draw. Roberts, a veteran of Arizona's bloody Pleasant Valley War, and a deputy sheriff of Yavapai County, happened to see the two men dash out of the bank, jump into an open-top automobile and roar away. Roberts did not know that the sack carried by one man contained $50,000 of the bank's money, but he did know that something was wrong and he reacted accordingly, which to him meant drawing his pistol and firing.

A shot caught Forrester in the head, causing the car to crash. Nelson was caught, convicted and sentenced to prison in Florence for a term of forty years. Later, he made a spectacular escape and after a chase half way across the state, he was captured. At this time he revealed that he was attempting to reach Stoneman Lake, where he said that he and his dead partner had hid several thousand dollars from a previous robbery. They had not wished to carry the money on them lest they should be picked up and questioned as they cased the Clarkdale bank job. He would give no further information.

Stoneman Lake is a large crater-like depression between precipitous walls and located in the heart of cow country and pine forests. So far as is known no treasure has ever been found there, although the area has been searched extensively. Nelson was paroled in November, 1942, and you can be certain that if he had any treasure buried there, he has long since made an attempt to recover it.

(36) Burt Alvord Treasure

VALUE: $60,000 in gold bullion and coin.

LOCATION: Somewhere along the old trail between Cochise and Willcox, Cochise County. It is generally believed that the treasure was hidden a few miles out of Cochise.

AUTHENTICATION: The hiding of the treasure by Burt
Alvord is a matter of historical record, but whether Alvord later recovered the treasure or not is not known.
It seems likely that Alvord would have been watched
closely by Wells Fargo agents after his release from
prison in the hope that he would lead them to the
treasure. There is no record of this.

On September 9, 1899, the westbound Southern Pacific
Express ground to a stop for water at the blistering hot little
town of Cochise, eleven miles southwest of Willcox. Two
masked men jumped from the trackside shadows, covered
the engine crew and ordered the engine and express car
cut from the train and pulled a short distance away. Mo-
ments later there was a shattering blast. When the smoke
cleared, one of the bandits entered the express car and threw
out several bags which were gathered and dragged into the
darkness. The sound of hoofbeats heralded the success of
the job and the escape of the outlaws.

In Willcox Constable Burt Alvord heard of the robbery
and raced to the scene. Soon he was back in Willcox and
organizing a posse with all the efficiency of a good law en-
forcement officer. The robbers had made away with a cool
$60,000 in gold coin and bullion, most of it comprising a
Wells Fargo shipment. Splitting his posse into three groups,
Alvord led one, while his two deputies, William N. "Billy"
Stiles, and William "Bob" Downing, rode off at the head of
the others.

When the outlaw trail was finally lost, the posse drifted
back to Willcox and disbanded. Only a resourceful Wells
Fargo detective named John Thacker refused to admit defeat. When word later reached Thacker that one of Alvord's
deputies, Bob Downing, was spending new $10 gold pieces
in the honky-tonks of Willcox, he began a quiet investigation. Soon he learned that all three of the Willcox officers
— Stiles, Downing and Alvord — had backgrounds that left
them open to suspicion. Despite the badges they wore, all
three had been involved in some form of outlawry.

Selecting the weakest of the trio, Billy Stiles, Thacker
went to work on him and soon had a confession. Stiles stated

that he, Alvord and Downing had, in fact, engineered the holdup, but only he, Stiles, and a cowboy named Burt Matts had carried it out. And Stiles revealed some of the startling details to detective Thacker.

Leaving the scene of the holdup, Stiles and Matts had ridden to an abandoned shack on the old trail from Willcox to Cochise. It was located, he said, only a short distance from Cochise. Here they met Alvord who brought them a change of clothing from Willcox. Alvord now gave each of the men $350 from the stolen loot and took out a like amount for Bob Downing. While Stiles and Matts waited, Alvord rode off a short distance with the money bags and hid them. Separately the three men rode back to Willcox, under instructions from Alvord to act natural and not to make a display of the gold.

It was now apparent to Thacker that only Alvord knew where the loot was hidden and he had to wrest the secret from him. Stiles agreed to assist the Wells Fargo agent. In due time Alvord, Downing and Matts were picked up and jailed. According to the plan, Alvord was placed in a cell with Stiles, but instead of carrying out his agreement with Thacker, Stiles spilled everything. With the aid of a gun smuggled into the cell, Stiles and Alvord made an escape. On their way out they released a notorious Mexican outlaw named Augustine Chacon, a man badly wanted by the newly-formed Arizona Rangers.

A few miles out of Willcox, Alvord abandoned Stiles and fled to Mexico with Chacon. It was not long before Alvord was wounded in a fight in Mexico and needed medical attention. When Arizona authorities learned of this they managed to get word to Alvord that he would be guaranteed a fair trial in Arizona if he would lure Chacon into Arizona where the Rangers could capture him. Alvord agreed and went through with the plan. Chacon was captured on Arizona soil and Alvord was brought to trial, receiving a ten-year sentence in the Territorial Prison at Yuma.

In an attempt to get Alvord to reveal where the $60,000 loot was hidden, his sentence was delayed from time to time. But Alvord persistently refused to talk and he was eventually locked up in Yuma. Meantime, the search for the treasure

81

was pressed, but without results. Even Stiles, released in return for the cooperation he had given Thacker, entered the search.

Alvord served his term and was released. Months later he turned up in Mexico, and later officials learned that he had died in Panama a wealthy man. Had he managed to elude the Wells Fargo agent who had dogged his trail after his release from prison, and reclaimed the treasure? Some believe he might have, but others think the loot from the Cochise robbery is still hidden along the old trail to Willcox.

(37) Rincon Cave Treasure

VALUE: Gold bullion and dust of an undetermined amount.

LOCATION: In a cave in the Rincon Mountains southeast of Tucson, Pima County.

AUTHENTICATION: The story is handed down by Mexicans. No documentary source is known.

Most of the Rincon Mountains are in Saguaro National Monument southeast of Tucson, and any treasure hunting done here will have to be cleared with the National Park Service. Traditionally the Park Service takes a dim view of such matters.

In a thick growth of manzanita on a steep, cliff-like side of the Rincons, there is a cave, large enough, it is said, to hold a herd of cattle. In this cave is a rich treasure consisting of gold bullion and dust, hidden there by a war party of Apache Indians.

According to the legend, a party of padres and a number of friendly Indians from Sonora were traveling through the Rincons in search of a friendly country in which to establish a *rancheria*. They found no place to their satisfaction, but they did find gold and they accumulated a great quantity of it which they packed on their horses for transport back to Sonora.

Weaving their way through the lower stretches of the Rincons on their return trip, they were suddenly attacked by a band of Apaches who were more interested in capturing horses than in stealing the gold. In the surprise of the attack, the animals were successfully driven off, but the heavily-armed Pima *conducta* put up such a stubborn fight that the Apaches were finally driven off.

Driving the stolen horses before them, the Apaches fled to the safety of a mountainside cave. From this stronghold they were able to hold out against the counter attack of the Mexicans and the Pimas.

The padres finally reached Sonora where they spread the news of the gold they had found and lost to the Apaches. They figured that the Apaches, having no use for the treasure, would leave it in the Rincon cave, but none in the party was interested in returning for it.

During the battle many of the Apaches had been killed, and their injured had been left in the cave to heal or die. Ricocheting bullets had also killed a number of the horses and cattle and they were, of course, left where they fell. The area around the cave, then, would be marked with the bleached bones of men and animals.

In modern times two Mexican cowboys were rounding up some cattle in the Rincons when a calf one of them was chasing suddenly disappeared behind a mazanita bush. An investigation led to the discovery of a cave entrance. The Mexicans cautiously entered it. Scattered over the floor were the bones of humans and animals. The *vaqueros* suspected that it was a treasure cave, but having the Mexican's dread superstition of treasure that does not belong to them, they rode away without further investigation.

When white ranchers heard of the cave, they conducted a search but found nothing. What happened to the gold taken from the padres' horses? Your guess is as good as mine, and mine is that there never was any.

(38) Lost Coyotero Mine

VALUE: Unknown.

LOCATION: Very vaguely placed in the northern end of Tonto Basin, close to the Mogollon Rim, Pinal County.

AUTHENTICATION: We have the word of certain members of the Aubrey party that they traded with the Coyoteros for free gold which these Indians seemed to have in unlimited quantities. It was assumed by the party that this gold was secured someplace in the vicinity. This is a broad assumption, for many Indians, after they learned of the white man's passion for gold, used it for trading purposes and may have carried it for that purpose from one end of the state to the other.

Felix (Francois Xavier) Aubrey had many hair-raising adventures on the plains of the early West, but is best remembered as the little Frenchman who wagered $1000 that he could ride horseback from Santa Fe, New Mexico, to Independence, Missouri, in eight days. He made it in three days less than that time, killing several horses enroute. Later, he repeated the feat in even less time and won some sort of notoriety as the "Skimmer of the Plains."

Aubrey was an experienced frontiersman and had survived many close brushes with hostile Indians. He should have known that the Coyotero (wolf-men) Apaches, no matter how outwardly friendly, were the sworn enemies of the white man and extremely treacherous. Nevertheless, while riding with a party of men through the Coyotero country, close to the Mogollon Rim in Tonto Basin, a land of wild and striking beauty, he mistook the actions of a band of Coyoteros and almost led his men into a fatal trap. Only the modern Colt pistols they were armed with saved their lives.

When a small group of stray Apaches later appeared at Aubrey's camp the white men were naturally suspicious of their real intentions. They wanted to trade for food, tobacco

84

and clothing and they had a supply of gold nuggets to offer in exchange. Aubrey wrote in his journal later that they received $1500 in nuggets for some cast-off rags.

There were stories among the frontiersmen that these and other Indians used gold bullets for hunting, and Aubrey tells of seeing an Indian put four gold bullets in a gun to shoot a rabbit. There is little doubt but that the Coyotero Apaches had a rich source of gold, but the story of gold bullets is as old as the invention of the gun. A lot of the early Westerners were well known masters of the art of tall-story telling. Gold carried by the Indians was usually in the form of free gold, meaning that it was picked up on the surface of placer deposits. Aware that it had a real trading value, the Indians naturally kept its source a tribal secret.

The theory has been argued that the Coyoteros' source of gold was that found by the Adams party, and then "lost" when the prospectors were driven away by the Indians. The mine became known as the Lost Adams Diggings and is one of the most famous of the Southwest's many lost mines. It may have been, but it lacks proof. Nor could the Aubrey party give the faintest clue where the Apaches they traded with secured their plentiful supply of gold. Anyone who searches for the Lost Coyotero Mine will have a lot of area to cover.

(39) John Nummel's Lost Mine

VALUE: A gold ledge of unknown value, but described as the richest ever seen by the finder.

LOCATION: Approximately in the center of a triangle with its points at Norton's Landing on the Colorado River, Yuma Wash and the old Red Cloud Mine, Yuma County.

AUTHENTICATION: The old miner who told this story spent half a lifetime searching for this mine which he found and lost. We have his word for it. He told the story to many old cronies who vouched for its truth.

John Nummel died in 1948, so the memory of his lost mine in the Chocolate Range north of Yuma is still fresh in the minds of a lot of people. He had come to Arizona from Germany in the late 1870's or early 1800's. Nobody was ever quite sure, nor does it make any difference. But whatever the date, and almost up to the time of his death, he worked in most of the mines in southwestern Yuma County, walking across the hot desert from one to another when he did not have a burro.

Nummel often worked for the Red Cloud Mine along the Colorado above Picacho, and for the La Fortuna Mine on the western slopes of the Gila Mountains southwest of Yuma. As he followed the old Red Cloud-Fortuna trail between the two mines, he prospected along the way, frequently straying many miles from the trail. Sometimes he found promising mineral leads.

Sometime between 1895 and 1900, Nummel left the employ of the Red Cloud and started out on the long walk to the Fortuna. It was a distance of about forty miles and there was little trail then to follow. Nummel later told the story. It was hot as blazes, he recalled. He sat down in a skimpy patch of shade cast by a palo verde tree for a swig of water from his canteen. Out of habit, and without thinking of what he was doing, he took out his hammer and broke off a chunk of a nearby ledge. To his amazement, it was richly colored with free gold. Without tools or supplies he could not immediately take advantage of his find, nor did he want to return to the Red Cloud, for he had quit in a huff.

He pocketed the piece of ore and made the decision to proceed to La Fortuna, take a job there and save enough money to develop his find. It was not long before he had a disagreement with the Fortuna foreman, however, so he quit and started back again for the Red Cloud, walking as usual. A series of circumstances now occurred which took

86

him from his usual route, and before he knew it his rich find was lost. He was offered a ride to Yuma and accepted, caught another ride on the California side to Picacho, crossed over to Red Cloud for a drink in the booming camp and went on a first-class drunk. To a miner this meant one that lasted until the last penny was gone.

Broke again, Nummel went to work for the Red Cloud, and here he stayed until he had managed to save enough money for supplies and tools. When he was finally ready to work the rich ledge, he could find no trace of it. He could not locate a single familiar marker. In a region that he had tramped many times, everything seemed to have changed. He could not explain it.

Between jobs he searched. He swore he could see that ledge just as it was — the trees and the rocks he had covered it with. Up until the very last years of his life he never gave up, and he never succeeded.

The Red Cloud Mine is located at the southern tip of the Trigo Mountains, west of the Chocolates and just north of Picacho, California. The La Fortuna Mine was on the west side of the Gila Mountains, about 16 miles southwest of Yuma. Norton's Landing is 52 miles north of Yuma, the landing place on the Colorado for freight for the Red Cloud Mine. In the center of a triangle drawn from Norton's Landing to the Red Cloud Mine to Yuma Wash where it enters the Colorado, you should be close to John Nummel's lost ledge of gold.

(40) Castle Dome Lost Mine

VALUE: Unknown quantity of gold ore assaying $3600 to the ton.

LOCATION: Somewhere between the old King of Arizona Mine and the site of Ehrenberg on the Colorado River, Yuma County.

AUTHENTICATION: None that can be traced and so far as this writer knows, few people have tried to.

An old Mexican spent many months prospecting around the Castle Dome Range north of Yuma. His success was very discouraging. One morning as he loafed at the old King of Arizona (Kofa) Mine, which was located about 15 miles northeast of Castle Dome Peak, he decided that he had had enough. He loaded his burro, gave it a kick in the rump and headed straight for Ehrenberg on the Colorado River.

In crossing a narrow gully the old prospector noticed an outcropping that looked interesting. He broke off a piece of the ore, placed it in his pocket and trudged on, an act that proved also that he had rocks in his head. Without making any notes on the landmarks in the region he simply renewed the journey to Ehrenberg. Oh, well, that's why we have so many lost mines!

Months later he was in California and still carrying that piece of ore. One day he got around to having it assayed, and it showed $3600 to the ton! Even the assayer liked that. He teamed up with the Mexican and the two made extensive plans for locating and mining the ore. Now the story falls flat on its face. The two partners just never got around to searching for that gold, which makes it the most unwanted lost mine we ever heard of.

(41) Buried Treasure of Bicuner

VALUE: Unknown quantity of mined placer gold in a raw-hide bag.

LOCATION: Near Squaw Peak in the Laguna Mountains not far distant from the Colorado River, Yuma County.

AUTHENTICATION: The history of the origin of this

gold is clouded with myth and tradition. There is some reason to believe that the Mission Bicuner did accumulate a considerable quantity of gold which would have been an easy thing to do, for it was located in an area that was rich in minerals and later produced millions. The story has been handed down, however, by Indians and Mexicans and many versions of it are found. Such persistency over the years would seem to indicate that there may be some basis of fact in the story. But even if the padres of Bicuner did accumulate the gold brought in by their Indian charges, there is a controversy as to its eventual fate. Some stories place the buried gold near the old mission site on the California side of the Colorado; some on the Arizona side, and some say that the hoard of gold was dumped into the river, in which case it is certainly lost for all time.

Late in the year 1780, the Spanish established the mission-pueblo of San Pedro y San Pablo de Bicuner on the California side of the Colorado River, a short distance below Laguna Dam and at a site that is now bisected by the All-American Canal. When the canal was constructed the ruins of Bicuner were uncovered, but nothing remains today.

Above the mission on the California side were the famous Potholes gold placers which produced at least $2,000,000, and across the river in Arizona was the even richer Laguna Placers, where the ground once was covered with gold, and it could be picked up by the bucketful. These two places are the traditional source of the Bicuner gold.

Less than a year after the founding of Bicuner, the Indians (Yumas who called themselves Quechans) burned and pillaged the infant mission, killed or drove off the soldiers and priests, and took all the women and children prisoners for later ransoming.

When the Franciscan historian, Father Zephryin Engelhardt, wrote of his visit to the mission site in 1886, he related the story of the gold as it was told to him by the Quechans. He seemed not to have believed the story, and this

90

would have been natural, for every mission in the South-west had its legend of a lost mine of buried treasure.

There is strong reason to believe that the Bicuner colonists did find the Potholes placers, and perhaps, too, the Laguna gold field. They could hardly have missed them. And the Spanish colonists were not the people to ignore gold. That is what they were here for in the first place.

Having accumulated a considerable quantity by the time of the revolt, the suddenness of the attack took the padres completely by surprise. Whether or not they had time to hide the gold at the mission, or whether the Indians found it and hid it later is a question of controversy. Some old stories have it that the gold was taken to the river and dumped to prevent it falling into the hands of the Indians. There hardly seems to be any point in this as the gold was then definitely lost.

According to other stories, the Indians transported the gold across the river, held a big pow-wow, and buried the gold wrapped in rawhide bags. After filling the hole they restored the ground around it to its natural condition so that it would blend into the surroundings. The question has been asked: Why did the Indians go to so much trouble to conceal this gold when other lay on the ground all around?

(42) Cienega Benders' Treasure

VALUE: $75,000, possibly more.

LOCATION: Near the old stage station of Cienega, which was in or near the present village of Pantano, on U. S. 80, about 30 miles southeast of Tucson, Pima County.

AUTHENTICATION: There is sufficient historic reason to believe that treasure was buried here at the old Cienega stage station, but whether or not it was found by the four mysterious men is a question only they — all long since departed from this world — could answer.

The most important station between Tucson, Arizona, and Silver City, New Mexico, on the old Butterfield stage route that connected El Paso and San Diego, was La Cienega, in the heart of a country infested with Indians and robbers. Not to be confused with another Cienega station located about three miles from the present railroad station in Pantano, La Cienega was located in a box canyon to the east of the station. This geographical location played directly into the hands of robbers. In 1872 La Cienega was operated by a small band of desperadoes known locally as "Benders," presumably from the many drunken sprees they held there. They were employees of the stage company until their depredations were discovered. Long since abandoned, the station site is difficult to locate without a local guide.

The mysteries surrounding the Cienega station have never been cleared up. Murders, robberies and holdups regularly occurred there with little or no interference from the authorities. On a little hill back of the station the outlaws kept a private cemetery for the benefit of their victims, and for many years a single shaft here marked the graves of 16 unknown dead.

Most of the crimes committed in the vicinity, and thought to have been the works of the Benders, were made to appear as outrages of the Apaches. When the Benders were finally killed off, Indian paraphernalia was found, which was said to have been donned by the outlaws when holding up stages. Their most widely known crime was the capture of $75,000 enroute from El Paso to San Diego and in charge of a small government guard. These were the funds of a U. S. Army paymaster. The three men who attempted to convoy it past the Cienega station in a buckboard were suddenly jumped by Indians. It turned out that the "Indians" were really Americans dressed in Indian costumes.

At the peak of their career it was impossible for the Benders to get out of the country with this loot and other wealth that they had acquired, so most of it was buried at a secret spot near the station.

92

While American authorities did little to prevent these horrible crimes that were blamed on the Apaches, the Indians took matters into their own hands in the fall of 1873. One dark night the Apaches gathered in the surrounding hills, and at daybreak swarmed down on the station and killed every man present. It was the last of the Benders.

Treasure hunters have made many vain efforts to locate the hidden treasure of the Cienega Benders. According to a story in an 1897 issue of the Yuma *Sentinel*, four men arrived in Yuma in that year. They said that they were from San Francisco, but said little else. They remained several days, ostensibly outfitting for an extensive expedition. One day they rode out of town toward the east.

Two weeks later the same four men arrived in Tucson, bringing with them several well-filled sacks which they said contained ore samples they had picked up in the Rincon Mountains. They disposed of their outfits and left for Los Angeles, taking their ore with them. The belief was general at the time that these sacks contained treasure from the Cienega stage station.

Several teamsters brought word to Tucson that four mysterious men had lived in the abandoned Cienega station for several days, during which time they had maintained a close guard over all passing traffic. As soon as they had departed in the night, some teamsters investigated the station and the nearby grounds. They found a number of holes both inside and outside the adobe structure. Some time later a party of ranchers probing the vicinity found $300 in American coins hidden under the stones of the old fireplace. This find stirred many other and more extensive searches, but as far as is known, nothing further was found.

If the four mystery men found the treasure, how did they know where to dig, since all the Benders were thought to have been killed by the Apaches? Old-timers thought for a long time that the treasure was still there, but they couldn't explain what the four strangers took with them in sacks to Los Angeles. Certainly it wasn't necessary to stage ore that distance!

It should be pointed out that some controversy exists as to the exact location of the La Cienega station. Conkling, an excellent authority, says that it was 1¼ miles west of Irene siding on the Southern Pacific railroad, and that the tracks are laid on the exact site of the old station, but that, in 1947, some nearby ruins were still visible. It should not be difficult to locate in any event, and a thorough electronic search here should prove interesting.

(43) Lost Mine of the Two Skeletons

VALUE: Gold ore of an unknown quantity, but assaying $35,000 to the ton.

LOCATION: A few miles north of the Superstition Mountains, on a straight line between the southern base of Mt. Ord and the northern slopes of the Superstitions. There are two Mt. Ords in Arizona. This story refers to the Mt. Ord on the Gila-Maricopa County line, in the Mazatzal Range.

AUTHENTICATION: There is little reason to believe that this is anything more than just another lost mine story.

A party of Pima Indians were returning from Mt. Ord, in the Mazatzal Mountains, to their reservation near the northern slopes of the Superstitions. They had escorted a party of eastern hunters to the Mazatzals, and were now riding leisurely homeward. They followed the Indian custom of traveling in as straight a line as possible.

A few miles north of the Superstition Mountains the Indian riders came upon the skeletons of two white men, bleached white by the sun and scattered over a wide area by predatory animals. In their midst the Indians found a shallow mining shaft, and in the vicinity were their tools, utensils, and a small pile of ore which the Indians found to be sprinkled generously with gold. They picked up a few of the larger pieces to take home with them.

94

Skirting the western side of the Superstitions, they came to a water hole at the north end of the San Tan (Santa Ana) Mountains where they stopped for the night. Later that evening an old prospector stopped at their water hole. After filling his water containers, he paused for a chat with the friendly Pimas. He noticed the few rocks they had brought with them and examined one with the true prospector's curiosity. He saw at once that it was rich in gold, but not wanting to arouse the Indians, he carelessly threw it aside, saying that it had no value.

That night the prospector camped a short distance away, and in the morning when he saw the Indians break camp and ride away, he returned to their campsite. As he had hoped, they had left a few pieces of the ore. He now examined the rocks thoroughly and verified his first opinion. Knowing that the Indians had come from Mt. Ord, he started to backtrack them. This was not difficult until he came to the high rocky country north of the Superstitions. There all signs were lost in the boulders. He had to give up for the moment.

In Phoenix the ore he had kept assayed $35,000 to the ton. He told no one where he had secured it. Soon he returned to the area and continued his search. The years passed and, as men do, he grew old. Still he searched, and then came the day when he could no longer stand the rigorous life. Now he told others. They searched, but never found the two skeletons and the lost shaft. It is now your turn.

(44) Lost Six-Shooter Mine

VALUE: An unknown quantity of gold ore assaying $25,000 to the ton.

LOCATION: Between Quartzsite and the old copper mining camp of Planet, which was 15 miles northeast of Parker on the (Bill) Williams River, Yuma County.

AUTHENTICATION: There is an almost identical lost mine story with its locale in California. There are two "lost six-shooter" mines in Arizona; one is a gold mine, the other silver. There appears to be no solid foundation of fact in any of them.

The first copper mine worked in Arizona by Americans is claimed to have been the Planet, discovered by a man named Ryland in 1863, near Planet Peak in the Buckskin Mountains. One day the superintendent of this mine had to escort a party of eastern stockholders to the stage station at Quartzsite. His mission ended, he was on his way back to the Planet when he was caught in a whipping sandstorm that blacked out the sun.

Both man and horse became lost in the storm and wandered aimlessly for several days. When further travel became pointless, he stopped to rest by a ledge of rock that protruded from the sand. It offered some welcome protection from the storm. He curled up at its base and pulled his coat over his head, wondering. if the storm would ever abate, and if he would have the strength to go on when it did.

When the storm finally blew itself out and he struggled to regain his feet, he noticed that the ledge was quartz and that it was sprinkled with free gold. He broke off a few pieces and put them in his pocket. Then he made a written description of the location which he also placed in his pocket. In order to mark the location for easy finding when he returned, he took off his two six-shooters, placed them on his coat and left them on the ledge.

Heading his weakened horse in what he supposed was the direction of the Planet Mine, the superintendent slumped into the saddle and tried to hold on. When the horse appeared at the mining settlement without its rider a search party left to locate the missing superintendent. His body was found on the desert where he had fallen from his horse. In his pockets they found the samples of ore taken from the ledge and the note describing its location. When the ore was assayed it showed $25,000 to the ton, but the Lost Six-Shooter Mine has never been found. Old-timers, who always have an explanation for such things, say that it is covered with sand.

In its details, this story fails to ring true. Any man acquainted with the desert, as the mine superintendent must have been, would never discard his coat if he expected to spend a night on the desert. Nor would any man leave his six-shooter to mark a ledge. This man left two!

(45) Sander's Lost Mine

VALUE: An extremely rich dike of gold-filled quartz.

LOCATION: On Coon Creek, about 10 miles from its head in the northern slopes of the Sierra Anchas, Gila County.

AUTHENTICATION: The Arizona *Star* reported this story in 1912. It was well known at the time, but has been almost forgotten in recent years. Whether or not it is merely an old-timers' tale — there were many of them — is difficult to determine. Efforts to locate any records of Sanders have failed.

In 1879 a soldier named Sanders was stationed at Fort Apache. Like most troops in that region he spent most of his time in the saddle chasing Indians. In September of that year he was detailed to scout a band of Indians suspected of stealing cattle from a ranch on the Salt River. His trail led him toward the Sierra Anchas (wide mountains), north of Roosevelt Lake in Gila County.

After skirting around the eastern end of the mountains he came to Coon Creek and traveled in its bed, now almost dry. About ten miles from its head he came to a waterfall over a ledge. The obstruction forced him to climb the steep canyon wall to get around it. Walking his horse up the incline, he came to a slight ridge and sat down to rest.

Soldiers were usually on the lookout for gold and silver

deposits, and Sanders was no different. He looked at the rock he was seated on and saw that it was a large block of quartz, and that the entire ridge was actually a quartz dike. He examined the rock and found that it contained gold. He realized that the ledge was part of the mother lode and proved this to himself by picking up rock after rock in the vicinity. It was rich in gold. Unable to believe his good luck, he packed all the ore he could carry and continued on his journey, careful to observe the country carefully for landmarks.

Back at Fort Apache, Sanders tried to obtain a discharge, but was told that he would have to serve out the remainder of his enlistment, about two years. His discharge finally came just as the expeditions were taking the field to search for Miner's Lost Mine. He feared that it might be his quartz dike they were seeking. In an effort to protect himself he joined a party of about 300 men and proceeded with them into the Sierra Anchas. When they came to a point near the head of Coon Creek, Sanders was fearful that someone in the large party might stumble upon his ledge.

While in this area one of the party was injured by a falling rock and the gang moved on to a better camp at Oak Springs. Sanders watched his chance and found an opportunity to sneak away. He found his ledge again and gathered some more ore specimens. He was not missed and he kept a strict silence regarding his find. When the Miner party moved out of the area, Sanders left it and went to Phoenix. It was here that he showed his specimens to several men, but revealed nothing of where the ore had been picked up.

Some six months after the Miner party disbanded (Miner was accused of being a fraud), Sanders left Phoenix for Fort McDowell with three other men. At old Camp Reno they met a party of soldiers who warned them to turn back because of a band of Indians on the warpath. Two members of the group heeded the advice, but Sanders and a lone companion proceeded on. Neither was ever seen alive again. About three weeks after their disappearance became known, a search party left Phoenix and trailed the two men to Walnut Springs in the western reaches of the Sierra Anchas. Here the trail was completely lost and the searchers gave up.

Years later two cattlemen were riding down Coon Creek

when they came upon a human skull. In searching for the rest of the skeleton, they found two partially buried skeletons which they took to be white men. Nearby they located the foundation and ruins of a cabin. Amid the ashes they uncovered half-burned timbers. Obviously the cabin had been fired by Indians.

In digging a grave for the remains of the two men, they dug up a rock that contained gold. This they took back to Phoenix with them and cleaned it of its crust of dirt. One side appeared to have been cut or ground with a hard substance, and one of the other sides presented a perfect surface of gold on which had been carved with a knife the letters: S A N D E R S.

(46) Treasure of Skeleton Canyon

VALUE: One of the dying bandits placed a value of $3,000,000 on the treasure which consists in part of a cigar box filled with diamonds, 39 solid bars of pure gold, 90,000 minted Mexican dollars (some say they were gold; others silver), and two life-sized statuary figures of pure gold.

LOCATION: Probably in Skeleton Canyon in the Peloncillo Mountains, Cochise County.

AUTHENTICATION: The story is full of many controversial points and becomes involved with another treasure story located in Texas. There is, nevertheless, considerable reason to believe that the treasure was actually buried. Whether it has been recovered or not is another question.

A sign in Apache, Arizona, reads: "SKELETON CANYON — 8 MILES," and this is the scene of one of the most persistent buried treasure stories in the Southwest. Through

100

Skeleton Canyon wound the old Smugglers' Trail from Sonora, across a corner of New Mexico and into southeastern Arizona. It was a trail of blood, murder and intrigue. Across this trail smugglers came with their stolen goods to be sold in Tucson and other markets. And along this trail American outlaws waylaid the smugglers to steal their riches.

In nearby wild and reckless Galeyville, now a ghost town, ruled the king of the outlaws, William Graham, alias Curly Bill Brocius. Posing as a cattleman, Curly Bill led his private band of raiders in their favorite pastime of robbing the Mexican smugglers. It was profitable work, too. On a hot July day in 1881, Curly Bill and his gang swooped down from the canyon walls, slaughtered the members of a smuggling train, killed all the pack animals and made off with $75,000 in silver, which they are said to have spent in the honkey-tonks of Galeyville in less than a month.

A few months after this successful haul, Jim Hughes, a Curly Bill henchman, returned from a spying trip into Sonora with the news that the Mexicans were about to send an unusually rich shipment of stolen merchandise through Skeleton Canyon. But when Hughes arrived in Galeyville to report to Curly Bill, the outlaw leader was away on a mysterious errand. No one knew when he would return.

As time drew near for the arrival of the smugglers in Skeleton Canyon, Hughes decided that he could no longer wait for Curly Bill if he was to intercept the Mexicans. He recruited seven of Galeyville's most unsavory characters and decided to pull the job himself. Among his crew of hijackers were Zwing (Richard) Hunt, a mule skinner turned outlaw, and a young desperado named Billy Grounds (Arthur Burcher). Hughes swore the seven men to secrecy.

When the Mexican pack train came winding down through the wooded canyon, the eight outlaws watched from their place of concealment along the canyon wall. Perhaps there were as many as thirty mules in the train, and riding on their backs was the richest treasure ever smuggled across the border. They plodded past the Devil's Kitchen rock formation, and near the western entrance to the canyon the leader of the 15-man train drew up and ordered a halt for lunch and a siesta.

The roar of gunfire suddenly exploding from the canyon wall took the Mexicans completely by surprise and they scattered in wild panic. Mules not yet relieved of their packs, stampeded in fright, scattering the contents of their packs across the canyon floor. Out of the ambush rode the outlaws in hot pursuit of the treasure. Accounts differ as to whether or not one or two of the Mexicans escaped. Of the outlaws, only Zwing Hunt received a slight wound.

After the far-scattered loot had been gathered up, there was such a huge quantity that hauling it to Galeyville on their horses was out of the question. At the mouth of the canyon the bandits dug an enormous hole and buried the treasure. They then rode to Galeyville to report their success.

Obviously such a great amount of treasure so carelessly buried was to appeal to the greed of the outlaws. Upon learning that Curly Bill was still absent from Galeyville, some of the boys began to get ideas about cutting the outlaw leader out. Jim Hunt presented a doublecross plan to Zwing Hunt and Billy Grounds. While he remained in Galeyville to allay suspicions, they were to ride to Skeleton Canyon and secretly re-bury the treasure. Then only the three would know of its hiding place. When they all returned with Curly Bill to recover the treasure from its original hiding place, they would feign amazement at its disappearance.

Accordingly, Zwing Hunt and Grounds secured an old Mexican with a wagon and two horses and they rode out to Skeleton Canyon, dug up the treasure, removed it to a new site, presumably in Skeleton Canyon, and reburied it in a deep hole dug by the Mexican laborer. When the hole had been filled, he was killed in cold blood and his body disposed of. Over the spot where the treasure was buried the two horses were killed and the wagon was burned. Now only Hunt and Grounds knew where the treasure was buried. Instead of returning immediately to Galeyville, they rode to Jack Chandler's ranch near Charleston. Here they were cornered by a posse and Billy Grounds was killed. Zwing Hunt was so badly wounded that he had to be hospitalized in Tombstone. The secret of the treasure was his alone.

When Jim Hughes learned of Hunt's plight, he rushed to Tombstone to protect his interest in the treasure. He did not know where the treasure was buried, and if Hunt should die, there was a good chance that he never would know where it was hidden. But when Hughes arrived in Tombstone, Hunt was gone. He had fled the hospital under circumstances that have never been cleared up. Hughes was now certain that he had been doublecrossed. Sometime later Hunt's brother, Hugh, showed up in Arizona and spread the word that he had assisted Zwing in fleeing the hospital. He described the escape and said further that Zwing had been killed when they were attacked by Apaches. Jim Hughes was one who doubted this story.

There are others who believe that Zwing Hunt was not killed at all, but had successfully made his way to his home in San Antonio, Texas. He was suffering terribly from his wounds, and the doctor despaired of saving his life. Hunt called an uncle to his bedside and related the whole story of the buried treasure. Before he died he drew a map and gave the uncle directions for locating the treasure.

The directions were simple: The treasure was buried near the foot of Davis Mountain, he said, from the summit of which could be seen an open stretch of New Mexico. A short distance from the mountain was a curving canyon, its west wall covered with wood, while the east wall was bare and rocky. Through the canyon meandered a small stream. A ten-foot drop in the canyon floor created a cascade in which he and Grounds had bathed after burying the treasure. Nearby were two springs, about a mile apart. One was called Silver, and the other Gum. The treasure was buried near Silver Spring. Twenty steps east of the actual treasure site, was a square-shaped rock about three feet high. On this rock they had chiseled two crosses, one above the other. Over the burial spot would be found the bones of two horses and the charred remains of a burned wagon.

All one had to do now was to find Davis Mountain and start from there. But it turned out that Hunt and Grounds themselves had named the mountain after a pal they had

103

buried there. It could have been any one of hundreds of peaks in the Peloncillos.

Hunt's uncle searched for the treasure and it is said that Hugh Hunt spent almost thirty years combing the mountains around Skeleton Canyon without success. The two springs have never been located, nor has the waterfall. Presumably they could have dried up. The remains of a burned wagon were found, but there was no treasure. A grave was located at the foot of Harris Mountain, but was this Davis?

A mysterious old German appeared in Skeleton Canyon in the 1890's. He built a little hut at the forks above the Devil's Kitchen and lived there alone. Who he was or what he was doing there was never known, except that he dug all over the canyon looking for buried treasure taken from Mexican smugglers. One day he simply vanished and was never seen again.

The contradictions are many, and the facts are few. But of this much we are sure. Outlaws did hold up smuggling trains passing through Skeleton Canyon. The bleached bones of dead smugglers and their mules are still occasionally seen in the western entrance to the canyon. Human skulls found along the valley floor were used as soap basins at the Ross Sloan ranch for many years, and an occasional Mexican dollar is still found. About ten years after the Hunt-Grounds attack on the smuggler train, a government official and a cowboy, while riding up Skeleton Canyon, chanced upon an old rawhide pouch. The cowboy gave it a reckless kick and out tumbled several thousand dollars in gold coins. We think there are few more potential treasure sites than Skeleton Canyon, provided, of course, that the treasure has not already been found.

(47) Frenchmen's Lost Mine

VALUE: Unknown.

LOCATION: In the Tenhachape Pass area of the Eagle Tail Mountains, northeast of Yuma, Yuma County. Other locations given, however, include the Harquahala, Little Harquahala, White Tank, Kofa, Palomas and Little Horn Mountains. It is evident that the mine is pretty well lost.

AUTHENTICATION: The evidence is the flimsiest kind and no two accounts are in agreement on the broadest details. Unless someone can turn up with the old records of Hooper & Co. (mercantile store in Yuma, later Hooper, Barney & Co., long out of business), it seems that the facts, if any, in this story can never be determined.

One day in 1864 (different accounts give different dates) a party of three roughly dressed Frenchmen stopped their pack animals in front of Hooper & Company's store in Yuma. Removing some sacks from their mules they stepped inside and deposited $8000 worth of gold. A few days later, after purchasing supplies, the strangers mounted and rode out of town toward the east. The strangers had not gone unnoticed in Yuma and when the word of their rich deposit got out, there was considerable speculation as to who the men were, and more particularly, where they had obtained their gold. Five Mexicans decided to find out. They trailed the Frenchmen east to Agua Caliente where they found them camped at the hot springs almost on the Yuma-Maricopa County line and directly south of the Eagle Tail Mountains, so named because of three columnar shafts resembling the tail of an eagle.

The following morning the three Frenchmen set out in a northerly direction, closely followed by the Mexicans. Suddenly they reversed their direction and faced the Mexi-

105

cans with the knowledge that they were being trailed. The Frenchmen then returned to Agua Caliente where they went through the motions of establishing a permanent camp. The ruse worked. During the night they silently packed and rode away, leaving the Mexicans fast asleep.

Not to be outsmarted, the Mexicans took up the trail as soon as the three Frenchmen were missed. They followed them into the Eagle Tail Mountains to a point where their tracks took off in three different directions. This was enough for the Mexicans. They returned to Yuma where they related their experience. The Frenchmen were never seen nor heard of again, nor did they ever reclaim their $8000 deposit at Hooper's store. It was assumed that they met with disaster of some kind.

In 1873 when King S. Woolsey, pioneer Indian fighter, was chasing a band of Apaches across western Arizona, his party passed through the Eagle Tails. Following the trail which crossed through Tenhachape Pass, they came upon a pile of rich ore. Obviously it had been placed there by parties unknown, and no attempt had been made to conceal it. The ore was taken to Yuma and there it was identified as the same type as deposited by the three Frenchmen several years previously. The only explanation was that the Frenchmen, suddenly overtaken by hostile Indians, had dumped their gold ore to better facilitate their escape. Had they not been chased down and killed, it was reasoned that they would have later recovered their ore.

In 1868, A. H. Peeples, a pioneer Arizona mining man, while passing through the Harquahala Mountains, straight north of the Eagle Tails, came upon three Frenchmen working a placer near their camp. Sometime later Peeples again passed through the region on his return trip and found the camp burned. He located one skeleton which he thought to be that of a white man, but was not sure. In the slopes of these mountains are several noted mines. There is no explanation in the discrepancy of the dates.

In the early part of 1889 a middle-aged Mexican arrived in Yuma and hired a local character known as Old Bill Bear to haul supplies and water into the Eagle Tail Mountains for him. He told Old Bill that he had run away from home

106

when a boy of twelve and had met a three-man pack train southbound out of the Eagle Tails. They gave him a job as a cook and later he went into the Eagle Tails with them to their permanent camp. Each morning the three men left and returned that evening with a collection of gold nuggets which they stored in cans. One day the boy followed the miners and found them busily engaged in working a placer about a quarter of a mile from the camp. His presence was discovered and he was punished. That evening they changed the hiding place of the cans of gold.

The Mexican boy stayed around a few days, but he was closely watched. Finally he slipped out of camp and returned to Mexico. He was now on his way to the mine which he thought he could find without any trouble. After an absence of some length, the Mexican and Old Bill returned to Yuma. He failed to locate the mine which is often thought to have been the mine of the three Frenchmen.

(48) Lost Mine of the Silver Stairway

VALUE: Unknown quantity of silver ore.

LOCATION: In a small depression on the desert floor between Quijotoa and Gunsight Wells, at the northern end of the Ajo Mountains, Pima County.

AUTHENTICATION: Too fantastic to really be considered.

After the Civil War an unnamed easterner went West to regain his health. This is a new twist; most of them left to get away from a nagging wife, some burdensome debts, or were simply staying a step ahead of the law. Others just wanted to feel their oats in new surroundings. Be that as it may, this frail little fellow, while waiting for nature to patch up his ails, planned to prospect for gold. He finally landed in Tucson and quickly took up with a partner. They outfitted and set out hopefully for the little mining camp of Quijotoa at the northern end of the Quijotoa Mountains.

Luck was with the partners and before long they found a rich claim from which they took considerable wealth. Soon they were so rich that they dissolved the partnership and each man struck out for himself. The frail man, having now regained his full health, was crossing the desert wastes between Gunsight (a camp named after the famed Lost Gunsight Mine in Death Valley, and now usually mapped as Gunsight Wells), when he was attracted to a large number of boulders scattered across the floor of a small depression. His examination disclosed that they were rich in silver. A search of the area revealed no ledge, and they were too scattered to have been dropped there by other miners. He broke the rocks up, packed them on mules and took them to Yuma. From there they were shipped down the Colorado River to the Gulf of California and transhipped to the east coast where they were milled.

The proceeds of the ore made the lucky prospector a rich man. He built a fine home and topped it off with a staircase of solid silver, made from the metal taken from those rocks. He was so pleased with this vulgar show of wealth that he never returned to Arizona to reclaim more of the marvelously rich ore that still waits today for another finder.

You can believe this bunk if you wish. This writer has no intention of passing it off as anything else.

(49) Geronimo's Lost Gold Mine

VALUE: A fabulously rich vein of gold in the side of a canyon wall and an unknown number of gold bars stored in the mine's tunnel.

108

LOCATION: In the Sycamore Canyon region, close to the Verde River, between Jerome and Perkinsville, Yavapai County.

AUTHENTICATION: In spite of the fact that Geronimo was a notorious liar, and we only have his word for it that he knew of rich gold deposits, it must be concluded that he probably did. His people had for centuries wandered the deserts and mountains of Arizona, and little escaped their searching eyes. It is almost certain that this tough, wily old chief knew where there was gold — not just one place, but several. Whether this is one of his gold "mines" or not is left to your judgment.

While a prisoner of the United States Government in Fort Sill, Oklahoma, in 1886, Geronimo offered to exchange his knowledge of gold deposits for his freedom. He had tricked the army so many times that the acceptance of his offer could not be considered. Furthermore, the military had no stomach for meeting his warriors in the mountain passes again. Some have tried to establish that he actually made a deal with certain officers at Fort Sill, but this seems unlikely. At least, he never secured his freedom.

Geronimo, of course, was not his real name, but one given to him by the Mexicans, a Spanish word which translates into Jerome. A full-blooded Apache, and extremely proud of it, he was born in Janos, Mexico, and given the Apache name of Goy-ath-lay, which, ironically enough, meant "one who yawns." Once he had declared war on the white man, he spent precious little time yawning.

It is said that Geronimo told a·friend at Fort Sill (if he had any friends there, they must have been fellow Indians), that his source of gold was located in the Verde River country. The vein, according to stories, was first found by the Apaches, and later seized by Spanish soldiers. The main body of these troops moved on to New Mexico, only a few remaining behind to build an *arrastre* and a smelter for refining the ore.

The angered Apaches could not stand up to the Spanish

109

weapons, so they fought a war of attrition. From the canyon walls, they rolled boulders into the camp. They attacked from ambush when they were certain of success. They made frightening sounds at night, and they generally did everything they could to keep the Spanish in a constant state of turmoil. Nevertheless, the Spaniards refused to be driven away. They tunneled into the canyon wall where the vein became so rich that the ore could be taken direct to the smelter.

When a large number of gold bars had been smelted, it was decided to carry them to Mexico on mules and return with sufficient force to drive the molesting Apaches from the canyon. In packing out of the canyon, the Indians attacked furiously, killing all of the Spaniards with the exception of two.

The two surviving miners waited their chance and returned to the canyon. They hid the bars of gold in the tunnel and closed the mine. At night they made their way out and finally reached Tubac, where they rested for the long trip to Mexico City. There they told of the mine and supplied maps to others. It is said that a party of prospectors later found the remains of an old stone building and evidence of mining activity in one of the many small canyons emptying into Sycamore Creek, but they found no mine.

Geronimo's lost mine pops up every place. It is in Texas It is in New Mexico, and a half-dozen locations in Arizona. Where do I think it is? Well, if there is one, I favor the Guadalupe Mountains of New Mexico, but I can contain my excitement.

(50) Treasure of the Mountain of Noise

VALUE: Thirty tons of silver ore in sacks in a mine with ore of unknown quantity and value.

LOCATION: Near Cerro Ruido Mountain in the Pajarito Range (now called Oro Blanco Mountains), or very near the International Border west of Nogales, Santa Cruz County.

AUTHENTICATION: This one frankly puzzles me. I would like to say it is authentic because there are a lot of substantiating facts. In 1958 one of the principals of this story appeared on a television series with which I was associated. He did not want to disclose his real identity, nor can I now. He was there and he verified this story. Still, I would like to see some additional proof.

To the Mexicans who live in the vicinity of Cerro Ruido (Noisy Mountain) the place is surrounded with superstitions and is to be avoided at all costs. One of the highest peaks (6000 feet) in the Pajarito (Little Bird) Range, Cerro Ruido's craggy summit emits strange, hard-to-describe sounds, sometimes like low, distant rumbling thunder; at others, like the rumble of empty wagons on rocks. Some have compared the sounds to the lowest notes of a far-distant pipe organ. Whatever the sound, Cerro Ruido's rocky canyons are filled with legend.

There is some evidence that the mission padres, in traveling from their stations in Sonora to those in southern Arizona, frequently took a shorter, but much rougher, trail through the Pajaritos and passed near the base of Cerro Ruido. Stories handed down by generations of Indians in the region say that a mine and a mission were hidden in the rugged reaches near Cerro Ruido. Men have spent many years in searching the Pajaritos and the slopes of Cerro Ruido for this mine.

In 1736, not far south of Cerro Ruido, the Spanish found the famed *planchas de plata* (planks of silver) ore which was one of the richest silver mines ever discovered in North America. It is not improbable that other mines, now lost, existed in the vicinity.

The story has persisted that a large amount of bullion was buried near the lost mission to prevent it from falling into the hands of Spanish soldiers who were sent to collect it for the Crown. This was the Royal Fifth, the percentage

111

claimed by the Spanish monarch. Failure to pay this tribute is said to have been one of the reasons why the Jesuit padres were eventually expelled from Spain's New World dominions.

Although there is no record of any mission founded by the padres in this area whose location has not been checked by careful historical research, it is entirely possible that one or more could have been founded, abandoned, and all historical record of it completely lost. Consider this: a chain of missions was established in northern Sonora, another chain in southern Arizona, both by the same group of missionaries. In the administration of these two closely-associated chains, there was considerable travel between the two regions. Standing squarely across the shortest route between these two chains of churches were the Pajarito Mountains. Padre Kino records in his diary that he traveled across these mountains at least once, and it seems quite likely that a trail, now obliterated and forgotten, once wound through the Pajaritos.

One day's journey south of the southernmost Arizona mission, Guevavi, would have placed a traveler in the vicinity of Cerro Ruido. Water was plentiful there, and it seems reasonable to assume that this would have been a logical place for a *visita,* a stopping or visiting place, where shelter could be had. It was a common practice to establish missions a day's journey apart. This was true in Arizona as well as California.

Shortly after World War I, two army veterans — their names they succeeded in keeping secret for some unknown reason — prospected in the region of Cerro Ruido. One carried a camera. One of the men had to go to Tucson for a week or so, but the other decided to stay in the mountains and look around for anything of interest that came along. After reminding each other of the danger of abandoned mine shafts and flash floods, they set a date and a place for their reunion and parted company.

At the appointed time the two partners met at the prearranged rendezvous. The man who had remained in the mountains reported that he had found a place where a large amount of dirt and rock at the base of a ledge had aroused

112

his curiosity. It appeared to have been put there by man. They agreed to investigate, but by the time they finally arrived at the spot, they were again short of provisions. It was agreed that while one worked at removing the earth and rocks, the other would make the short trip to Nogales for supplies. Again they separated, agreeing to meet a few days later.

When the partner returned from Nogales, he found his companion asleep at the base of an oak tree. His clothing was torn, and his face and arms were badly scratched. He had a harrowing tale to relate.

He had labored all day with pick and shovel and he had succeeded in removing the pile of dirt and rock. At the base of the ledge he had uncovered a small opening into solid rock. On the following morning he had enlarged the opening enough to permit his body to slip through. The opening led to a dark, but dry and dusty tunnel. He had used his carbide light to progress further into the tunnel, finally coming to a pile of shapeless sacks stacked along one side. He kicked one of the sacks and it broke open, revealing pieces of glittering ore. He counted the crude rawhide sacks, lifted several pieces of the heavy ore and estimated that the pile contained about thirty tons.

Exploring further, he had judged the tunnel to be about 400 feet long, with several shafts running off of either side. He left the tunnel, taking some of the ore with him. To his surprise the ore was not gold, but silver of exceeding richness. As nothing more could be accomplished by himself in the mine, he had decided to further explore the canyon. On the following day he made his way up the canyon, climbed its wall, and crossed over into another canyon. He followed up this canyon until he came to a small opening covered with shrubs and dried yellow grass. It was surrounded with trees and his eyes were taking in the beautiful sight when he spotted the remains of an ancient church. Its walls were crumbled and broken, but it was clear and distinct in outline. Mesquite all but covered the details of the roofless interior, but there was enough to tell the astonished prospector that he had found a lost mission — and this explained the mine.

113

Night was approaching so the prospector made camp. Before he had fallen asleep, a strange feeling of unexplained fear had gripped him. He felt the suddenness of impending danger upon him. Suddenly the silence of the little glen was pierced with a horrifying scream. He had plunged headlong down the canyon, tearing through thorny brush and stumbling over boulders in the darkness.

Upon reaching his camp at the mine, he had collapsed. It was here that the returning companion from Nogales found him, exhausted and shaken. Interest in the mine took precedence over that of the mission, and during the following day they surveyed the mine again and determined that it was still rich in unmined ore. They had stumbled upon a bonanza, but they were not certain whether it was in the United States or Mexico. They would guess that it was north of the border and act accordingly.

At this point the man who had experienced the frightening night, recalled that he had had his camera with him and had actually snapped some pictures of the mission ruins. There was one unexposed frame on the roll of film. Developed, these would prove once and for all whether or not he had had a nightmare as his partner suggested.

It was decided now that some of the ore should be taken to Tucson for an assay. Nogales, although much closer, was ruled out because it would be much more difficult to keep their secret there than in the larger city. The man who had undergone the frightful experience again elected to stay at the mine while his partner made the trip to Tucson. Packing some of the ore from the mine, and with the camera safely in his pack, the partner headed down the trail. In the far distance the sky was darkening with heavy clouds. He shouted a warning back to his friend to seek high ground if a storm came up.

All that afternoon the clouds twisted and rolled. But the man on the trail to Tucson soon passed out of their path. Looking back late in the afternoon, he could see that they were centered over Cerro Ruido. He drew the camera from his pack and snapped a picture of the storm on the last unexposed frame.

In Tucson the prospector learned that the storm had

swept the entire border region with torrents of rain and several minor floods had resulted. He felt some concern for his partner. As soon as he had secured the assay and picked up the developed pictures, he headed back for the mountains. In his haste, he did not pause to examine the pictures.

Back in the mountains he saw the marks left by the storm on all sides. Trees were uprooted. New gullies cut across the trail. In places it was blocked with landslides. At the camp there was no sign of his friend. He settled down for the night, and in the morning he was still alone. Two days passed and still his partner did not appear. Alarmed, he went to Nogales and secured horses and help. For days the Pajaritos and the slopes of Cerro Ruido were scoured. It was weeks before they gave up, and by this time they could find neither the man, the mine nor the mission.

During the search for his partner, the prospector had completely overlooked the pictures. He examined them now and what he saw paled him. There was unmistakable evidence on film of the ruins of an old mission building, half-covered with twisted mesquite. Another showed the entrance to a tunnel piercing a solid wall of rock. And there was the picture he had shot on the trail — the storm over the faint outline of Cerro Ruido. Had this storm engulfed his partner and destroyed the mission ruins? He never knew, for his partner was never found, nor were the mission remains and the tunnel to the silver mine.

One must admit that this is one of the most dramatic of all lost mine stories. Does Cerro Ruido, as the Mexicans say, harbor evil spirits? What about the piercing screams heard at the mission ruins? Is the mine there?

(51) Lost Mine of Coconino

VALUE: Unknown quantity of unmined gold ore and bars of smelted gold.

LOCATION: In the extreme southwestern corner of Coconino County, about 20 miles southwest of Flagstaff.

AUTHENTICATION: Veteran prospectors in this section of Arizona are said to be convinced that the lost mine and city actually exist. Be that as it may, there has not yet been any evidence presented to support the story.

In 1582 Antonio de Espejo, an adventure-loving Spaniard of considerable wealth, led a small expedition into what is now New Mexico in search of three missionaries who had been abandoned by Spanish soldiers. At the same time, Espejo was also searching for precious metals. Educated as a mining engineer in Cordova, Spain, he had accumulated his wealth through successful mining ventures in Mexico, and he was interested in running down rumors that large quantities of gold and silver existed in the region.

Espejo traveled north as far as Zuni, New Mexico, and then swung west into Arizona, going as far as the Bill Williams Fork west of Prescott. Here, it is recorded in his own journals, he found silver, samples of the ore of which he took to Mexico with him on his return journey.

The foregoing is historical fact, but from this point on, the story becomes hopelessly involved in legend.

It is told that a party of Espejo's men, unbeknown to him, found gold in the southwest corner of Coconino County. They took samples of the ore, made location maps, and left Espejo to return to Mexico City. When news of the gold reached the ears of certain Church officials, an exploring party was sent north to locate it. This it did, and then made the trip back to Mexico to report success.

About 1720, so the story goes, a party of padres, accompanied by a squad of soldiers, several Spanish families and 200 Opata Indian workers, journeyed to the region and constructed a small village. The Indians were used as forced workers. As they brought out the ore it was smelted into bars, some of which were transported to Mexico City over a route which took them through Tucson. The remainder was kept stored in or near the mine.

116

In 1760 the mine and city were mysteriously abandoned
and the Spanish never again returned to it. Where was it
located? Bancroft thought it to be near Bill Williams Mountain; others say that it was in the Santa Maria Mountains
where Walnut Creek flows into Chino Creek. I haven't
the slightest idea where it was, and with no more evidence
to go on than the above, I never intend to concern myself
with trying to find it.

(52) Lost Silver Mine of Monument Valley

VALUE: Unknown quantity of silver ore assaying $800 to
the ton.

LOCATION: In the Arizona section of Monument Valley,
probably in the vicinity of Mitchell and Merrick buttes,
which are just south of the Utah border. Both are visible
from Arizona Route 47, Navajo or Apache County.

AUTHENTICATION: There are two separate and conflicting stories about the movements of Mitchell and
Merrick. It is a fact of record that the two prospectors
were slain in Monument Valley either because (1) they
had discovered silver there, or (2) they were in a dis-
pute over the use of water belonging to the Indians.

In 1864, Kit Carson and a party of soldiers marched the
entire length of Arizona's Canyon de Chelly, rounding up
7000 Navajo Indians for the "Long Walk" to the Bosque
Redondo in New Mexico. Two of the men in this military
party were named Mitchell and Merrick. They noted the
abundance of silver jewelry and adornments worn by some
of the Indian captives and guessed that it came from the
Navajo lands to the northwest. Many of the Indians who

117

had sought refuge in Canyon de Chelly were from the Monument Valley region. Mitchell and Merrick asked questions and came to the conclusion that since all the Indians from Monument Valley were richly draped in silver there must be a source of silver in the land of monuments, an isolated country where rose-colored "monuments" loomed above the desert floor like Greek temples.

At the end of the "Long Walk" the enlistment terms of Mitchell and Merrick were up and they were mustered out of service. Posing as trappers, they entered Monument Valley and went through the motions of operating trap lines while they actually were searching for the Navajo silver. Observed in the area, they were warned to leave by aging Chief Hoskininni. The white men agreed to leave, but once out of sight of the Indians, they continued their search.

At length Mitchell and Merrick found the silver mine of the Navajos. After taking out samples of the rich ore which they concealed in their packs, they started to leave, but had not gone far when they were again stopped by the Indians. Told that they had been seen taking out the ore, they were given permission to keep it, but warned that if they were seen in the region again they would be killed.

The two prospectors went directly to Cortez, Colorado, where they told of their rich find and showed samples to prove it. They were financially unable to develop the mine, they said, and were ready to team up with a few partners. They found no backers. They went to Mancos and told their story, but with negative results. They repeated it in Dolores. Nobody wanted anything to do with a mine in the Navajo country.

It was not until 1879 that an interested party approached them. He was James Jarvis, a new arrival in Cortez. He had the original samples assayed and the ore ran $800 to the ton. Jarvis now proposed to back the prospectors with $4000 provided they returned to the mine and brought additional ore to substantiate their story. If they brought back the same kind of ore, he would then put up the money for a fifty per cent interest.

Mitchell and Merrick returned to Monument Valley. Although several years had passed since they had last been

118

there, they had no difficulty in locating the ore. They saw no Indians. Could they have left Monument Valley?

When they had mined all the ore they could pack, they set out again for Colorado. One night they made camp at the base of a great red butte. Their campfire glowed brightly. They were no longer afraid of Indians. In the shadows the red men waited in silence for the signal to attack. Unseen by the prospectors, the Indians had watched their every move.

One of the prospectors had not yet fallen asleep. He thought he heard a faint unfamiliar night sound. He threw out an arm to rouse his partner. At that moment the lurking Indians swarmed upon them. Both men jumped to their feet, but Merrick was immediately killed. Mitchell, painfully wounded, managed to reach the shadows and disappeared into the darkness. Somehow he managed to crawl through the night, crossing four miles of sand to the talus base of another great butte. Sunrise found him huddled among some rocks, and there the Indians put him out of his misery. Both prospectors had met death at the base of a red butte. Today one is known as Mitchell Butte, the other as Merrick Butte. Monuments to a lost mine?

When Mitchell and Merrick did not return to Cortez, Jarvis, their intended backer, made inquiries. He heard rumors that they had been killed, that they had been wounded, that they were lost, that they were running out on him. Finally Jarvis formed a party of 22 men and they rode into Monument Valley to investigate. They talked to the Navajos who said little, but led them to two separate graves four miles apart. The bodies were exhumed and identified as those of Mitchell and Merrick. At the base of Merrick Butte they found the rich ore samples and some of the prospectors' belongings.

Charged with murdering the two white men, the Navajos denied it vehemently and laid the blame on a party of Paiutes. The two prospectors had stopped one morning at the hogan of Chief Hoskininni, they said, and had demanded mutton. They were supplied with it and directed to a place where they could secure water for their horses and fill their canteens. That night they camped at the base of a red butte. On the following morning the Paiutes rode into their camp

119

and accused the white men of taking water that did not belong to them. The prospectors replied that Chief Hoskininni had directed them to the water. The Indians went into a huddle.

Suddenly one of the bucks turned to Merrick and asked him for a chew of tobacco. As Merrick reached into his pocket, the Indian grabbed his rifle and killed him. Mitchell made a dash for freedom, managed to get away and reached another red butte. Here he was found and wounded, but not killed. Death occurred from starvation.

After re-burying the bodies of the two men, the Jarvis party, unhindered by the Indians, made a futile search for the lost mine before it returned to Colorado. After this incident the Indians are believed to have thoroughly obliterated all traces of the mine lest it attract an influx of white men into the region.

This, then, is the popular version of the lost Navajo silver mine. Another story has it that Merrick (his name is given as Jack), heard of silver in Monument Valley while he was working as a miner in Colorado. He outfitted for a search, found the mine and returned to Durango where the ore assayed $800 to the ton. Here he met Mitchell, who had recently arrived from the east. They teamed up and made a return trip to the mine in 1880. Other details of the story are in general the same. Still a third version of the story differs in many little details.

The murder of Mitchell and Merrick is a matter of historical record, but whether or not they found silver in Monument Valley is a point still argued. However, some people in a position to know some of the first-hand facts, believe that they did. One of these is Harry Goulding, operator of Goulding's Trading Post in Monument Valley. He probably knows the Navajos in this region better than any other white man. The Indians trust him. It would be interesting to know what, if anything, they have told him. He has searched for silver in Monument Valley.

Hoskininni-begay, son of old Chief Hoskininni, told Charles Kelly (now superintendent of Capitol Reef National Monument, Utah), that he remembered the two prospectors and the incident of their death at the hands of the Paiutes.

120

He stated that the two white men had with them "sacks of rocks." When Kelly asked Hoskininni-begay if it was true that the Navajos had a secret silver mine, he said: "It is true." He went on to explain that only seven tribal members knew its exact location. One by one they grew old and died, but just before the death of the last survivor, he called in his son and passed along the secret. The son was never able to locate the mine, and so in this manner, the mine was lost even to the Navajos.

Warning! No prospecting is allowed in Monument Valley without permission of the tribal council which is located in Window Rock.

(53) Black Burro Lost Mine

VALUE: Gold ore of unknown value but described at the time as being of "incredible richness."

LOCATION: The mule was found along the old Mansfield Trail where it paralleled the San Francisco River close to the Arizona-New Mexico line in Greenlee County. It was assumed that the mule had not traveled far and, therefore, the gold must have come from the area near the junction of the San Francisco and Blue rivers, northeast of Clifton. Although this is the region in which most searches have been made, others have roamed for a hundred miles around in search of the Lost Black Burro Mine.

AUTHENTICATION: Although the original author of this story, so far as can be determined, was a man who ranched in the vicinity of Kingston, New Mexico, and was well acquainted with the history of the region, there is no evidence other than his word that the mine ever existed.

121

The Old Mansfield Trail ran from the San Francisco River in Catron County, New Mexico, to the headwaters of Eagle Creek in Graham County, Arizona. It was more of a mule path than a trail and today hardly any trace of it remains. But Old Man Mansfield, a prospector of whom very little is known, operated a mine (now also lost) and packed his ore over this path into eastern Arizona. It was a region of wild Apache bands, and many a prospector, including Mansfield, fell a victim of Apache ferocity.

One day in 1826 a party of three travelers were picking their way along the old trail when they came upon a black burro idly grazing some distance from the path. They were about to pass it by when one of the party noted that the animal seemed to be bearing a pack. They rode up to investigate and to inquire directions of its owner. The burro was indeed bearing a packsaddle that looked to be new, and lashed to each side was a large rawhide sack. They looked about but could find no owner. They shouted but received no answer. Thinking that the owner might have strayed away in search of game, they settled down to wait for his return. But why had he left his pack animal untethered?

With the passing of several hours the men became alarmed that some misfortune had befallen the missing man and they searched the area for some sign of him. Nothing was found to indicate that there was a human within miles. Now, for the first time, they investigated the rawhide sacks and found that they contained gold ore which they later described to be of "incredible richness."

Nightfall came and the travelers made camp, determined to wait until morning before taking the mule and its burden into their possession. During the night strange sounds were heard, but fearing that it might be Apaches, the men remained quiet. They were up with the breaking of dawn and made another search of the area, but turned up nothing. It was now concluded that the owner of the mule was nowhere in the vicinity. Whatever fate had overtaken him could have occurred many miles away. Placing the black burro in their own pack train, the travelers proceeded on their journey, certain that somewhere in the area was a mine of fabulous richness, its owner probably killed by Apaches.

122

Nearing the end of the Mansfield Trail, the party of three were themselves attacked by Indians and two of the men were instantly killed, the third managing to escape into a thicket where he concealed himself under a narrow ledge until the Apaches left the vicinity. When he dared venture out he could find no trace of animals, including the mysterious black burro. But scattered on the ground where the attack had occurred was the gold ore which the Indians, finding worthless for their needs, had thrown away.

The lone survivor of the sudden attack eventually made his way safely to a small Mexican settlement where he told the story of the black burro and the gold. No immediate search was made for the source of the gold, and the sole witness to the episode drifted on, never to be heard of again.

In later years when many prospectors roamed the area, they learned the story of the black burro from the Mexicans and many searches were made for the mine which now bears the name of the Lost Black Burro. Whether there is any truth to this story is for you to decide for vourself. The facts, if any, are extremely vague.

(54) Apache Girl Lost Mine

VALUE: Gold ore of unknown value, but said to have been the richest ever seen by a number of experienced prospectors, one of whom estimated the value at $88,000 per ton.

LOCATION: Generally considered to be in the Dos Cabezas Mountains, Cochise County, and sometimes pinpointed as being directly west of the site of old Fort Bowie.

AUTHENTICATION: Although this story is now well established in the lore of Arizona lost mines, and it has been repeated time and countless time again as being "true," there are actually no facts to substantiate it other than the word of one nameless old prospector, dead these many years. It is quite possible that this story is but a variation of one of many lost mine stories in which the principal part is played by an Indian girl.

It was a hot day in 1852, blazingly hot for it was July and the searing desert sun was at its worst. As the old prospector trudged, parched and panting into the southeastern slopes of the Dos Cabezas in search of water, it appeared that he could not go on much longer. Gold was of no importance to him now, and he would have exchanged all that he ever hoped to find for one little bubbling spring, or one little trickle of a stream. He was not only without food and water, but he was lost. His equipment had been cast aside piece by piece, and some miles back his burro had wandered away, leaving him without the strength to recover it.

If there was water in these mountains, it would more than likely be marked by a little clump of green. He knew this, and his burning eyes scanned the area around him. Ahead was a great rock protruding into the canyon he was following. It would at least offer some shade while he regained his strength to push on in one more desperate attempt at survival. He reached the rock and fell exhausted, hardly noticing, until she moved, that an Indian girl was crouched there beside him.

Aware that the old man was about to collapse from thirst, the girl raised an arm and pointed. When it was obvious that her intentions were not understood, she arose and walked away. Presently she returned and held out a hand before him. It was dripping with water. Again she pointed and the prospector knew now that she was directing him to water. He followed her and they came to a tiny trickle of water that flowed from a crevice in the rock wall. It was not much, but it was constant and it saved his life.

Returning to the shade, the two sat down, the girl some distance away. Only now did he note that she was very young, perhaps no more than seventeen. She did not ap-

124

pear to be in distress. When he approached her, she moved away, always maintaining a certain distance between them. He spoke to her and she replied in her native tongue which he could not understand. Only now and then could he catch a word of Spanish that had found its way into her vocabulary, but not enough to carry on a conversation.

Presently the girl arose again, and walking a short distance away, recovered a bundle which she had concealed in the rocks. Taking it to his side, she untied the cord that held the colored piece of cloth into a container for its contents. Spread out before them, it revealed a quantity of desert nuts and what the prospector later judged to be about a quart of gold nuggets ranging in size from tiny beads to much larger ones. She handed him a handful of the nuts, but when he indicated that he wanted to see the gold, she withdrew and closed the bundle.

Toward evening when the sun had diminished in fury, she got up, and taking her bundle, started to walk away. From a distance she looked back and motioned him to follow. Ranging deeper into the mountains, they traveled until nightfall, halting then at another spring. Obviously the girl knew her way, and although the prospector did not know where she was leading him, he determined to follow her.

For three days the pair moved only during the cooler hours of evening and morning, always camping near water at night, always subsisting upon food which she miraculously supplied. On one occasion, when the bundle of nuts and gold was opened, she handed him one of the larger pieces. When he asked her in Spanish where the gold came from she pointed in the direction in which they had come. When he inquired if there was more of the gold, she made motions which he interpreted to mean that there were "heaps" of it, although he could not be sure.

On the evening of the third day they came to a trail at the edge of the mountains overlooking a broad valley. In the distance could be seen the scattered buildings of a small community. She pointed and motioned for him to go. After failing to persuade her to go with him, he started out alone and eventually came to a small settlement the name of which is not given in any known account of the story.

Recovered completely from his experience, the prospector made inquiries and found that a girl answering the description of the Apache who had saved his life frequently came alone to the village and exchanged gold nuggets for certain supplies. Always she disappeared in the night and no attempt to follow her had ever been successful. It was assumed that she was acting as an agent for the members of her tribe, and that any attempt to follow her into the mountains, even if successful, would be highly dangerous.

After much persuasion the old prospector induced a small party of men to join him in a search for the Apache girl's gold, and they headed into the Dos Cabezas range to retrace his footsteps. They were well provisioned and equipped for any emergency, and they had no trouble in following the mountain trail over which the girl had led him.

On the second day, when hopes were high that the gold would be found in the vicinity of the first tiny spring, they came upon the body of an Apache girl who had apparently been dead for several days. She had been shot and left to die where she had fallen. Beside her was a piece of colorful cloth, a cord, a few desert nuts — but no gold nuggets. All agreed that this was the Apache girl who had saved the prospector's life. Who had killed her? Her own people to preserve the secret of the gold? A prospector who had stumbled upon her and failed to force the secret location of the mine from her? The question has never been answered.

Fearful to probe deeper into the Apache country, the searchers returned to the village and abandoned the search. The old prospector is said to have conducted searches at a later date, and from one of these journeys he never returned. Whether or not there is a semblance of truth to this story, is, as we have said, for you to decide. We think it belongs in the campfire variety, where good stories do not necessarily have to be true.

(55) Sublett's Lost Gold Mine

VALUE: There is no way of knowing the value of the ore left in this mine, but Sublett once said that he could take out more than $10,000 in less than a week.

LOCATION: There is more or less general agreement that Sublett secured his gold in the Guadalupe Mountains or southeastern New Mexico or western Texas. This rugged, pine-crested range, wild and desolate, starts in Otero County, near Lincoln, New Mexico, and extends in a northwest to southeast direction across the southwestern corner of Chaves County, and into Culberson County, Texas, where they merge into the Delaware Mountains. From their northern foothills to their southern extremity is a distance of about 100 miles, a very large area, indeed, in which to pinpoint a hole in the ground no larger than a mine shaft. One school of thought places the mine in the New Mexico section of the range; another in the Texas extension. Still others locate the mine near a seep spring in the Rustler Hills, foothill extensions of the Guadalupes in Texas. A granddaughter of Old Ben Sublett who originally found the mine, told the writer in 1958: "I do not think it is the Guadalupes — it could have been anywhere in southern New Mexico." I could not learn the reason for this conclusion. Based upon all the information this writer has been able to locate, it is his opinion — and opinion only — that the mine is located in the Guadalupe Mountains close to the New Mexico-Texas border, and probably in New Mexico.

AUTHENTICATION: The story of the Lost Sublett Mine has become a legend of the Southwest; and although the legend has probably strayed far from the original story due to careless writing and far too little research, there remains much to support the belief that Bill (he was never called "Ben" as most accounts state)

Sublett did find and periodically work a mine in the Guadalupe Mountains. At least two persons, living until recent years, saw that mine, and there are several still living who knew those two men and heard from them first-hand accounts of the mine. It is the opinion of the writer, who believes that his research on the subject is probably more extensive than any other, that the Lost Sublett Mine actually exists.

Heretofore, much of the common version of the Sublett Mine story is traceable to J. Frank Dobie, that grand teller of tales of the Southwest. Dobie has recorded the story of the mine as he heard it from old-timers. He did not present the story as fact, but as a folktale. Other writers, however, pounced upon the Dobie story, elaborated and twisted the story to suit their own purposes, and presented their product as a "true" account. Let it be understood that the complete facts are not yet known, but that Dobie's much copied version is not consistent with information now available.

The tradition of gold in the Guadalupe Mountains goes back almost to the time of Coronado, and the belief among white men that the rugged Guadalupes contain great riches is as old as the first pioneers to reach the region. There are those who will say, however, that the geologic structure of the Guadalupes precludes any possibility of extensive mineralization. Didn't they ever hear that "Gold is where you find it"?

It is said that the Mescalero Apaches, on their reservation near the northern extremities of the Guadalupes, admit to knowing of gold in the mountains, but they themselves never do any mining, and they have a tradition dating back centuries of never revealing to a white man where gold can be found. This may well be. Nobody knows better than the Apaches that little was to be gained, and much could be lost, by giving out this kind of information.

The notorious Apache leader, Geronimo, once said that the richest gold deposits in the United States were in the Guadalupes. This region was his ancestral home and he and his people knew its vast stretches better than any people before or since. Yet Geronimo was a liar and he was deal-

129

ing for his freedom when this statement was made. Who knows whether or not he was sincere?

When Lew Wallace was Governor of New Mexico Territory, he is said to have uncovered a Spanish document in the archives at Santa Fe, which proved that the Spanish mined gold in the northern Guadalupes previous to their departure in 1680. The writer has had no success in his search for this document.

One of the earliest Americans known to have searched for gold in the Guadalupes was William Caldwell Sublett, who is frequently and erroneously referred to as Ben Sublett. The matter of his name has had a lot of abuse by writers. First, there is no final "e" on his surname. It is Sublett, not Sublette. His middle name is frequently given as Colum; it is Caldwell. And he was known as Bill, not Ben. These points have all been verified through his living descendents.

It appears that William Caldwell Sublett had drifted west with his frail wife and two (some say three) small children. They settled in the small, sun-baked town of Monahans in West Texas, where the Texas & Pacific railroad was then under construction. Sublett took various odd jobs with the railroad construction contractor, but remained only long enough to get together a small stake. Then he would disappear into the mountains in search of gold. When his funds were gone, he would return. For a while he served as a water witch, roaming far and wide with a forked stick, looking for sources of underground water. This job must have been to his liking, for he seems to have been a perpetual drifter. It would have been easy for his travels to have taken him into the Guadalupes.

The Texas & Pacific railroad almost parallels U. S. 80 across West Texas from El Paso to Fort Worth. At Van Horn it is but 55 miles to Guadalupe Pass in the heart of the Texas section of the Guadalupes. It is certainly not unreasonable to believe that Sublett's straying footsteps took him into these mountains. He was looking for gold, and he told everybody so. He had probably heard the Apache legends. Occasionally he came home with a lone nugget to show for his travels. People are said to have pitied him, but their real concern was for his ailing wife and his neglected

130

children. They had to shift for themselves when Bill Sublett was away on his many jaunts.

Eventually Sublett's wife succumbed to her ailments and the strain of many hardships. Finally the father took the motherless children to Odessa, Texas, and placed them in the homes of sympathetic neighbors. With the children off his hands, Sublett disappeared again into the mountains. Weeks later he returned empty-handed to renew his quest for credit from merchants and saloonkeepers.

Bill Sublett became known as the "crazy man." What little respect a few people had for him faded when they saw him dissipate his last dime for liquor while his children lived off the kindness of friends. He could talk of nothing but the gold that he would find some day. Often he made veiled remarks about the Guadalupes, but never revealed any definite information as to where his mysterious trips took him.

One day he returned to Odessa after an absence of several weeks, and it was immediately obvious that his luck had changed. He swaggered into a saloon where his credit had been shut off and ordered drinks for the house. The bartender paid no attention. Sublett repeated his order. "Drinks for everybody!" he shouted. "I'm rich! I've found gold!" He slapped a sizeable poke of nuggets on the bar and got service.

From this day on Sublett delighted in tantalizing his fair-weather friends with tales of his secret mine, but he told them no more. His trip to the mountains became more frequent. Always he returned with a bag of nuggets. He spent freely until they were gone, and again he vanished. Some say that he continued to let friends take care of his children, but the truth seems to be that he built a house for them and hired a caretaker.

No amount of persuasion could induce Sublett to give out any information about his mine, except that it was "very, very rich." Once when he was offered $10,000 for an interest in his mine, he scornfully said, "I can take out more gold than that in less than a week!" Nor could any amount of whiskey loosen his tongue. He only became more cautious. Many attempts were made to follow him, but none were

131

successful. The snoopy individual who approached the mountains behind him was discouraged with a rifle. "Go and find it like I did," was Sublett's stock answer, "but don't try to follow me!"

The story of Sublett's secret mine swept the country. Men resorted to any means to trail the old prospector or to wheedle the information from him. When he was pressured into taking in a financial partner to develop his mine, Sublett frequently agreed, but at the last minute he always found a convenient excuse to delay the trip. It is said that he actually did take an old friend and drinking crony, Mike Wilson, to his secret location and allowed him to bring out a sack or two of ore. But back in Odessa with his new wealth, Wilson went on such a prolonged drunk that he completely forgot how to get to the mine again, nor would Sublett tell him a second time. Wilson said the mine was in the Guadalupes. That was all he knew — or would tell.

Some believed that Sublett had made friends with the Apaches, and that they had taken him to an old Spanish mine. Sublett always denied it. He denied everything. He admitted nothing. In 1887, Sublett's son, Rolth (most accounts give his name wrongly as Ross), was nine years of age. In that year the old prospector took him into the mountains and showed him the mine. The boy, of course, was too young to remember the location of the mine. In later years he made many attempts to learn the secret from his father, but Sublett would only say, "Boy, if you want the mine, go out and find it like I did."

When Rolth was later a resident of Carlsbad and Artesia, New Mexico, he made frequent search trips into the Guadalupes, but never with any success. He once stated that he recalled distinctly seeing his father climb down a rope ladder into a crevice or a cave from which he took the gold. Rolth also said once that he believed the mine to be located in the Rustler Hills, branches of the Guadalupes in Texas, but he was never sure.

Rolth Sublett, who most certainly saw the lost mine, died in 1953 or 1954. This would place his birth in 1872 or 1873, and if his father took him to the mine in 1887, as it is said, he would have been 14 or 15 years of age, not nine as most

132

accounts state. These few years would have made a great deal of difference in what the youth could remember of the trip.

William Caldwell Sublett, according to most accounts, died in Odessa, Texas, in 1892, at anywhere from 80 to 90 years of age. I prefer the word of his granddaughter, Mrs. Ethel Pitt Lovelady, of Santa Fe, New Mexico, who has given me these facts. Sublett was born September 25, 1835. He died January 6, 1892. He was, then, not yet 57 years of age at the time of his death and far from the "old man" of most accounts. Mrs. Lovelady also doubts that he died in Odessa, but was later taken there for burial by his daughter, Jennie, and her husband, Sidney Pitt.

Mrs. Lovelady says of Rolth Sublett: "My Uncle Rolth spent his life searching for it. He never in his life worked at anything longer than it would take to get a grubstake to start a fresh search for the mine. Mama (Jennie Sublett Pitt) claimed that she didn't think that Rolth had ever been to the mine. He thought he had, but the time he tells about, he was only *nine* years of age. Mama said that was before the mine was discovered, she thought. But there was a mine, and a rich one. Mama said Grandpa (William Caldwell Sublett) carried with him a gold nugget that was the size of a robin's egg."

Jennie Sublett married Sidney Pitt (not Pitts, as many accounts state). Of this marriage, three grandchildren of William Caldwell Sublett still survive: William F. Pitt, Crownpoint, New Mexico; Mrs. C. M. Davenport, House, New Mexico; and Mrs. Ethel Pitt Lovelady, Santa Fe, New Mexico. In searching for the facts about the Lost Sublett Mine, I have been in contact with all of these and some distant relatives. From their combined accounts, I am convinced that Bill Sublett did have a source of gold; if not a mine, then some other source; and that he died with the secret, which is held today only by the Guadalupe Mountains — and possibly by a few close-mouthed Mescalero Apaches.

(56) Belle McKeever Lost Mine

VALUE: Unknown quantity of quartz ore valued at $1800 per ton.

LOCATION: Believed to be in the Granite Wash Mountains, northern Yuma County.

AUTHENTICATION: The incident leading to the discovery of the ore is well authenticated. The approximate location is involved in a tangle of controversy. McClintock says that this is one of the best authenticated of all lost mine tales. It had little embellishment, and in part, may be true. This historian called the mine the "Lost Soldier," although it is referred to today as the "Belle McKeever."

In 1869 Abner McKeever and his family operated a ranch near the Big Bend of the Gila River, near the present town of Gila Bend. It is an area where mountains rise abruptly from the desert, and massed against each other, appear like dark storm clouds on the horizon; hazy blue and purple and seeming to belong to the sky more than to the land.

One day McKeever and his young daughter, Belle, were working on a small placer claim some distance from the protection of the ranch. For a moment the father relaxed his guard, a fatal mistake in a country where the Apache roamed almost at will. A small band swept down from the hills and seized the pair. They seemed not to be interested in old Abner and let him go. With the screaming girl they rode away to the north, shouting back tormenting words which the girl's helpless father did not understand.

Pursuit without help was out of the question, and although it cost precious time. Abner rode with all possible speed to Fort Yuma where there was a garrison of soldiers. To Abner it seemed that it took the soldiers forever to saddle up and give chase, but eventually they were mounted and rode away in a cloud of dust.

Sighting the approach of the soldiers, the Apaches broke up into small bands and fled in different directions. Not knowing which band held the captive girl, the soldiers also divided and gave chase to all. In one of these detachments was a sergeant named Crossthwaite, and under him were two privates, Joe Wormley and Eugene Flannigan. The band of Indians they followed rapidly disappeared in a northwesterly direction. Soon they had lost the Indians and it wasn't long before they had managed to lose themselves in the rocky hills. They are thought today to have traveled in a general northerly direction through a region dreaded by early travelers for its lack of water.

First, their provisions ran out; and then, one by one, their horses dropped of exhaustion. They struggled on afoot in a desperate search for water, the girl all but forgotten. Wormley became delirious and it was all his companions could do to keep him from wandering off by himself. As it appeared that all were about to collapse, they came to a small spring of water which is generally placed in the Granite Wash Mountains of northern Yuma County. That night they camped beside the spring and were fortunate enough to kill some small game on which they feasted. In the morning they felt able to travel again and it was agreed that they would take turns riding the only surviving horse. While washing in the spring, Crossthwaite was amazed to find some gold nuggets. The three men pocketed those that they could pick off the surface.

Knowing enough about prospecting to look for a vein or outcropping, the three men turned their attention to the surrounding region. Above the spring a short distance away they located not one vein, but two; one narrow and the other about 16 feet in width. With their knives they dug out about 50 pounds of the rich ore, loaded it on the remaining horse and set out in the direction of the Gila to the south.

But the return journey was fraught with equal hardships, and in a few days they were all again delirious with thirst. Less than a day's journey from the river the horse dropped dead. Soon Crossthwaite was unable to stagger on and dropped by the wayside. Flannigan was next, and Wormley half-crawled, half-walked on alone. Eventually he managed to reach the river where he was rescued in the nick of time. From his almost incoherent babblings, the rescuers finally pieced together the story and started off in search of Crossthwaite and Flannigan. When they found Flannigan he was more dead than alive, but they managed to pull him through. Crossthwaite was dead. They found the body of the horse and from its saddlebags took out the 50 pounds of ore which was later assayed at $50 to the ton.

Later, when Flannigan and Wormley were fully recovered, they related the story in detail and gave directions as best they could for locating the rich outcroppings. Flannigan refused to return to the area for all the gold in Arizona. He died in Phoenix in 1880. Wormley led several searches for the lost springs and the ore above it, but all were fruitless. Among the many others who believed in the lost mine was Harold Bell Wright, the author, who is said to have sought it persistently. His interest in lost mines and buried treasure is well known and his book, *Mine With the Iron Door* (Appleton, 1923), was based on the famous lost mine of that name.

The Belle McKeever mine, so far as is known, has never been found — and neither has the girl, but then the search for the little girl was never as intensive as that for the gold.

(57) Lost Nigger Bill Mine

VALUE: Gold ore of unknown value, but said to have assayed from $80,000 to $92,000 per ton.

LOCATION: It is generally agreed that the find made by Seminole Bill was in southern Brewster County, probably in the section that is now a part of Big Bend National Park, Texas, and it is usually placed at the mouth of Reagan Canyon. This is a land of rugged beauty where legends of lost mines and hidden treasures are many.

AUTHENTICATION: While there is no available documentary evidence to establish beyond a doubt that the colored cowboy actually found a rich source of gold while riding for the Reagan brothers, there is considerable reason to believe that the story has some basis in fact. These facts, if any, however, are enveloped in a mass of conflicting accounts, hardly any two of which agree even in the simplest of details.

This much we know for certain: the Reagan brothers — Lee, Jim, John and Frank — did operate a ranch southwest of Sanderson in the late 1880's, and they were well known in Sanderson and Dryden, where they frequently traded. It was one of the Reagan boys who first heard and told the story of Seminole Bill's find. Although the Reagans did not at first believe the story, they later spent many years in searching for the lost mine.

Seminole Bill's real name was supposedly Bill Kelley (or Kelly), although he was generally known as "Seminole Bill," "Nigger Bill," or, as he is said to have sometimes called himself, "Santa Rosa." It was assumed that he was a native of Mexico, coming to Texas from the region south of Del Rio.

Accounts do not agree as to where and under what circumstances the Reagans met Seminole Bill, but the popular story is that Seminole Bill approached Lee Reagan in Sanderson. He said that he was broke and wanted a job. Lee Reagan hired him and he eventually showed up at the Reagan camp in the Big Bend country at the mouth of a canyon now named after the Reagans.

One night around the campfire Seminole Bill calmly announced that he had found a gold mine that day while out rounding up some stray horses. The remark brought only roars of laughter, so Bill refrained from showing the samples of ore he had brought to the camp. Later he took Lee Reagan aside and tried to convince him he really had found gold. Reagan remained unconvinced. Nothing more was said of the matter until a few days afterward, when Lee Reagan and Seminole Bill were riding together at the base of a long, rocky ridge. "Right over that ridge," Bill told his boss, "is

137

where I found the gold." Reagan had other things on his mind and all but ignored the statement.

Having found no one who placed any credence in his story, Seminole Bill did not mention the subject again. One day, some weeks later, he borrowed a horse, rode away and was never seen again by members of the Reagan outfit. He had been on friendly terms with the Reagans and his disappearance was puzzling, but soon forgotten. Cowboys came and went. The next time the Reagans heard of Seminole Bill, they were not so sure that he had not found gold, but where was he, and where was the gold? All they knew for certain was that the mine, or ledge, or whatever it was, was probably located some seven or eight miles from the old camping place at the mouth of Reagan Canyon.

After leaving the Reagan camp it seems that Seminole Bill rode into Sanderson, disposed of the horse and caught a freight train into San Antonio. Here he attempted to locate a man named Lock Campbell whom, it seems, Seminole Bill had once known. Campbell was a conductor on the Southern Pacific and was away at the time on his run. Bill located a friend of the railroader and left with him samples of gold ore with specific instructions that they were to be turned over to Lock Campbell upon his return to San Antonio. The reason for Seminole Bill's haste has never been satisfactorily explained, but after this act he secured a horse and rode out of town. His subsequent fate has been a matter of considerable conjecture. It has been claimed that he was killed in a fight in Mexico, that he died a natural death in Louisiana, and that he settled down in Monterrey, Mexico. At any rate his sudden disappearance seems to have been complete and final, for no amount of searching could later locate him.

In due time Lock Campbell is said to have had Seminole Bill's ore samples assayed, and that the report came back that the ore was worth a fabulous $80,000 to the ton, although the Reagans claimed later that it was $92,000. These assay records, if available, would lend strong credence to the Negro's story, but all efforts to locate them have failed.

When Campbell learned of the startling value of Seminole Bill's gold, he began a frantic search for the missing

138

cowboy, first trying to reach him by letter at the Reagan ranch, where he presumed he might have returned. When this brought no results, he advertised widely, offering to pay a high reward for any information leading to the Negro's whereabouts. He learned nothing. Campbell is said to have thereafter spent a great deal of time in searching the area around the mouth of Reagan Canyon, and when he could no longer devote his time to this, to have grubstaked prospectors to search for him.

Of course, it was not long before the Reagans heard the news of Campbell's search for Seminole Bill. Now they regretted that they had practically laughed the Negro out of their camp and began a frantic search for the only man who knew the secret of the lost mine. They were no more successful than Campbell. It is said that they spent twenty years in a fruitless search for the gold "just over that ridge."

The Lost Nigger Bill Mine is sometimes known as the "Lost Apache Mine," after an Indian who called himself Solito Gonzales. He was deaf and in 1924 he came to Dr. Daniel McCall in Texas for treatment. Although the Indian was penniless, Dr. McCall treated him. When Gonzales left, the doctor soon forgot the matter. Some time later the Indian again appeared at Dr. McCall's place. His hearing had been restored and he wished to express his gratitude. Showing the doctor a ring he was wearing, he said that he had hammered it out of crude gold and that there was much more gold where that had come from. In order to repay the doctor for his services, he told him where the gold could be found and offered to take him there.

Eventually Dr. McCall and the Indian left for the Big Bend country. When they arrived in the vicinity of Maravillas Springs after much difficult traveling, the Indian pointed out a spot and said that the gold was 45 feet straight down. Before McCall could take any action the Indian became ill and the doctor felt obliged to hurry him to San Saba for treatment. But the Indian soon died and McCall temporarily gave up the search. Some ten years later he returned to the site, found some low grade ore, but nothing of the value described by the Indian.

If there is any connection between the gold supposedly

139

found by Solito Gonzales, and that found by Seminole Bill, it is a thin thread, indeed.

(58) The Mysterious Treasure of Karl Steinheimer

VALUE: Ten mule loads of gold and silver buried in one location and a "package" of gold buried in another. How much is a mule load of gold? There has been much speculation on this subject, and nobody agrees on the answer. There are far too many intangibles for this writer to attempt a guess. The treasure herein is otherwise described as being worth "millions."

LOCATION: The search for Steinheimer's fabulous treasure has taken place at many locations, but the burial sites are popularly agreed to be in Bell County, Texas, the main hoard near the junction point of three streams. These streams are named as the Leon, Lampasas, and Salado which unite south of Belton to form the Little River. The smaller portion of gold is said to have been buried about fifteen miles south of the stream junction, in a group of hills locally known as the "Knobs."

AUTHENTICATION: There has been an "authentic" Steinheimer map in existence for many years, and a great many people have searched for the Steinheimer treasure. Yet, strangely, little is known of the principal character in this story, and none of the so-called "facts" have ever been satisfactorily substantiated. This in itself does not, of course, prove that the treasure does not exist. It does make one wonder, however, if there can be any truth behind such vague details.

Karl Steinheimer, according to pure legend, was born

140

in Germany in 1793. At the age of eleven (remember this point) he ran away from home and became a sailor. Among the pirate commanders he served was one Luis de Aury, who specialized in running black slaves into America. It is a matter of record that Aury became military and civil governor of Texas, and in 1816 moved his headquarters to Galveston. Steinheimer is said to have accompanied him to the Texas port, and to have been placed in charge there of the slave running activities.

Some time after the move to Galveston, Steinheimer and Aury had a falling out and the German left for the interior of Mexico, where he soon became involved in a series of mining ventures. Here he prospered and is said to have amassed a great fortune in gold and silver, remaining until 1838, when his sudden departure was brought about by a piece of startling news that reached his ears.

It will be remembered that Steinheimer had left Germany at the tender age of eleven. But now, in the process of growing wealthier by the day, he heard that the sweetheart he had left behind in Germany was in St. Louis, and that she was not married! Such was his devotion to this girl whom he had not seen since the age of eleven, that he decided to give up everything, rush to her and ask for her hand in marriage. Accordingly he disposed of all of his Mexican interests, packed his gold and silver on ten mules and, with but two trusted companions, started out across the deserts and mountains, bound for his childhood love in St. Louis. It is your privilege to believe this incredible story, and it is ours to disbelieve it, which we do.

At any rate, the Steinheimer pack train eventually arrived safely at San Antonio on the plains of Texas. To the north was dangerous Indian country, and Steinheimer delayed the journey while debating the wisdom of risking his fortune and life in the inhospitable land. But after a delay of several weeks the decision was made to push on, Indians or no Indians. He wanted to see that childhood sweetheart.

Avoiding all traveled trails, and moving only at night, the little party of three and the ten treasure-laden mules eventually arrived at a place where three small streams joined into a single river. Here Steinheimer decided that his luck

141

must soon run out, and he did not want anything to happen to his fortune. There was only one thing to do — bury it and return for it later. Keeping aside one small sack of gold for traveling expenses, the major portion of the fortune was secreted or buried near the place where the Leon, Lampasas and Salado join to form the Little River. How would he know where to find the treasure when he returned? Well, the streams would be there forever, but just to be on the safe side, he drove a brass spike into an oak tree about fifty feet from the actual hiding place. Now the mules were turned loose and the three men set out on their horses in a southeasterly direction.

After about fifteen miles of relaxed travel the little party came to a group of hills rising above the broad prairie. To the east was a great valley ringed with trees. While resting here, Steinheimer and his companions were suddenly attacked by a party of Indians. Two of the men were immediately killed but Steinheimer, although badly wounded, managed to find concealment in some brush atop one of the hills. In his flight he had not had time to secure his horse, and he was now afoot, surrounded for all he knew, by hostile Indians. During the day he buried his sack of gold, keeping out only a few coins. With nightfall, and in spite of his pain, he crept out and started in a northward direction.

Afraid to shoot any game lest he attract the attention of Indians, and barely able to walk, he nevertheless pushed on, sustained only by his determination to reach his childhood love in St. Louis. He eventually arrived at a trail and was soon overtaken by a party of eastbound travelers. They were friendly and offered help, but by this time Steinheimer realized that his wound was going to be fatal. He told his full story to members of the party, and drawing a crude map of the treasure site, elicited the promise that the map and message would be delivered to his sweetheart in St. Louis. Some time after the departure of the strangers, Steinheimer died at a place unknown.

In due time, and true to their word, the strangers found Steinheimer's sweetheart in St. Louis and delivered the dying man's message to her. In spite of the huge fortune waiting

142

for her at the place indicated on the map, it was many years before the young lady got around to having relatives make a search for the brass spike embedded in the trunk of an oak tree near the junction place of three streams. It was concluded that the treasure was buried near a place now known as Three Forks, and that the smaller package of gold was hidden in the Knobs two or three miles from the present town of Rogers — but no treasure was found at either site. Nor has any of the many searches made later, so far as is known, produced a single gold piece of Steinheimer's fabulous hidden wealth.

This and little more is known of the man named Karl Steinheimer. Less is known of his sweetheart, whose very name has escaped history. Nothing is known of the men who delivered the dying German's message. Was there any Steinheimer gold to begin with? No one knows that for certain either, but the devotion of this man for the sweetheart whom he had not seen for thirty-four years, and then when he was but eleven years of age, must go down in the annals of love as a classic.

(59) Bandit Treasure of Colossal Cave

VALUE: $62,000 in gold coins . . . or nothing.

LOCATION: In Colossal Cave about 27 miles southeast ot Tucson. The cave is in a Pima County Park, well-kept and worth seeing, even if the treasure isn't there.

AUTHENTICATION: Historical records substantiate that the bandits took the treasure into the cave. The question is: was it taken out again? Evidence seems to indicate that it was.

In 1884 four masked bandits held up a Southern Pacific passenger train as it stopped at the little tank town of Pantano for water. The town is still there, and still a tank town.

143

Overpowering the armed Wells Fargo guards, the outlaws successfully made away with $62,000 in gold coins consigned to meet Tucson payrolls and the troops stationed at Fort Lowell.

When Sheriff Robert Leatherwood and his posse took up the trail of the bandits, they soon learned that the masked men had fled in the direction of Rincon Peak. They took off in pursuit and followed the robbers to the ranch of a Negro named Crane, where they learned that the fleeing men had secured fresh horses at gunpoint. Angry over the forced loss of his horses, Crane had watched the bandits ride away and saw them tether their mounts in a thicket and disappear into a "hole in the ground." He gave the Sheriff's party full directions and again the posse rode away in pursuit.

Shortly the possemen found Crane's "hole in the ground." It turned out to be a cave, a colossal cave, as a matter of fact, on the south slope of Wromg Mountain in the Rincon Range. The first eager law officer to stick his head in the small entrance drew a fusillade of shots. He withdrew in a hurry and a council of war was called. Sheriff Leatherwood now made a safe and sane observation. The bandits would have to come out sooner or later and they would have to emerge by the same entrance. All the possemen had to do was to wait for the outlaws to run out of food and water and pick them off as they tried to escape. It might be a long wait so a party was sent to Tucson to secure food and supplies for the vigil.

Several days passed. Patience waned. Men began to wonder why the bandits did not appear. One week slipped by. Two weeks, and Leatherwood determined to investigate. Selecting a small party, he cautiously entered the cave, progressing through a dry labyrinth of passages until their eyes met complete blackness and barred further advance. There was not a sign of the robbers. Unless you have experienced the sensation of total absence of light you cannot imagine the utter helplessness that confronted the lawmen. They withdrew.

While the bewildered posse was trying to decide whether or not to give up the chase, a cowboy rode into the camp

144

with the news that four men were throwing gold coins around in the saloons of Willcox, and they were boasting about the manner in which they had outwitted a sheriff's posse. Bob Leatherwood rode for Willcox, recruited some local peace officers and located the four strangers. In the wild gun battle that followed an attempt to question them, three of the bandits were killed. The surviving outlaw was eventually convicted and sentenced to a 28-year term in the Territorial Prison at Yuma. He steadfastly refused to reveal where the stolen gold had been hidden, there having been very little found on the captives. He did, however, take delight in revealing how the bandits had made their exit from the cave. They had probed around in the darkness until they had come upon a second entrance. Finally the lone survivor said that the sacks of gold had been buried in the cave by the other three men while he was guarding the entrance. They had been killed without telling him of the hiding place.

Colossal Cave, as it is now known, was not systematically explored until 1922. The exploration party went about 39 miles into the mountain and never reached the end of the ancient dried-up underground waterway. The cave has not been thoroughly explored to this day, although the second entrance has been found. It is a completely dry (dead) cave without a drop of moisture. Natural ventilation keeps the air fresh. The temperature remains steady the year round at 72 degrees.

Wells Fargo did not believe the story told by the imprisoned bandit. When he was released an agent quietly shadowed him. The freed man went immediately to Tucson. Close behind him was Agent James Westphal. Here the outlaw remained a few days before giving Westphal the slip. Certain that the missing man would head immediately for the cave to recover the gold, Westphal lost no time in rushing there. He found no trace of the outlaw and no indication that anything had been removed from the cave. A three-day search of the cave turned up nothing.

Several years later some empty money sacks were found in the depths of the cave. Wells Fargo identified them as the same kind that contained the shipment of gold coins.

145

Who had recovered the treasure? Where was the remainder of it? These are questions Wells Fargo (the company still exists) would like to know. As you take a guided tour through Colossal Cave today, the guide obligingly points out where the money sacks were found and slyly suggests that more may be hidden there. Even if you ever have the opportunity, don't try to wander around in Colossal Cave without a competent guide. It is easy to miss the treasure and find death in its maze of dark passageways, chambers, caverns and silent rooms.

(60) Yuma's Lost Mine

VALUE: Gold ore assertedly assaying almost $51,000 to the ton.

LOCATION: Near the junction of the Gila and San Pedro rivers in Gila or Pinal County.

AUTHENTICATION: With ore of this value involved, it's a pity a stamp of authenticity can't be placed upon it.

Why some writers fail to give the real name of the principal character in this story is puzzling. This writer sees no point in withholding the identity of a man dead some 90 years, and especially the name of a man who figured so prominently in one of the better known lost mine tales of the Southwest.

His name was Thomas McLean (McLain), a man of high character until he became involved, through his own contrivance, or that of others, in a scandal at old Fort Yuma on the Colorado River. He was a graduate of West Point, where his heavy head of bushy black hair earned for him the nickname of "Buffalo Tom." It is said that he came from a fine Eastern family of long-standing military traditions.

146

In 1849 McLean showed up in the gold camps of California. A few years later he appeared in Arizona as Lieutenant McLean, acting quartermaster in charge of all army supplies shipped into Yuma by boat and then transshipped to the many inland military posts. The quantity of supplies passing through Fort Yuma was enormous, and the temptation to increase one's meager army pay must have been great. McLean did not long resist it, but whether or not he concocted the scheme to defraud the government, or was the innocent tool of crooked army contractors, is not clear. Several attempts to clear the matter up with army historical records in Washington have produced absolutely nothing. Whatever the circumstances, the story has it that Lieutenant McLean was court-martialed and discharged from the army in disgrace.

It seems that McLean now turned his back on white men and did everything in his power to become an Indian. He took up his residence with Yumas in the vicinity of the fort. He married the daughter of a chief and was made a full tribal member. From this period on, he never used his true name, but was known to white and red men alike as "Yuma."

Among the Yumas and the Papagos he was trusted as one of their own, and even the Apaches condescended to trade with him. With his wife serving as a safe passport among the various Indian tribes of southwestern Arizona, he traveled back and forth between Yuma and Tucson, carrying on a profitable trade with the red men. His pack mules were loaded with firearms, ammunition, calico, beads, and such other articles as the Indians cherished. He passed through hostile country where other white men dared not go alone. In trade he received coin and gold nuggets.

From his Indian wife, Yuma learned that a local group of Apaches known as the Aravaipas, possessed a rich mine from which they secured the gold to carry on their trading. As they needed the gold they took it out, otherwise keeping the source covered with gravel and brush. The chief *rancheria* of the Aravaipas was located about five miles from old Camp Grant, which was situated at the junction point of the San Pedro River and Aravaipa Creek, a few miles

147

southwest of Winkleman in Pinal County. It was near here that Yuma guessed from the information given him by his wife, that the rich Aravaipa placer was located.

When Yuma met Es-kim-en-zin, chief of the Aravaipas, he asked to see the mine, presenting the argument that, as a member of the tribe in good standing, he was only asking for his right to be let in on the secret. The Aravaipa chief was reluctant at first, but finally succumbed to Yuma's argument and agreed to take him to the place where the gold was picked up. They traveled in a northwesterly direction from the Aravaipa camp, climbed a long rocky ridge and kept on its crest for about three miles until they came to a range that overlooked San Pedro Valley to the east. Proceeding northward for another six miles, the chief suddenly stopped and announced that this was the place.

From the floor of a depression they were standing in, Yuma scraped away the loose earth with his hands and there was the ore! While digging out a generous sample with his knife, Yuma carefully observed the surrounding country, making mental notes of any landmarks. They returned to the Aravaipa camp and Yuma remained there several days to avert any suspicion that he was in a hurry to leave. When he eventually took leave, he did not return to the mine, but rode straight to Tucson.

Up to this point the various accounts of the tale are in general agreement. One story has it that Yuma returned to the mine in 1860 with a General Walker. (Whether this was Joseph R. Walker, or John D. Walker is not clear. Both were prominent in southwestern Arizona about that time.) They supposedly filled their saddlebags with the rich ore which they took to Tucson and publicly displayed. There was a lot of excitement, but they told their secret to no one.

In 1861, following the Indian troubles at Camp Grant (a white massacre of the reds), Yuma went into the Papago country to round up the cattle he grazed there. He feared a raid by the Apaches and planned to move his herd to safer country. The Papagos took this move to mean that he was joining up with the Apaches, their bitter enemies. As he slept in the shade of a mesquite, they crept up on him and clubbed him to death.

With the death of Yuma, the secret of the gold mine was now General Walker's. Continued fear of the Apaches kept him away from the gold, and in 1865 he died of tuberculosis. Before his death, however, he passed on the secret of the mine to a friend, John Sweeney. Sweeney was a heavy boozer and was more interested in the bars in Tucson than all the gold in Arizona. For the price of a few whiskeys he told the secret to one Charles O Brown, but the directions to the mine were so garbled that Brown was never able to locate the gold.

Now for a second version of the story. When Yuma returned to Tucson, he promptly looked up an old friend, John J. Crittenden, who operated a freighting business between Fort Yuma and Tucson. Yuma offered to take Crittenden in on an even share. Together they traveled to the Aravaipa mine, dug out all the ore they could carry in a few hours and returned at once to Tucson. For the thirty pounds of ore they had received they received $1200, which indicated that the ore assayed about $51,000 to the ton based on the present gold price.

News like this could not be kept quiet any place, let alone in Tucson, which was filled with gold seekers. Yuma and Crittenden decided to return to their respective occupations until the excitement abated. Yuma left on a trading trip to the Papago country west of Tucson. It was a routine trip for him except that now he was accompanied by his Indian wife. Crittenden made a freighting trip or two and then waited in Tucson for his partner to return. As the months went by and Yuma did not appear, he became uneasy. Yuma and his wife were never seen again. Crittenden believed that either the Papago or the Aravaipas had killed Yuma, and possibly his wife.

Crittenden finally worked up enough nerve to make another trip to the Aravaipa mine. Leaving Camp Grant, where he had secured supplies, he announced that he was going hunting. He never returned and it is assumed that the Apaches caught him near the mine and killed him.

Soon after the disappearance of Crittenden, a band of white-inspired Papagos and Mexicans swooped down upon the sleeping Aravaipa camp at Camp Grant and butchered

150

every adult man and woman. With this band of Aravaipa Apaches wiped out, it is believed that the secret location of the mine was lost, even to the Indians.

These are the two versions of the Yuma Lost Mine story. Neither one can be authenticated.

(61) Major Peeples' Lost Mine

VALUE: Unknown.

LOCATION: Probably in the area east and a little south of Congress Junction, in the hills extending to the Hassayampa River, Yavapai County.

AUTHENTICATION: Part of this story is absolutely authentic and attested to by several Arizona pioneers of unquestioned integrity. But it does not prove that the mine was there (the Indian may have been lying), or that it was not found by other parties at a later date. The location most generally given was in an area of intensive prospecting, and it seems unlikely that it could have been passed over all these years. On the other hand, it could have been covered up in the process of the erosive forces which are constantly changing the surface of the earth.

In 1862 Major Abraham H. Peeples, a prominent Arizona pioneer, was engaged in prospecting and mining at La Paz and other points along the Colorado River in western Arizona. The northern and central parts of Arizona at that time were occupied by large numbers of individual and distinct tribes of Indians, many of them under the rule of strict and able leaders. The interior Indians fraternized more or less freely with the Indians along the river, and many of them were tolerant of the white men, even though sometimes reluctantly so. From the interior the mountain

151

Indians came to La Paz to make purchases from the white traders, paying for their merchandise with gold, which they seemed to have in unlimited quantities.

The gold nuggets which the Indians offered in trade naturally aroused the interest and greed of the white prospectors, who used every trick and stratagem to learn the source from the Indians. About the only information an Indian ever gave was that he was forbidden under penalty of death by their chief to tell.

Major Peeples finally gained the confidence of one of these mountain Indians, and in exchange for a number of mules, he agreed to lead Peeples to one of the places where the gold was secured. At an agreed upon time the Indian was to meet Major Peeples at a secret rendezvous. From here they were to leave together for the gold field. Peeples, meantime, told the plan to Jack (Joseph Walker) Swilling, who, with two or three others taken in on the scheme, were to secretly follow Peeples and the Indian. However, the Indian did not meet Peeples as arranged. When Peeples next saw him, the Indian pleaded that he failed to show up because he feared the vengeance of his tribe if he revealed the location of the gold.

Further persuasion and some additional bribes finally reduced the Indian's fear and he agreed to leading the entire party on the mission. They left La Paz and crossed the desert in a northeasterly direction toward a range of mountains. At the last camp before reaching the mountains, the Indian refused to move another inch, insisting that he would certainly be killed by his tribe if he was seen in the region with the white men.

Jack Swilling, who minced no words, informed the Indian guide that he would surely be killed by the white men if he went back on his word. The Indian appealed to Major Peeples who promised protection only if he would reveal where the gold was located. That evening the red man confided to Peeples that they were very near the gold, which, he said, was scattered over the floor of a small canyon. This description was the very best Peeples could get out of the Indian. That night he disappeared from the camp.

When the Indian's absence was discovered the following

152

morning, the party of white men decided to push on. They did so with extreme caution lest they walk into an Apache ambush. Without incident, however, they finally reached the mountains. On the afternoon of the second day in the mountains they came to a small gulch through which ran a creek. They followed this creek to the foot of the highest peak in the range and made camp for the night. Saddle horses and mules were turned out to graze under the care of a Mexican who was the party's packer. The animals were soon grazing up the mountain slope, and when time came to bring them in for the night, they had rounded the mountain shoulder and were feeding on the opposite side.

The Mexican herder figured that by going to the top of the mountain he could not only see to locate the animals easier, but he could get a good view of the surrounding country. Perhaps he could also flush a deer. He reached the mountain top and there before his eyes, in a slight depression, he found the rocks and earth practically covered with nuggets and slugs of native gold. It was scattered over the whole surface and wedged into the crevices between rocks. Picking up several of the larger nuggets, he proceeded down the mountain, rounded up his horses and mules, and returned to the camp where he told his story and exhibited the gold.

Preparations were made at once to move the camp to the top of the hill. They gathered nuggets — some worth $500 to $600 each — until each man had a considerable fortune. That hill became known as Rich Hill, visible today to one's right while traveling east on U. S. 89, between Congress Junction and Peeples' Valley. It is said that Rich Hill yielded $500,000 in less than one year, and all taken from the surface in an area no larger than a single acre. Before its riches gave out it had produced a total of $70,000,000!

Major Peeples had found riches enough for any man, but he was never convinced that they had found the gold the Indian had agreed to take them to. For several years he kept prospecting parties searching for the lost mine of the Apache. It must be admitted that Peeples was no fool. He was a mining man of integrity. He knew the country. So far as is known, the gold referred to by the Indian has never

153

been found, although the whole region has been much explored and several rich mines have been found and worked. Only that long-dead Apache could tell whether his gold was ever found.

(62) Lost Squaw Mine

VALUE: Unknown.

LOCATION: Someplace between Yuma and Phoenix, or Yuma and Wickenburg, Maricopa or Yuma County.

AUTHENTICATION: If Ed Schieffelin thought the old squaw had found a rich deposit of gold, it's good enough for me.

Ed Schieffelin, one of Arizona's most noted — and successful — prospectors, after finding the great Tombstone bonanza, spent many years in roaming around North America in search of another rich strike. One day in Yuma he heard of an old squaw who had found a very rich deposit of gold. Many had tried to pry the secret from the old woman, but all had failed. Schieffelin decided to try his luck with her.

He located the squaw's hogan along the Colorado River and he spent hours in talking to her there. When the conversation was over, he knew no more than before. Schieffelin did not give up, however. He talked to the squaw again and again. Finally she gave him a brief description of a place that could have fitted almost any spot in southwestern Arizona. She did say, however, that it was along the trail between Yuma and Wickenburg. Schieffelin knew that country well. He knew it far too well to attempt any search over such a vast area. But she would not define the area closer, and Schieffelin finally gave up in disgust and started chasing down other rumors.

Next the old squaw was approached by a small group of

154

Mexican prospectors who had heard of the hidden deposit. When she refused to reveal anything to them, they applied some pressure. Still she would not talk. They threatened violence and went away, saying that they would be back. In the meantime the old squaw consulted the tribe. It was agreed that the Mexicans should be given some directions — false directions.

When the Mexicans returned, the old squaw and two bucks offered to take them part way to the deposit. They left and traveled to the northern end of the Harqua Hala Mountains. Here she stopped and refused to go further. The Mexicans beat her and when her tribesmen interceded, they were killed. Held a prisoner by the Mexicans, she resisted all efforts to force the secret from her. One night she managed to escape and returned to her people. Thereafter she refused to talk even to her own tribe about the gold.

When an immensely rich strike was made in the Harqua Halas sometime later, Ed Schieffelin visited the place and declared that it fitted the description given him by the Indian woman. He was convinced that it was the lost Squaw Mine. Others didn't agree. Maybe it was, and maybe it wasn't. To Ed Schieffelin it shouldn't have made any difference. He made a million dollars out of the Tombstone find.

(63) Walnut Grave Dam Treasure

VALUE: $6,500, mostly in gold coin.

LOCATION: In or along the old course of the fabled Hassayampa River, someplace between Wickenburg and its mouth. Maricopa or Yuma County.

AUTHENTICATION: This is a relatively small treasure, but the treasure seeker can take heart in that it is almost a certainty — unless, of course, it has been found.

155

In 1888 the Walnut Grove Water Storage Company built a loose rock, dirt-encased, mortar-lined dam across the Hassayampa River about 40 miles above Wickenburg. One hundred and ten feet high, 400 feet across the top, it backed up a lake of water two miles long, used in hydraulic mining in the Walnut Grove area, and to irrigate a small acreage. Twenty miles down stream a smaller dam was constructed to control the runoff from the larger dam. The dam was being rushed to completion when the rains came.

In the winter of 1889-1890, a great quantity of snow fell in the Bradshaw Mountains, followed by warm rains in February. Almost immediately the entire winter's accumulation of snow was turned into torrents of water which drained into the Hassayampa. In a short time the big lake back of the main dam was filled to capacity and overflowing out of control.

Early on the morning of Saturday, February 22, 1890, the big dam collapsed with a deafening roar and a hundred-foot wall of water cascaded down the canyon toward the smaller dam, which it reached in less than an hour. This dam was swept aside as if it had not been there.

It was known that the dam was weak and the fear that it might give way under the pressure of heavy rains was prevalent. When it was obvious that it could not hold, a rider was sent to warn the people below. He stopped at a saloon (one authority says it was Boulder Pat's place, but most agree that it was Bob Brow's Saloon at Fool's Gulch, the construction camp about 15 miles below the small dam) to spread the news, but was laughed at. Piqued with the reception given him, the rider stayed and joined the others in the revelry. Soon he, too, was drunk.

The loss of life in the flood was never established, but 83 bodies were later recovered, some as many as 25 years later when their skeletons were found in the sand along the Hassayampa. Out of this tragedy came a treasure that many people have searched for.

In the Conger Store at Seymore, $1500 was hidden in the rafters of the building. This was swept away together with $5000 in gold kept in a heavy iron safe in Bob Brow's

156

Saloon. The Hassayampa empties into the Gila at Palo Verde, and the Gila into the Colorado at Yuma, and the Colorado, of course, empties into the Gulf of California. The treasure safe could conceivably be any place between Wickenburg and the Gulf, but likely the heavy safe would not carry that far. Below the canyon the Hassayampa was over its banks for miles, so it is reasonable to assume that the heavy safe could have been covered by sand and left on dry ground after the waters receded.

(64) Lincoln—Glanton Treasure

VALUE: $50,000 to $80,000 in silver and gold coins was the sum believed to have been hidden by Lincoln. Glanton's fortune was believed to have been equal to this, or greater, also in coins. So this amounts to the tidy little sum of $100,000 to $180,000.

LOCATION: Some place in the near vicinity of Yuma, Yuma County. The caches would be in two parts as they were hidden separately. Glanton's share is conceivably buried on the California side of the Colorado.

AUTHENTICATION: Rarely is a treasure story so well documented as this. The facts are absolutely in the records. Nor has this story been widely publicized. The only question to concern the treasure seeker is whether the treasure has been found and kept a secret.

He signed his name "A. Lincoln," although it is believed that he was no relation to Abraham Lincoln. He was better known as "Doctor" Able B. Lincoln. He was serving in the army in the War With Mexico when he heard of the gold rush in California and decided to go there when discharged. He boarded a boat in Vera Cruz. After a long, tedious voyage, he disembarked at the mouth of the Rio Grande and made his way overland to Yuma Crossing (now Yuma, Arizona),

157

where he intended to cross the Colorado River into California.

At this time Yuma Crossing was claimed by California. Two ferries were operating across the river and both were doing a lucrative business, swelled by the increasing numbers of men rushing to the gold fields. Lincoln saw the money to be made at Yuma and purchased one of the ferries.

According to his own words, written in a letter to his parents, he began making money immediately. In his first three months of operating, he wrote that he had ferried 20,000 people across the river at the rate of more than 200 per day. During this time he grossed more than $60,000, charging $1 per man, $2 per horse or mule, another $1 for a pack, 50c for a packsaddle, and 25c for a saddle. He stated that he had 22 Americans in his employ, but, nevertheless, he did not expect to stay at Yuma Crossing longer than six months, possibly only another month, because the place was "unsafe to live in." How provocative his letter was! In less than a month he was involved with one of the bloodiest characters in Arizona history — John Glanton.

John Glanton was also a veteran of the Mexican War, having served as a member of the Texas Cavalry in General Taylor's army. Glanton seems always to have been in trouble, but he first came to attention officially when he murdered a helpless Mexican while in the army. The crime was so revolting that General Taylor ordered Glanton placed in irons. He escaped, returned to service and was mustered out in 1848.

After the war, Glanton turned up in San Antonio, Texas, where he made himself so obnoxious that he was lucky to escape to Mexico with his life. He next appeared in Chihuahua, where he became a professional scalp hunter, getting together a crew of equally desperate characters.

The Mexican government, eager to wipe out the Apaches, paid a bounty of from $50 to $500 per scalp, depending upon what kind of a deal could be made with the officials. Glanton led his band of murderers on expeditions and delivered scalps literally by the bale. When he ran out of Apaches, he found that he could trim the scalps of Mexicans to resemble Apache headpieces. In this fashion he sold

158

the Mexican officials the scalps of their own people. This continued until the Mexicans began to wonder why they found the bodies of so many scalped Mexicans in a country where there were no longer any Apaches. When the finger of suspicion pointed to Glanton, he left for California in a hurry.

At Yuma Crossing John Glanton met up with ferryman Able Lincoln. The ex-scalp hunter was not long in appraising the ferry business as a sure source of quick wealth. He went to work for Lincoln, and in some unexplained manner he soon pushed Lincoln aside as manager of the ferry and took over. He raised prices that were already prohibitive for many unfortunate travelers, abused the Yuma Indians who operated the second ferry down the river at Algodones, and generally made himself a most unpopular and despicable character. He is even accused of robbing emigrants who displayed any wealth while paying their tolls.

Not content with the enormous profits from Lincoln's ferry, Glanton decided to put the Indian ferry out of business. It thrived on mostly Mexicans headed for the California gold fields, and was operated by an American named Callaghan, employed by the Yumas. One night Callaghan was shot and killed. The ferry was cut loose from its moorings and drifted aimlessly down the river.

Suspecting Glanton, the Indians came to question him. Glanton greeted them by attacking their chief with a club. With a threat to kill an Indian for each Mexican they ferried across the river, Glanton threw the delegation out. Shortly after this incident, Glanton and some cronies went to San Diego to secure supplies. When they returned to Yuma Crossing, they threw a big celebration and all got drunk.

During the absence of Glanton, the Indians met and decided to meet his ruthless tactics with actions of their own. As the drunken white men lay sleeping off their spree, the Indians struck with vengeance in a surprise attack. Having no opportunity to escape or to defend themselves, the eleven Americans were killed, including Glanton and Lincoln. Glanton's head was split open by the chief whom he had insulted and clubbed. Able Lincoln had taken no part in the

159

drunken spree, but lay asleep in his cabin. He was clubbed to death in this place where it was "unsafe to live."

William Carr, one of three ferrymen to escape the attack, said later he knew that Lincoln had $50,000 in silver and between $20,000 and $30,000 in gold. He did not mention the bounty money Glanton is said to have buried under a mesquite tree. To this day no one really knows what became of this treasure.

Jeremiah Hill, an emigrant who arrived at Yuma Crossing a few days after the massacre, claimed that the Indians found Lincoln's treasure, but he said nothing of Glanton's. One of the Yuma chiefs, according to Hill, told him that the Yumas found three bags of silver, each of which was three feet high and two feet thick; and one bag of gold a foot high and a foot thick. The chief could not count, but indicated the size of the bags with his hands. He said that he distributed the coins among the members of his tribe. There is no record in Yuma, as far as this writer can learn, of the Yumas displaying the sudden wealth this windfall would have brought to them.

Glanton's treasure — the combined income from his scalping venture, his share of the ferry business, and from his sideline of robbery, seems quite likely to have exceeded that of Lincoln's. We have no knowledge of how he kept it, other than the report that it was buried under a mesquite tree. On the west bank of the Colorado, at that time, there was a grove of hundreds of acres of mesquite trees, according to the chronicles of travelers who crossed there during the gold rush. It has been speculated that, in the absence of any banking facilities, Glanton may have used this grove as a burial place for his treasure.

It is interesting to note that the State of California took official note of treasure hidden by Glanton and Lincoln. After the massacre of the ferrymen, Governor Burnett ordered the sheriffs of Los Angeles and San Diego counties to raise a militia of 40 and 20 men respectively, and to dispatch them to Yuma Crossing to protect travelers, to punish the Indians involved in the bloody affair, *and to recover as much as possible of the treasure that Lincoln and Glanton were supposed to have hidden away.*

160

The size of the militia was later increased to 100 men, but 142 actually made the trip to Yuma. At that time it was probably the best paid military force in history — and the State of California had trouble in finally paying the bill. Privates received $5 per day, corporals $6, sergeants $7, lieutenants $10, and all received their provisions. If a man supplied his own horse, he received an additional $1 a day for its use.

The Gila Expedition, as the California military party was called, consumed an incredible four years. Nobody was punished and absolutely nothing was accomplished. In the end it cost the State of California $113,482.25, which was more than the treasury contained! To meet part of the cost of the expedition, $99,000 worth of bonds were issued — and the expedition did not find the treasure.

(65) Lost Gold of Camel's Tank

VALUE: Unknown.

LOCATION: In the Tank Mountains northeast of Yuma, Yuma County.

AUTHENTICATION: A good tale to tell around the campfire; and that's probably where this one started.

John Gordon, a Scotsman, and Juan Perea, a Mexican, were as strange a pair of prospecting partners as ever saw a mirage. They had worked their way up the Colorado Desert north of the Gila, and their luck had been miserable every step of the way. The heat was furnace-hot. They were out of food. They were desperately short of water. Bilingually, they cursed the day they were born.

Had the Mexican not known the ways of the desert, they most certainly would have met their Maker then and there. "Look for a *tinaja!*" the Mexican said, aware that a *tinaja* (tank) is a natural bowl in the rocks that catches and holds water. They looked and they saw nothing but the simmering heat waves of the desert floor.

They came to a huge boulder that offered some welcome shade. They settled down by it to ponder their fate . . . death by dehydration. "Look!" shouted the Mexican, his swollen eyes set upon the form of an animal approaching from the nearby hills. "It can't be . . . but it is . . . a camel!"

And sure enough it was a camel — a stray from Lt. Beale's experiment in desert transportation. But the suffering prospectors knew nothing of this, and the strange sight only added to their delirium. The pleasantly contented-looking animal came nearer, walked right by them and disappeared around the rocks.

"*Madre de Dios!*" cried the Mexican. "He looks for water!" They struggled to their feet and took out after the lumbering beast. And it led them straight to a small *tinaja*.

Not until some time after they had quenched their thirst did the thankful prospectors notice that the ground around the tank was literally covered with gold nuggets. They gathered up all they could carry, filled their canteens with water, and returned happily to Yuma.

Just why the prospectors could never again find their way back to the camel's drinking place in the Tank Mountains is not clear, but they didn't. But then anything can happen when a Scotsman and a Mexican team up.

(66) The Treasure of Doubtful Canyon

VALUE: $28,000 to $30,000 in gold.

LOCATION: In Doubtful Canyon, in the Peloncillo (sometimes called Stein's Peak) Range of mountains, Hidalgo County.

162

AUTHENTICATION: The authenticity of the robbery is substantiated by old Butterfield Stage records still in existence. Whether or not the robbers found the money they were seeking is the question that has never been determined, and there is always the possibility that one of the many seekers for the treasure may have found it.

Stein's Peak Station was the last stage stop in New Mexico on the Butterfield route going west. It was a large stone-fortified station where meals could be had and horses changed before entering the most dangerous section of the route through Doubtful Canyon. It was here in Doubtful Canyon that stage passengers were offered the climax in excitement. There were places where the rim walls were so close that the stage barely cleared, yet the horses were whipped through on the dead run to avoid the possibility of being hit by rocks which were often hurled down by Indians from above.

The location of Doubtful Canyon, astride the New Mexico-Arizona border, was a notorious haunt of both Apaches and renegade whites. It was considered to be the single most dangerous stretch along the full 2800-mile length of the Butterfield route. An alternate route across Stein's Pass was used when Apaches were known to be in the area, but Doubtful Canyon was the most direct route, and most drivers preferred it in spite of the dangers it offered.

The station itself was situated in the eastern reaches of Doubtful Canyon, at the foot of Stein's Peak; its ruins are still visible, making the exact location easy to find.

On April 28, 1861, a party of seven Texans on their way from San Antonio to California, were waylaid by a band of renegade outlaws about one mile west of the station, in the wild and magnificent mountain pass. All seven of the Texans were killed.

The leader of the party of Texans was John James Giddings. He had been manager of the Texas Division of the Butterfield Stage Line, and at the outbreak of the Civil War, he had received orders to take all of the company's

163

money and proceed to its California terminal. He carried with them in the wagon between $28,000 and $30,000 in gold which he managed to hide among the rocks at the outset of the attack.

A short time after the massacre, a passing wagon train found the charred remains of the Butterfield wagon and five bodies. The bodies of Giddings and one other were not among those found. About a month later, an eastbound wagon train camped near the scene of the attack, and on the following morning, members of this party found the remains of Giddings and the other missing man in the rocks just outside their camp. A few scattered gold coins were found nearby, leading to the speculation that Giddings had managed to hide the gold before being killed.

Giddings and his companion were buried in graves near the point where their bodies had been found, but all traces of these graves have now disappeared. Near these now-lost graves the treasure probably rests — if indeed, the bandits did not secure it.

(67) Father La Rue's Lost Mine

VALUE: Unknown. The story goes that the rich mine was worked for several years and that all the gold recovered was refined into bars and stored in the mine with the exception of that portion used for the purchase of supplies and equipment, and possibly 96 bars taken out in modern times.

LOCATION: Two locations for this mine are usually given, but they are reasonably close together. One source places the mine in the Organ Mountains in Dona Ana County. Another source says the mine is located in a cavern on Soledad Peak in the San Andres Mountains. This would place the mine in the extreme southern end of Sierra County, but very close to the Dona Ana County line.

AUTHENTICATION: This is another story supposedly documented in old church records, but local people in the area are inclined to believe that the story was invented as part of a stock selling scheme.

Father La Rue (or La Ruz, as his name is sometimes given), a native of France, was one of a small band of priests who volunteered for service in Mexico. Father La Rue took up his work among the Indians and peons at a large hacienda near what is now the city of Chihuahua, arriving there in 1798.

From the people at the hacienda, Father La Rue heard tales of rich minerals to be found in the mountains to the north. If he was concerned with these stories of riches, he did not reveal it, for he went about his work caring for the physical and spiritual needs of his people, among whom there was an old man who had been a soldier of fortune during his younger days and had traveled far and wide in the surrounding country.

Father La Rue cared for the ailing man and the two became close friends. One day the good padre asked the old man about the tales of riches to the north. In reply, his patient said if it was gold he was seeking, he knew of a rich deposit high in the mountains, about two day's travel to the north of El Paseo del Norte (present day El Paso, Texas.)

"After one day's travel to the north of El Paseo del Norte," the old man explained, "you will come to three small peaks yet further to the north. Upon first sight of these peaks, turn to the east and cross the desert toward the mountains. In the mountains you will find a basin in which there is a spring at the foot of a solitary (Soledad) peak. On this peak there is a rich vein of gold." Shortly after making this statement the ailing man died.

Not until the hacienda was faced with a crop failure did Father La Rue again think of the solitary peak with

165

the gold. He called his people together and asked them if they would follow him to the north. They agreed and finally, the little party, carrying what possessions they could, started on the journey. They came to El Paseo del Norte and followed the Rio Grande to the little settlement of La Mesilla. North of there they sighted the three peaks and turned east across the dreaded Jornado del Muerto, arriving at last in the San Andres Range. In time they located a basin in the mountains and in it was a spring at the foot of a solitary peak, just as the old man had said there would be. The basin is popularly said to be Hembrillo Basin and the peak known on maps today as Soledad Peak.

After establishing a crude camp, Father La Rue sent the men out in search of the gold, and on the side of the peak they found a rich vein. They tunneled into the mountain, following the vein, and worked the mine for many years. All of the refined gold, except that used for the purchase of supplies and equipment in La Mesilla, they stored in a cavern which was a part of the mine.

Word reached the Church officials in Mexico City that Father La Rue and his entire colony was missing, the hacienda abandoned. A troop of soldiers was dispatched to trace the missing padre and his people.

One day when Father La Rue's men were in Mesilla, word arrived that Spanish soldiers were approaching. The miners rushed back to their camp and spread the alarm. Father La Rue, fearful that the soldiers would punish his people for abandoning the hacienda, knew also that he had not delivered the Royal Fifth from the mine. He immediately ordered all traces of the mine entrance concealed.

When the soldiers arrived, they were already aware of the mining activities, having heard of the purchases made in Mesilla with gold. They demanded to know where the gold came from, but Father La Rue stubbornly refused to tell. When a search of the area failed to disclose the location of the mine, the soldiers opened fire on the colonists. They fought back as best they could, but outnumbered and without weapons, they were soon overwhelmed. Father La Rue and most of his people were killed. A few escaped into the mountains and were never heard of again. Still fewer

166

were taken prisoners, but they permitted themselves to be beaten to death rather than reveal their secret. With the slaughter complete, the Spanish left the mountains and Father La Rue's mine was lost to the world — until, possibly, in 1937.

In November 1937 a resident of Hatch, New Mexico, E. M. Noss, was deer hunting in the San Andres. Making his way down the slope of Hembrillo Basin toward the spring, he hoped that a deer would bound into the open. Having no luck, he decided to climb nearby Soledad Peak to get a better view of the surrounding country. A light rain began to fall and he sought shelter under an overhanging ledge. While waiting for the weather to clear, he noticed a small crevice nearby and wriggled his way into it. Soon he found himself in a tunnel which led to a small room, where his flashlight revealed crude drawings on its walls. Progressing further, he came to a large boulder that blocked further movement. It appeared to Noss that the boulder had been deliberately placed there to impede further entrance. Removing some small rocks and dirt, Noss was soon able to crawl past the large boulder and here he found himself in another passageway that led to a large room. It was now late in the afternoon, and Noss left the cave and returned to Hatch.

Keeping the secret of Soledad Peak to himself, Noss soon returned for further exploration. He discovered the passageway to be a nearly vertical fault, extending down about 300 feet and leveling off into a series of caves. In the main cavern he found the mummified remains of 27 bodies and many articles indicating that a mining operation had once been conducted there. Further on, he came across some yellowed and musty papers and a neatly stacked pile of bars which he judged to be lead. Taking three bars and the papers with him, he concealed the entrance and left.

Later, Noss discovered that the bars were not lead, but gold! Still he kept the secret to himself. Among the papers taken from the cavern was a document dated 1797 and signed by Father La Rue. The full realization of his discovery now dawned on Noss. He had stumbled upon a fortune that had been resting there for some 200 years! He

167

hired a Mexican boy and removed some more bars of gold, but progress was very slow, and in blasting away a particularly annoying ledge, he succeeded only in blocking the passage completely and sealing off the remainder of the treasure.

During 1937, Noss is said to have taken 96 bars of gold from the cave, each having a value of $4500, or a total of $432,000. Finally in 1938 Noss sought help from friends to explore the cave further, but they made no progress. In 1939 he hired an engineer, but something went wrong with a blasting charge placed in the troublesome area of the passageway, and this sealed solid the entrance to the treasure room with hundreds of tons of rock. Further attempts to reach the gold bars were made in 1940, and in 1941 a company composed of about 40 people was formed to raise money to clear the passage and bring out the treasure which Noss estimated to amount to several million dollars. Having already recovered $432,000 worth of gold bars, it is hard to understand why Noss required further financing.

When World War II came along, the area encompassing Soledad Peak was closed to the public and made part of a bombing range. This stopped all further attempts to secure the treasure.

In 1949 Noss was foreman for a mining company owned by Charles Ryan of Hatch, New Mexico and Alice, Texas. On March 25, 1949 Noss and Ryan became involved in a quarrel and Noss was killed. The details of the argument have never been made clear, but presumably it occurred over the money Ryan had advanced to Noss to secure the treasure in Soledad Peak. Ryan is also said to have had an interest in the 96 gold bars supposedly recovered by Noss, but which Noss would not produce on Ryan's insistence.

(68) Simeon Turley's
Lost Mine

VALUE: Unknown

LOCATION: Two miles west of the village of Arroyo
Hondo will be found the remains of Turley's Mill
and Distillery. Somewhere in the vicinity of this mill
Simeon Turley found a source of gold.

AUTHENTICATION: This story is documented beyond
any question by letters written by Simeon Turley, and
still in the possession of the Turley family. This lost
mine is not only an authentic one, but in the belief of
the writer, has never been the subject of any search.

In 1827 Simeon Turley went to Santa Fe, then a part of
Old Mexico. Three years later, he had the most flourishing
ranch and trading center in the Taos district. Two miles
from the village of Arroyo Hondo, and about 12 miles from
Taos Pueblo, he threw a dam across the Hondo River, built
a grist mill, distillery (the famous "Taos Lightning" was
made here), a store and a general trading post. The remains
of these buildings can be seen today.

Turley's extensive ranch had herds of cattle and sheep,
and supplied all their wheat and corn. Later he added
looms and spinning wheels, and all the things necessary for
a comfortable and civilized life on the frontier were made
available to his family and the people working for him,
mostly Pueblo Indians and Mexicans.

Turley married a Mexican girl and raised a family of
several children. He was a king, but he was also a kind,
generous and jolly man who never turned a needy person
away from his door empty-handed. So far as he knew he did
not have an enemy in the world and, therefore, he was not

169

unduly alarmed one day in 1847 when a rider brought word that a party of insurrectos was marching on his ranch.

He knew of course, that Charles Bent, Governor of the newly-formed New Mexico Territory, had been killed on January 19, 1847, along with other Americans, by an uprising of Pueblo Indians and Mexicans in an attempt to break American rule of the country. It was with reluctance that he finally yielded to the pleas of the nine Americans at his mill and built a barricade for their protection. It was unthinkable to Turley that the Indians and Mexicans, all his friends, would harm the husband of a good Mexican wife.

But Turley underestimated the fury of the mob. They arrived and demanded surrender of the ranch and the nine Americans, although they did consent to let him remain unharmed. He refused to betray his American friends, and the siege of Turley's Mill began.

For three days the battle raged, and Turley held his own until the mill was set afire. Enveloped by smoke, he and another man escaped into a canyon, and although Turley was a cripple, they managed to work their way north. On their way into the mountains, Turley met a Mexican friend who advised the fleeing men to take shelter in an abandoned ranch. On the following night he promised to return with food and mules. Then, the good samaritan rode straight to the mill and informed the raiders of Turley's hiding place. That night, thirty men rode to the abandoned ranch, called Turley by name, and when he appeared, riddled him with bullets.

At that time it was known only to a few members of Turley's family in Missouri that he had a secret source of gold. In a letter dated April 18, 1841, Turley wrote to his brother Jesse, and said in part, "I expect to send to the lower country this fall with robes and blankets as I had no choice to send in the robes. Send me word if any kind of stock will do to drive to the States, money is so scarce it is hard for me to get holt (sic) of it, I shall try hard to get the gold mine worked this summer as I think there is plenty clost (sic) to me but as I have got to be such a cripple I am not able to attend to aney (sic) business."

170

In another letter dated in 1843, he wrote, "I send to your wife some gold that was got out close to my house to make what ever she pleases of and pleased to write to me what gold is worth by the ounce as I have it in my power to get some quantity of it, it is here worth 19 per Am. Oz."

Part of this gold which Turley sent to Missouri was made into a ring which (in May 1958) was still in possession of Miss Jesse Turley of Blackwater, Missouri, then almost 90 years of age.

To the best knowledge of the writer, this is the first time the story of Simeon Turley's gold mine has appeared in print.

(69) The Hidden Gold of Madame Barcelo

VALUE: Gold coins worth $150,000 when minted in the 1830s, but probably worth more than twice that today.

LOCATION: Near a rock "half as large as a house" about 40 miles east of Taos, Colfax County.

AUTHENTICATION: The threads from which this story is woven are pretty thin. If such a person as Madame Barcelo ever existed, a diligent search in New Mexico has failed to reveal it.

Madame Barcelo was said to have dealt monte in her dancehall and saloon in Santa Fe when the country still belonged to Old Mexico. Her place was popular with freighters, traders, trappers and adventurers. She prospered, and in a day when there were no banks in which to deposit one's wealth, she decided that it would be prudent to ship her accumulation of 25 bags of gold coins to New York for safekeeping. The freighting firm of Cortez and De Grazi told

171

her that they did not handle valuables, but Madame made such a lucrative offer that they could not turn it down.

The slow line of pack mules left Santa Fe at dawn, ten of them carrying Madame Barcelo's fortune. No extra guards accompanied the train lest this be a tip-off that valuables were being carried. By noon, De Grazi's suspicions were aroused when he spotted a cloud of dust behind them. No question about it, he told his partner, they were being followed. Selecting a place where they could defend themselves, they stopped and waited. The cloud of dust disappeared and, with lightened hearts, they moved on.

Just as they were making camp that night, the cloud of dust appeared again and the packers hurriedly prepared to fight off the attackers. They waited with loaded guns, but no attack came. Presently the sound of galloping horses was heard on the ridge to the north, and in the fading light the figures of eight riders could be made out. Cortez was certain that the bandits were racing ahead to select a place of ambush of their own choosing. The long night passed uneventfully, and at daybreak the train was moved out, tightly grouped in anticipation of the attack that might come at any moment.

At noon, as they approached three large rocks, one of which was later described as "half as large as a house," they were suddenly fired upon. The siege lasted all afternoon and into the night. But under the cover of darkness the bandits improved their position, and two of the Mexican packers were killed. Early in the morning the tethered mules broke loose and bolted. Madame Barcelo's gold was safe, however, having been unpacked and placed in temporary hiding.

Cortez, aware that their position afoot would lead to eventual annihilation, ordered two separate holes dug. When this was completed, the bodies of the two dead men were placed in one, and the bags of gold in the other. Over the pit containing the gold a fire was built in the hopes that their attackers would not suspect that the treasure was buried there.

The battle continued all that day, but toward evening, DeGrazi and Cortez asked for a truce. Their attackers, re-

172

vealed now to be a band of Mexicans, immediately demanded the gold. Cortez insisted that the shipment of Madame Barcelo's gold had been delayed and would be carried by the next train. This infuriated the Mexicans and the fight was renewed. Soon only Cortez remained alive.

What to do with Cortez? If they killed him, the Mexicans reasoned, they might never know where the gold was hidden, for they were certain that it had left Santa Fe on this train. Finally the decision was made to take Cortez to Mexico with them. One night as they slept, Cortez managed to reach a horse and escaped. After days of riding, he finally reached Santa Fe, exhausted and almost at the point of collapse. He told his story to Madame Barcelo and drew a crude map of the treasure site, indicating the grave at the base of three large rocks.

Without delay Madame Barcelo sent a party of armed men to recover her gold, supplying them with the map. After several days when they did not return, another party went out in search of them. They were all found massacred and scalped. No trace of the single treasure map was found.

Periodic searches were made for the three rocks for many years, but they were never located — nor was the treasure — if it ever existed.

(70) The Many Treasures of Sam Bass

VALUE: The total value of the Sam Bass treasures, said to be buried in eight widely scattered spots in Texas, amounts to $355,000. However, all available records prove that Bass and his gang secured, at the most, only $70,000 from their hauls, and that $25,000 of this was recovered. This left a mere $45,000 to be divided among members of the gang.

LOCATION: The eight locations usually given, and the amount attributed to each are: 1) Near Springtown,

173

Parker County, amount unknown; 2) Northwest of Denton, Montague County, $30,000; 3) In a cave near McNeil, Travis County, $30,000; 4) Near Dallas, Dallas County, $30,000; 5) In a cave on Packsaddle Mountain, Brewster County, amount unknown; 6) Near Rosston, Wise County, $200,000; 7) Near Costell, Llano County, $60,000; 8) Near Breckenridge, Stephens County, $5,000.

AUTHENTICATION: As an outlaw, Sam Bass didn't cut much of a swath, but he left a big mark in the book of Texas legends. The stories of his buried treasures seem to be a part of them.

Sam Bass was an orphan boy who came to Texas from Indiana, longing for the exciting life of a cowboy. He stayed to become a hero, an outlaw and a legend.

Sam was nineteen when he reached Denton County in 1870. He found work on a ranch, but after a while he found that kind of excitement tiresome. In time, he went to work in the town of Denton and finally became the "hired man" of the sheriff who also operated a freighting business. Bass frequently accompanied the hauler, and in this manner acquired a large acquaintance among the people of north Texas and a great knowledge of the trails and roads.

Pony racing was in vogue in Denton and this sport offered Sam the excitement he was looking for. In time, he bought a mare and was soon winning races from the Red River to the Mexican border. There was some talk that Sam's races weren't always honest.

A friend, Joel Collins, talked Sam into investing his race winnings in a herd of cattle before it was consumed in liquor. In 1877, Bass and Collins combined their herds and drove them to Dodge City, then the center for the trail herds out of Texas. The market was unfavorable when they arrived there, so they continued on to Deadwood, Dakota Territory, then in a mining boom. Here the herd was sold for a good profit, and the two trail drivers decided on a

174

night's celebration before heading back for Texas. By morning, the two young Texans were broke, having lost the money from the sale of their herd at the gaming tables.

Sam and Joel now organized a small band of robbers and attempted to recoup their losses by holding up stagecoaches. After several successful jobs in which their haul was disgustingly small, Sam decided that they would never recover their losses and get back to Texas unless they pulled a really big job.

On September 18, 1877, Sam and four men rode into the tiny station at Big Springs, Nebraska, on the Union Pacific Railroad. When the eastbound passenger train pulled in that night and stopped for water, the five armed men overwhelmed the engine crew and forced the opening of the express car. Much to their surprise, and quite by accident, they found a pouch filled with 3000 freshly-minted $20 gold pieces. After relieving the passengers of their valuables, the robbers mounted their horses and rode away.

A short distance out of Big Springs, the gang halted, divided the loot, and split up into pairs, fully aware that officers would soon be on their trail, and that the coins bearing an 1877 date would be a dead giveaway if they were caught. A few days later, Joel Collins was overtaken by a posse and killed. In his saddlebags the officers found $25,000 of the stolen loot.

Following a devious route, Sam finally made his way back to Texas and set up a hideout in Cove Hollow, a lonely spot thickly covered with trees and brush about thirty miles from Denton. Shortly, Bass had organized another gang and before long they were preying on stagecoaches in the area Sam knew so well. Then, in a period of forty days, and within thirty miles of Denton, they held up four trains. The name of Sam Bass was on every lip in Texas, particularly the members of the famed Texas Rangers.

Sam was a sort of a Robin Hood to the Texas folks. He never stole from them, and payed them with good, hard cash — nice, new $20 gold pieces. In return, they hid him and tipped him off when the Rangers got closer than comfort permitted. Anyway, who much cared if the railroads were robbed? Weren't they just robbers of another sort?

175

Inevitably, the Rangers slowly moved in on Sam and the members of the gang. Sam replied by moving the gang southward, deciding to rob the Williamson County bank at the little town of Round Rock. Just before the robbery, a new member, Jim Murphy, joined the gang, but he was a traitor, already committed to tip the Rangers off about the time and place of the robbery.

When Sam, Seab Barnes and Frank Jackson arrived in Round Rock on the appointed day, the Rangers were already there waiting for them. In the street gunbattle that followed, Barnes was killed, Sam was critically wounded, and only Jackson escaped. They found Sam the next morning, dying beneath a tree. He was brought into Round Rock where he breathed his last on his twenty-seventh birthday, having found the excitement he had been seeking. On the stone put up to mark his grave, they carved these words: "He was a brave man. Why was he not true?"

Sam Bass was no sooner buried than the legends regarding his treasure were born. Some say Sam spent the last of the 1877 $20 gold pieces in a Waco saloon. Others say that the last of the Big Springs holdup money was spent on a new gun for Jim Murphy, the traitor who led Sam to his death. Still, there are many others who believe that Sam buried part of his loot and could not get to it, forcing him to attempt the Round Rock robbery to secure funds.

With part of his loot reportedly buried in so many location in Texas, was any of it ever found? No one can be sure. Perhaps a young farmer, Henry Chapman, who lived near Springtown, Parker County, came close to it. One day he was riding a mule through the woods from Harrison's gin, at the pool on Clear Fork, to Miller's place near the mouth of Salt Creek. At a point near Skeen's Peak, his mule shied and broke the saddle girth. While he was dismounted, mending the girth, he discovered a pile of fresh earth covered with brush. He supposed at first that it was the grave of a slain person, but he was curious and removed the brush and fresh earth.

Within a few minutes, Chapman uncovered a wooden box big enough, he said later, to hold a bushel and a half. It was filled to the top with gold and silver coins, many of

176

them $20 gold pieces. He was filling a sack with coins when he looked up and saw eight riders approaching in the distance. He hastily mounted and rode away. He never saw the men again, but he was sure they were surviving members of Sam Bass' gang, returning to recover the treasure they had helped the outlaw bury.

Hardly a year passes that does not produce a report of Sam's gold being found. So far as is known, these reports are never verified. The legend of Sam Bass lives on — man-sized.

(71) Treasure of El Muerto Springs

VALUE: Church jewels and gold ingots and coins with a total value placed in excess of $2,000,000.

LOCATION: In a cave in the Davis Mountains near El Muerto Springs, Jeff Davis County.

AUTHENTICATION: There is considerable reason to believe that this huge treasure actually exists. It is a documented fact that the Red Curly gang did conduct a raid on Monterrey, Mexico, and did make off with a fabulous treasure which they probably had to bury.

In 1879, there came to the Davis Mountains in Jeff Davis County, Texas, four Arizona bandits on their way to the Big Bend country. Led by Red Curly, whose real name was Andrew ("Sandy") King, the others consisted of Zwing Hunt, Jim Hughes, and John ("Doc") Neal, who is said to have been a doctor. For several years, this group had operated in New Mexico and Arizona, making frequent raids into Mexico. Planning their biggest foray yet into Mexico, they needed help, and they were looking for Juan Estrada, a Mexican outlaw who led a gang specializing in raids on both sides of the border in the Big Bend region.

For the project Red Curly had in mind, tne gang needed mules to carry back the loot they expected to seize in a bold robbery of the mint in Monterrey, Mexico. Here in the Davis Mountains they camped near Fort Davis, an army post rehabilitated that year to control rampaging Apache warriors. As Red Curly knew, wherever there was an army post, there were bound to be mules.

Hiding in the underbrush at the edge of a hayfield near Lobo, the four bandits watched a detachment of colored troops harvest the meadow, as a hundred or more long-eared mules grazed nearby. Carefully watching for their chance, the bandits finally caught the troops off guard, and suddenly poured volley after volley into their ranks, completely demoralizing the soldiers who fled afoot in all directions. Hurriedly, Curly's gang rounded up sixty mules and herded them south toward the border. That night, a downpour of rain obliterated their trail. Three nights later they rode into Presidio, a small town of sun-baked adobe buildings squatting in the shade of giant cottonwood trees along the Rio Grande.

It was not long before Juan Estrada was located in Ojinaga, the Mexican town across the river at the head of the Chihuahua Trail, one of the main freight routes into Mexico. Would he join Curly's gang in a raid on Monterrey? Estrada was delighted to throw in with the Americans, especially after Red Curly convinced him that an enormous amount of loot was just waiting there to be taken, and that he would receive a generous split for he and his 21 men.

Their pack mules loaded with a supply of empty burlap sacks, the train of 26 men and a long string of mules started south. Two days out of Presidio, they stopped at a group of bat caves and filled the bags with guano. This, Red Curly explained, was to give them a reason to be seen in Monterrey without arousing suspicions. They were traders, bringing fertilizer to sell to the peons.

Two weeks later, the bandit gang made camp on the outskirts of Monterrey, a rich cathedral town and the capital of Nuevo Leon. On the following day, the fertilizer was sold in the public market place and the bandits were free to

178

revel unmolested in the saloons, their presence freely accepted.

No federal troops were stationed in Monterrey, the nearest garrison being located some 140 miles away. The guarding of the gold smelter and mint, both located in the center of town, was trusted to local rurales, a small group of peons just recently converted into police officials. On the evening before the big strike was to be made, these guards were wined and dined by Red Curly and Juan Estrada until each was drunk and out of commission.

At midnight the bandits stormed the mint, easily killing off the few remaining guards. The great vault where the gold coins and bars were stored was blasted open and the enormous treasure loaded onto the waiting pack mules. Simultaneously, another group of the outlaws raided the cathedral, making off with a solid gold Virgin Mary and an assortment of precious stones.

When the outlaws rode unchallenged out of Monterrey, each of 28 mules carried 150 pounds of treasure; the remaining mules traveled unburdened, to take over the load on the following day. This plan was conceived to permit a rapid escape northward.

Reentering Texas at the mouth of Reagan Canyon, the train made its way northwest to the Davis Mountains where Red Curly had selected a cave near El Muerto Springs as the hiding place for the loot. Some twenty miles from their destination, Curly told Estrada that he and his men would ride ahead to scout the country. Elated with his riches, the Mexican leader agreed that it was a smart move.

As Estrada and his men hearded the mules through a narrow rock-walled canyon, they suddenly ran into a rain of bullets, and one by one they were slaughtered. Gathering the frightened mules, Red Curly's men herded the treasure-laden animals toward the El Muerto Springs cave where the loot was unloaded and concealed after each man had stuffed his pockets with all he could carry. Filling the entrance to the cave, the bandits rode away to spend their gold coins in the dives of New Mexico and Arizona.

In 1881 the same gang returned to El Muerto Springs with more treasure and four Mexicans they had hired to dig

179

a deep hole. When the pit was 12 feet deep, the Monterrey treasure was removed from the cave and, together with the new loot from an Arizona train robbery, was dumped into the freshly-dug hole. The four Mexicans were then killed and toppled into the hole they had just dug. When the treasure was carefully covered and tamped down, its surface was cleverly cemented over. That is supposedly the last ever seen of the enormous loot of Monterrey.

Back in Arizona the bandits finally got into trouble over the shooting of a man who refused to have a drink with them. Doc Neal was killed by a sheriff's posse. Zwing Hunt was captured, taken to Tombstone and jailed, only to escape and be killed by Apaches. Red Curly and Russina Bill, who later joined the gang, were caught in Shakespeare, New Mexico and hanged from the rafters of the Pioneer House dining room. Jim Hughes escaped and for a while ran a saloon in Lordsburg, New Mexico where he was killed in a brawl with a drunk.

As for the treasure of Monterrey, it supposedly reposes in its Davis Mountain hideaway. If it was ever found, no report of it was made public.

(72) The Lost Treasure of Palo Duro

VALUE: $20,000 in newly-minted $20 gold coins.

LOCATION: In Palo Duro Canyon, Randall or Armstrong County, Texas Panhandle.

AUTHENTICATION: There is a considerable semblance of truth to this story.

During the California gold rush, John Casner and three grown sons immigrated from the East along with thousands of others, hoping to strike it rich. The Casners were among

180

the few hopefuls who amassed wealth, but they tired of prospecting and decided that they wanted to go into the sheep-
raising business, selecting the relatively unsettled Panhandle
section of Texas as their most likely prospect.

Taking their small fortune in mined gold to the United
States mint in Carson City, Nevada, they had it minted into
$20 gold pieces — 1000 of them. Separating here, the father
and one son, Lew, headed southward through Southern California, intending to prospect the area, as well as Arizona and
New Mexico, on their way. The other two sons, with two
yoke of oxen pulling a wagon containing their belongings
and the gold, headed east through southern Colorado, purchasing sheep to add to their herd along the way. They
crossed the high plains of northeast New Mexico, over the
Staked Plains to the headwaters of the Red River in the
Palo Duro Canyon, a wild gorge through the placid prairie
land.

In time, the Casner brothers had established a home in
the canyon and employed a Navajo boy to herd their flocks.
They were expecting the arrival of their father and brother
when Sostenes Archiveque, a notorious outlaw, rode into
their camp with a Mexican boy from Tascosa. Sostenes had
been run out of the settlements along the Rio Grande. He
carried an undying hatred of all Americans, said to have
stemmed from the fact that his father had been killed by an
American when he was a boy. He swore to kill every American he met, and old timers claimed that he had slain twenty-
three.

Approaching the Casners in a friendly manner, Sostenes
induced one of them to accompany him on a hunt down the
canyon. As they passed along the trail through a thicket,
Sostenes dropped back and shot the American through the
head. Returning to the camp, Sostenes got the drop on the
other brother and killed him. He then ordered the Mexican
boy to kill the Navajo lad working for the Casners. The
young Mexican, however, mounted Sostenes' horse and rode
swiftly to Tascosa where he reported the killings to Colas
Martinez, an old Indian trader and sheepman.

Forced to walk the forty-odd miles to Tascosa, Sostenes
arrived one night and went directly to the home of Colas

181

Martinez. Angered by the unjustified killings, Colas and some friends stabbed Sostenes to death and buried him on a little eminence where they marked the grave with a cross.

About a week later, Leigh Dyer, brother-in-law of Charles Goodnight, and trail boss of the Goodnight herds, and James T. Hughes, son of the author of "Tom Brown's School Days," and herd rider for Goodnight, happened to be exploring the upper reaches of Palo Duro Canyon when they came upon the Casner herd, attended by the faithful dog of the Navajo boy who also had been slain by Sostenes. Nearby, they found the body of one of the Casner brothers.

When Charles Goodnight later came to the canyon, he learned of the murders and searched the bodies, but found no identification. In Pueblo, he gave the story of the local papers and requested that western newspapers carry the story along with a description of the property, in the hope that relatives might see the item.

John Casner and his son Lew were prospecting near Silver City, New Mexico, with two men named Berry and Bell. Neither of the Casners could read, but when one dropped into town for provisions, a storekeeper wrapped some of his purchases in a paper containing the story of the Casner murders in Palo Duro Canyon. Back at the camp, the purchases were unwrapped and the paper thrown away. Berry picked it up and happened to read the account aloud. John Casner recognized the description of the property and knew that the murdered boys were his sons. With Berry and Bell, the Casners struck out for Texas where they convinced Charles Goodnight that the property was theirs.

Positive that his sons had hidden the $20,000 in gold some place near their camp in the canyon, Casner made a thorough search, but found nothing. He swore to kill all the Mexicans in the region. Goodnight pleaded with the angry father that further murders would only create additional trouble between the Americans and Mexicans, but Casner was determined.

The Casners rode into Tascosa where they killed old Colas Martinez, unaware that he was not a Mexican, but an Indian, and that he had avenged the murder of his sons by killing Sostenes Archiveque. They hung his wife up by

182

the thumbs, trying to make her reveal something of which she had no knowledge — the murderer of the Casner brothers. Finally they cut her down and rode away. The Casners were never seen again in the Texas Panhandle.

Palo Duro is now a state park, and treasure hunting is frowned upon, but someone may just accidentally kick up the Casner treasure someday, for it is almost certainly there if it has not yet been found.

(73) Pirate Treasure of Hendricks Lake

VALUE: $2,000,000 in Spanish silver bullion bars.

LOCATION: In Hendricks Lake, near Tatum, Harrison County.

AUTHENTICATION: Since pirate treasure is invariably immersed in legend, one would suspect that this is true of the Hendricks Lake treasure, except for the persistent attempts to bring this vast amount of silver to the surface and the wealth spent in the endeavor to do so. One would have to surmise that these treasure seekers must be urged on by some kind of documentary evidence that the treasure is there. If such evidence exists, it has never come to the attention of this writer.

The story starts with Jean Lafitte, the "Gentleman Pirate" of the Gulf, whose exploits are surely known to all treasure hunters. Having finally been driven from his Galveston Island headquarters, where he had operated unmolested for many years, Lafitte moved southwestward into the less protected waters of Corpus Christi Bay. Here his ships continued their acts of piracy against the Spanish treasure ships transporting the wealth of Mexico to Havana and then on to Spain.

183

In 1816, the Spanish ship "Santa Rosa," having been blown off her usual course, was at anchor in Matagorda Bay, preparing to set sail for Havana with her cargo valued at $2,000,000 — all in silver bullion bars — destined for the Spanish treasury in Madrid. The vessel was just under way when Lafitte's crewmen attacked. After an exchange of shots, the "Santa Rosa" surrendered and was boarded.

Knowing that his days of piracy in Texas waters were numbered, Lafitte decided that his immense haul should be shipped to St. Louis at once for safe keeping. Accordingly, he hired an unsavory character named Gaspar Trammel, who operated a freight line over the old Trammel Trace, to transport the "Santa Rosa's" silver out of the reach of Mexican authorities.

The wagon train had covered about 200 miles and was camped at a little lake fed by the headwaters of the Sabine River when a rider galloped in with word that Mexican troops were approaching. Hurriedly, Trammel ordered the treasure wagons containing the silver bars rolled into the lake which is now known as Hendricks Lake. Minutes later, the Mexicans appeared and soon a pitched battle was in progress. Trammel and most of his men were killed, only two or three making their escape into the timbered wilderness of East Texas.

Not realizing that six of the wagons were missing, the Mexicans pulled the remaining wagons back to San Antonio before making the discovery that the silver-laden wagons had been rolled into the lake. Racing back to recover the treasure, they found that spring rains had raised the lake several feet above its normal level, making any salvage work impossible. They returned to San Antonio and as far as the Mexicans were concerned, the search for the "Santa Rosa's" silver was ended.

Not so the Spanish, however. About 79 years later, three Spaniards from Mexico came to East Texas and tried their luck at draining the lake. They found this to be impossible because of underground springs that fed the lake as fast as it could be drained off. Eventually the Spaniards gave up in disgust and returned to Mexico.

One of the two or three men in Gaspar Trammel's party

184

to escape massacre at the hands of the Mexicans was named Robert Dawson. He actually reached St. Louis where he told the story to any who would listen, but knowing exactly where the six silver-laden wagons were rolled into the lake, it is strange that Dawson, so far as is known, never made any attempt to recover the treasure. Fox Tatum, an early settler after whom the town of Tatum was named, reportedly made an unsuccessful try at draining the lake in 1855.

The treasure of Hendricks Lake seemed to have been forgotten until the late 1920's, when three fishermen are said to have fished up three silver bars. Although no one seems to know who the fishermen were, nor where they were from, or ever saw the silver bars, the story created wide interest in the treasure.

In 1959, a Houston drilling company dynamited the lake and recovered a six-foot high wagon wheel which was said to have been some 100 years old. This, of course, has been accepted as positive evidence that the treasure is there — and well it may be. Other pieces of wood have been brought up and metal locators are said to indicate the presence of metal on the bottom of Hendricks Lake.

As this is written, no doubt other attempts to recover the pirate treasure of Hendricks Lake are being planned.

(74) Empire Stagecoach Treasure

VALUE: $60,000 in gold bullion.

LOCATION: Between the Nevada State Prison at Carson City and Empire, Ormsby County.

AUTHENTICATION: The records of the Nevada State Prison do not support the so-called facts of this story of which several versions are told.

Sometime in the early days of Nevada — the date given varies between 1870 and 1890 — a stage carrying $60,000 worth of gold bullion left Virginia City for the United States Mint at Carson City. The driver had passed through Empire City (now called Empire) and was rattling along through the sagebrush flats when four armed men appeared from concealment and ordered the driver to pull up. Quickly the bandits secured the strongbox and rode off.

One version of the story reports that guards fired on the bandits, killing two while the third escaped. Another version states that the four men made their getaway, but were later surrounded by a posse and three were killed while the fourth, a Mexican, was captured.

In either case, the outlaws found it impossible to flee with the bullion, supposedly weighing 234 pounds, and hurriedly buried it in the sage covered hills northeast of Carson City. In the first version of the story, the lone surviving bandit immediately went to a Carson City saloon and was promptly recognized and arrested. In either case, the surviving holdup man was convicted and sentenced to a term in the Nevada State Prison, then located on the south-eastern outskirts of Carson City.

Both stories now agree that the prisoner asked for and was given a cell from which he could look out over the open country toward the spot where the stagecoach loot was hidden. This fine cooperation upon the part of the prison authorities was not reciprocated by the prisoner, for throughout his confinement he stubbornly refused to tell where he had buried the $60,000.

After serving eight years of his term, Wells Fargo, in whose care the bullion had been entrusted, influenced the governor to grant the prisoner a full pardon, the hope being that the free man would lead Wells Fargo agents to the treasure. Contradicting this, the second version of the story relates that the prisoner served his full term with substantial time off for good behavior, but just before his release, he took ill and died.

More melodramatic still is another version of the story. The prisoner was pardoned and released, but he was suffering from tuberculosis. He was befriended and taken in by a German butcher who tried to learn the secret hiding place of the gold from the ailing man. Eventually, the pardoned

186

man agreed to take the butcher with him to dig up the gold. All preparations for the trip were made, but as the bandit started to mount his horse, he fell dead.

It is said that the warden of the Nevada State Prison in 1935 considered suggestions that convicts be allowed to search for the stolen gold, but no action was taken. It has been suggested that convicts with illegal gold in their possession may have been the reason the project was never carried out. It is our opinion that the warden had better sense than to send his prisoners through the desert hills to search for a chest of gold that likely never existed.

(75) Duckett Lost Mine

VALUE: An outcropping of gold ore said to have a value of $15,000 per ton.

LOCATION: Three or four miles from Black Spring (also known as Pillar Spring), Nye County.

AUTHENTICATION: There is little or no documentary evidence to support this lost mine story, but it has persisted for many years.

In 1871, a French-Canadian prospector named Louis Duckett left the mining camp of Belmont on horseback, leading another horse carrying his pack. He was headed for the Colorado River where he planned to prospect a new region. As nearly as can be determined, he was near Pillar Spring without being aware of it when he found himself running out of water. He climbed a small juniper-covered hill to get a better view of the country when he came face to face with a lone Paiute Indian. With signs, he finally made the Indian understand that he was searching for water, and the redman led him along a faint trail that came to a large ravine. Part way down the ravine, they came to the spring.

After he had replenished his water supply, and had given his horses a chance to drink their fill, he asked the friendly Indian if he knew where there was any gold. After some time the Indian finally understood and grunted that he knew "plenty gold." He produced some samples and showed them to Duckett, but he played very dumb when the prospector tried to find out where the gold came from. Finally, the Indian offered to take him to the gold in exchange for the horse Duckett was riding. The trade completed, they rode away together.

At a distance said to have been no more than three or four miles, the Indian pointed to an outcropping and immediately rode away. Duckett gathered about 15 pounds of the ore and returned to the spring to make camp for the night. Next morning, he started out for Belmont, but had not traveled far when he spotted two Indians on his trail. They soon overtook him and angrily charged him with stealing their gold. In return they demanded his remaining horse. Seeing that the Indians· were determined to put him afoot, Duckett shot one from his horse, and after a short encounter with the other, managed to drop him also.

In the struggle with the Indians, Duckett had lost all but four pounds of ore, but this he had assayed in Belmont and it ran $14,000 to the ton, enough to create excitement in any mining camp. Just why Duckett waited three years to return to the outcropping is something of a mystery, but that is the way the story is told.

In 1874, Duckett and two companions headed south from Hamilton, intending to approach Pillar Spring from the east. A short distance west of Hiko they were stopped by a band of Paiutes and warned to turn back. Outnumbered and faced with a group determined to keep white men out of the region, the Duckett party returned to Hamilton.

Duckett is said to have made several later attempts to locate the outcropping, but always met with failure. Eventually, he was attracted to the great strike at Cripple Creek, Colorado and from there he dropped out of sight. He is said to have left a map of the lost mine area with a man in Ely, Nevada, but he, too, was never able to locate the outcropping.

188

If the lost Duckett mine is close to Pillar Spring, give up any thought of searching for it. The area is a Government bombing and gunnery range where rigid restrictions against any travel are enforced.

(76) Lost Breyfogle Mine

VALUE: Gold ore said to have assayed about $6000 to the ton.

LOCATION: There are as many locations as there are versions of the story, but it is generally considered to be within sight of Daylight Springs in Death Valley.

AUTHENTICATION: It must be concluded from all the available evidence at hand that Breyfogle did find a rich gold ledge. Whether or not the Breyfogle gold has been found is another matter; there have been many claims.

Jacob Breyfogle is the name usually given the California prospector who left a big mark in the annals of lost mines. However, evidence almost conclusively proves that his real name was Charles C. Breyfogle. He came to California from Ohio in the gold rush days and settled in Oakland, where he was elected Alameda County accessor (1854-1857) and county treasurer (1857-1859). In the latter position he was accused of defalcation of office, and although his offense seems to have been one of negligence rather than criminal intent, he was dismissed from office. There is no record that he served a prison sentence, as some accounts state.

Breyfogle was in Los Angeles in 1863 or 1864, having stopped there on his way back from Arizona, where he led a party of Confederate sympathizers. It was while in Los Angeles that Breyfogle heard stories of gold picked up in Death Valley by the California-bound Forty-Niners. These

189

stories created a great deal of excitement and prompted many searches for the Dealth Valley gold. Breyfogle caught the fever.

Joining up with two other prospectors, O'Bannion and McLeod, about whom little or nothing is known, he decided to prospect Death Valley. Leaving Los Angeles late in the summer, they spent their first night at San Fernando Mission, passed through Mint Canyon and emerged on the Mojave Desert. They trudged across the desert, skirted the southern spurs of the Argus Mountains, then, climbing the western slopes of the Panamints, they reached the summit and started the descent into Death Valley. Someplace on the eastern slopes of the Panamints, near a small spring or waterhole, they camped for the night.

Because of the roughness of the ground, it was impossible for the prospectors to bed down in a small group, so Breyfogle prepared his resting place some distance from that of O'Bannion and McLeod. Sometime during the night Breyfogle heard screams, and realized that the Indians were killing his partners. Grabbing nothing but his shoes — he was fully clothed otherwise — he ran barefooted through the darkness, picking his way as well as he could across rock and thorny desert growth.

At dawn, Breyfogle found himself on the desert floor at the eastern base of the Panamints. Fearing that the Indians might still overtake him, he found a depression in the sand and hid for several hours. But with the fierce sun beating down upon him, he began traveling again, arriving that afternoon at a shallow, filled with alkali water. He drank and it made him terribly sick, but he plodded on.

On the following day he saw a spot of green on the mountain range to the east. Judging this to be vegetation around a spring, he headed toward it. It was on this leg of his journey that he saw float rock of a grayish-white color. He examined it and found it to be rich in gold. Although almost maddened with thirst, he paused to pick up several pieces of the float and placed them in his bandana. Shortly after resuming his search for water, he came upon the vein from which the float had broken off and washed away. It was pink feldspar, and being much richer than the float he

190

carried, he threw away the float and filled his bandana with the pink ore.

When Breyfogle arrived at the patch of green, he found it was a mesquite bush covered with green beans. There was no water. He later said that at this point his mind went blank, and that he remembered nothing until a rancher named Wilson picked him up in Big Smoky Valley, Nevada. How he had arrived there, Breyfogle could never explain.

After recuperating at Wilson's ranch, Breyfogle made his way to Austin, Nevada, still carrying his bandana full of gold ore. There, he went to work in the quartz mill of a friend, Jake Gooding. He told Gooding of his frightful experience and showed him the pink feldspar. Realizing that ore of this value would cause a rush to Death Valley, the men kept the news to themselves, but quietly solicited the aid of five or six trusted men to return to Death Valley with them. Breyfogle was positive he could lead them to the place.

Late in the fall of 1864 the little party rode out of Austin, quietly and without arousing excitement. They reached the Funeral Range and were about to cross into Death Valley when they met a strong band of hostile Indians who turned them back. They returned to Austin.

In the spring of 1865, the Breyfogle-Gooding party succeeded in reaching the spot where Breyfogle had become ill from drinking the brackish water, but they failed to locate the patch of green made by the mesquite bush which, according to Breyfogle, was the key to the location of the gold. Discouraged, Breyfogle's companions gave up and returned to Austin.

Over the next dozen years or more, Breyfogle organized party after party to scour the burning reaches of Death Valley, and he made repeated trips alone, convinced always that continued search would one day reveal the vein of rich gold that he had once found. Eventually, Charles Breyfogle disappeared and there seems to be no record of his fate.

Periodically, there are reports that the Breyfogle mine has been found. It is indeed true that rich strikes have been made by men searching for the lost Breyfogle, but whether or not one of these was the original Breyfogle is anybody's guess. Certainly no mine has been found in the region described by Breyfogle as the location of his find.

(77) Old Man Lee's Lost Mine

VALUE: Gold ore of unknown quantity and value.

LOCATION: Popularly said to be in the Bullion Mountains, which are in the south central part of San Bernardino County.

AUTHENTICATION: When one examines the details of this story in the light of history, it falls apart. If Old Man Lee was well known around San Bernardino, as is stated, he has left no record behind indicating that he had ever been here. Old Man Lee (his first name is unknown) should not be confused with John D. Lee, the Mormon of Mountain Meadows Massacre fame, who definitely did have a mine that is now lost near Lee's Ferry on the Colorado River in Arizona.

Old Man Lee, so the story goes, was a well-known character around San Bernardino in the 1870s. He made frequent prospecting trips in the vast desert expanses south and east of San Bernardino, and one day he came to town and filed a claim. Before long, he hired a man to help him sink a shaft, build a windlass and an arrastra for grinding the ore. At frequent intervals thereafter, Lee came to San Bernardino to sell his bullion and to buy provisions and supplies.

Unlike most other prospectors, however, Lee made no effort to conceal the location of his mine, which supposedly was in the Bullion Mountains east of San Bernardino, but actually went out of his way to advertise the fact that he had a producing mine and would take anyone to it who was interested in purchasing a share. A number of people are said

192

to have been interested in the offer but negotiations always ended short of an inspection tour for various and sundry reasons. But one who finally did go to the mine with Lee was R. W. Waterman who later became governor of California. In view of subsequent incidents, however, nothing seems to have come of his visit to the mine.

One day, when Lee was in San Bernardino for supplies, he told a storekeeper that he had to hurry back to his mine because his helper was almost out of provisions. He left town that night, and the following morning his body was found not many miles away. A bullet through the head revealed the manner of the murder, but robbery as a motive was ruled out when his watch and money were found on his body. The mystery was never solved.

Recalling Lee's statement that his helper was about out of provisions, the storekeeper organized a . party and they went into the Bullions to rescue the man. In spite of the fact that Lee supposedly had told many people of the location of the mine, this party failed to locate the mine or Lee's helper. The hired hand was never seen again. Presumably he just stayed there at the mine and starved to death.

If you agree that this seems rather incredible, consider this next development. Many years later, Waterman, whom you will recall had *actually seen the mine,* made a search for it and failed. Having turned down an offer to purchase an interest in the mine, he then made a standing offer of $40,000 for a half interest in the mine should anyone find it. None of the people who knew the mine's location stepped forward to claim the $40,000! Nor did anyone think of going to the recorder's office to get the exact location of the mine (remember, Lee had filed his claim).

This writer did go to the San Bernardino County Recorder's Office, and was informed that "Old Man" Lee never filed a claim, and that they wished lost mine hunters would quit bothering them with this question. Anyone who searches for Old Man Lee's lost gold mine has little else to do.

(78) San Marcos Pass Treasure

VALUE: Actually, this consists of two separate treasures. One is a cache of an unknown number of octagonal $20 gold pieces, the value of which has increased immensely since they were minted. The second treasure consists of an unknown amount of stagecoach loot.

LOCATION: The traditional site of the $20 gold coins is in the vicinity of the old apple orchard on the Pat Kinevan ranch, near the summit of San Marcos Pass between Santa Barbara and Los Olivos. The second cache is supposed to be buried near Cold Spring Tavern on the San Marcos Pass Road, at a place known as Slippery Rock, where the wheel-ruts made by the stages a hundred years ago are still visible. The area is thickly covered with a tangle of brush.

AUTHENTICATION: The writer has talked to many people in this area, and while none can say with certainty that either treasure actually exists, practically everyone in the region believes that both treasures are there.

Before a railroad line fully covered the distance between Los Angeles and San Francisco, northward travelers were obliged to leave the train at the end of the line at Santa Barbara and take the stage over San Marcos Pass to Los Olivos where they again boarded a train for the remainder of the trip. All four relay stations on this 45-mile stage run still stand; one of the original coaches is still preserved in Santa Barbara. It is hard to find any place in the United States where more visible evidence of this romantic period of overland transportation is still to be seen.

This stage route, which existed until 1901, carried many passengers and attracted many road agents. The route up San Marcos Pass and across the rugged southern slopes of the Santa Ynez Range was strewn with boulders and manzanita clumps, making it an ideal place for stage holdups.

194

Near the summit of the 2250-foot pass, and about two miles from the main road today, was a cave (now known as Painted Cave) where outlaws are said to have hidden between robberies.

On one occasion, the stage was held up near Cold Springs where a stop was made for lunch. The loot from this robbery is said to have been buried near Slippery Rock, and if one pokes through the brush in this area, the excavations left by many treasure seekers may be uncovered.

Almost at the top of the summit and about one-quarter mile off the present paved road which leads down into a timbered gulch, still stands the old Post Station operated by Patrick Kinevan in the 1860s. Here the six-team horses were changed and the toll collected. Tom Kinevan, son of Pat, was well past 80 years of age when the writer interviewed him in 1956, and has since died. He was the source for much of the material in this story.

According to Tom Kinevan, who was an authority on the early history of this region, a member of Joaquin Murrieta's gang, dying in prison in 1909, confessed that he had participated in a stage robbery in San Marcos Pass, and that the bandits secured a large quantity of octagonal $20 gold pieces which they buried "at the creek fork south of San Marcos Pass summit." The only place fitting this description is the apple orchard on the old Kinevan ranch. One day in 1912, when Tom was plowing between the creek forks, he turned up a single gold octagonal minted in 1849. No one knows for certain that this was a coin from the San Marcos holdup, but it gave credence to the treasure story and many treasure seekers have searched the area.

(79) Smugglers' Mystery Gold

VALUE: $20,000,000. To the best knowledge of the writer, this hoard of gold, valued by its owner at $20,000,000, is the richest "buried" treasure in the United States.

LOCATION: Publicity given this story when it was the subject of a Federal Grand Jury investigation in Los Angeles, in October, 1952, placed it in Southern California or the Southwestern United States; but, the Assistant United States District Attorney at the time, presenting the case to the Grand Jury, informed the writer, and again verified the statement in 1960, that the testimony presented to the judicial body behind closed doors placed the treasure somewhere in "northwestern New Mexico." This story is cloaked in bureaucratic secrecy, but this writer believes that a vast treasure of gold does exist somewhere in the southwestern part of the United States.

DOCUMENTATION: After making an investigation of this story, the United States Secret Service presented enough evidence to the United States District Attorney in Los Angeles to prompt the Federal court to ask for a Federal Grand Jury investigation. This would seem to indicate that, at the time at least, the United States Government placed considerable credence in the story. The writer discussed this story in detail with Federal investigators in Los Angeles, and pledged not to reveal his sources of information. It is the opinion of this writer that a tremendous treasure, perhaps the largest in the United States, does exist someplace in the southwestern United States, and we will go along with the "northwestern New Mexico" location.

In the fall of 1952, a prominent Los Angeles cattleman and political leader, E. George Luckey, revealed to the United States Secret Service that he had been approached in 1950 by Bruce Clews, a California public relations man, in the presence of an attorney, Prentiss Moore, and asked to serve as an intermediary to help arrange the sale of $20,000,000 worth of gold to the United States mint in San Francisco. Clews stated that he had been approached in the matter by Isadore M. Nobel, Los Angeles business man, and Martin Hougen, a mining engineer.

196

Hougen, holding power of attorney from the legal owner, sought to sell the gold through an escrow set up with the First National Bank of Ontario, California, where he placed on file an affidavit that he had actually seen the gold.

The gold was reportedly brought into the United States shortly before the Gold Confiscation Act of 1934 became effective. This act required that all gold in paper or metal form be turned into the United States Treasury in exchange for Federal Reserve Notes. Any gold not turned in became subject to seizure and its owner liable to punishment. Instead of turning this $20,000,000 in gold into the Treasury, its owner chose to bury it.

The gold, in ingot form, was supposedly smuggled into the United States because of uncertain conditions in Mexico at the time. Just how it was possible to move this much gold past border patrols and custom officials is a matter of conjecture.

The plan to sell the gold without penalties to the Treasury fell through when officials revealed that it would be necessary to seize the gold under the 1934 Act, then bring suit to determine its legal owner. Under the law, penalties would then have to be assessed.

None of the fiindings of the Federal Grand Jury investigation have been made available to the public and requests to see the transcript have been denied. The case was suddenly dropped, however, and Angus D. McEachen, Assistant United States District Attorney at the time, who brought the case before the Grand Jury, has said "unofficially" that the case "blew up" in the government's face.

The writer's interviews with most of the principals in this strange case has produced little information of value. Nobody is talking. If there is any basis of fact in the story — and the Federal Government obviously thought there was at one time — neither the principals nor Government officials are revealing it.

If the gold does not exist, what was the purpose of the attempt to negotiate a deal with the Treasury? Why did the Federal Grand Jury suddenly drop the case? Why, after a barrage of publicity at the start of the case, did the Federal Government suddenly clam up?

(80) Van Duzen Lost Mine

VALUE: Unknown

LOCATION: In or near Van Duzen Canyon in the San Bernardino Mountains, San Bernardino County.

AUTHENTICATION: There is considerable reason to believe this story is basically substantiated, although some of the details are confusing.

In May, 1860, the first mining claim was staked out in Holcomb Valley north of Big Bear Lake and shortly afterwards thousands of prospectors swarmed into the area. Among these hopefuls was a man named Van Duzen, his first name unknown. He worked some of the northern regions and then moved down the deep, twisting canyon from Upper Holcomb to Big Bear Valley and into the canyon now bearing his name.

Van Duzen possessed a working knowledge of mining and geology and went about his business in a thorough manner. Somewhere during his prospecting trips Van Duzen acquired a partner about whom very little is known, and together they built a little cabin in what is now known as Van Duzen Canyon. They prospected diligently and suddenly they began showing up at the trading centers with gold dust and nuggets in such quantity as to attract attention. Everyone assumed that they had struck it rich, and unsuccessful attempts were made to follow them.

Van Duzen did confide to a friend, however, the·barest details of making a rich find of almost free gold. He said further that their gold was being stored in a secret place until they were ready to pack it out to San Bernardino. Therefore, no suspicions were aroused when Van Duzen's partner was later seen heading for San Barnardino with a string of pack animals. But after several weeks, when neither man showed up in their usual drinking places around Holcomb Valley, a party rode out to see if the prospectors were in trouble. They found Van Duzen's body

198

sprawled on the dirt floor of the cabin. It was then assumed that Van Duzen had been murdered by his partner who had escaped with their accumulated gold.

A search was made for the secret mine, but nothing was found. Then, in the summer of 1868, there appeared in Holcomb Valley a middle-aged Frenchman and a younger man named Stebbins. They appeared to be partners, yet the Frenchman went on many lone prospecting forays, leaving Stebbins to shift for himself.

The Frenchman centered his activities in the northern reaches of Van Duzen Canyon and before long it was apparent that he, too, had struck it rich. It was noted that the gold he spent in the trading places was amazingly like that displayed by Van Duzen several years earlier. Had he found the Van Duzen mine? Many thought he had, but the Frenchman wasn't talking.

Suddenly, and without apparent reason, the Frenchman vanished. When young Stebbins was questioned, he denied all knowledge of the Frenchman's disappearance, saying that he was just as puzzled as anyone. After a few weeks, Stebbins mysteriously dropped from sight.

Fifty years or so passed and the Van Duzen mine was all but forgotten. Then there appeared in Holcomb Valley an aged man who said his name was Stebbins — the same Stebbins who had worked with the Frenchman in Van Duzen Canyon. After outfitting himself, Stebbins left for Van Duzen Canyon, stating that he was determined to find the Frenchman's lost mine which he thought had originally been Van Duzen's.

Stebbins searched the entire summer, but always reported that he found nothing. He complained that the landmarks he had once known and associated with the lost mine were no longer to be found. Failing health finally forced him to abandon the search. He left the region and was never heard of again.

These facts are beyond question: there was a man named Van Duzen, and he did have a source of free gold; he was found dead in his cabin in the canyon bearing his name. Also, there was a Frenchman who had an equally rich source of similar gold, and he had a young partner named Stebbins. A man claiming to be Stebbins did appear fifty years later and did conduct an extensive search for a mine he thought to have been discovered originally by Van Duzen, and later by the Frenchman. All this would certainly indicate that Van Duzen Canyon still holds the secret of a lost mine, all traces of which might have been destroyed by an earthquake.

(81) Vallecito Stage Station Treasure

VALUE: $65,000 in gold, presumably in an iron box, just as taken from the stage.

LOCATION: Somewhere along the old Butterfield Overland Mail route through Vallecito Wash and, more precisely, between the ruins of the old stage station at Carrizo and the restore station of Vallecito to its west, in San Diego County.

AUTHENTICATION: The old stage station of Vallecito is alive with tales of ghosts, buried treasure, deeds of violence and deeds of heroism. One story persists of a ghostly stage that rattles in at midnight and stops to give its gold-seeking passengers a rest from the weary ride. If you believe in ghost stories, perhaps you can believe one of the two versions of this treasure tale.

Through the heavy sands of Vallecito Wash, the Concord stage rolled along as the six lathered mules kept the traces taut. Good time was being made and the driver looked forward to a rest at Carrizo before proceeding.

Suddenly, from behind concealment of a clump of desert bushes, four mounted men appeared and blocked the stage's path. Taken completely by surprise, and facing four leveled guns, the driver pulled up. Automatically, he threw his

200

hands skyward and waited for the command to throw down the strongbox. It came from the leader, a man named O'Hara, who was mounted on a white horse. Relieving the passengers of their valuables, the riders picked up the strongbox, mounted and rode away in the direction of Carrizo.

Before the bandits had traveled more than a short distance, the driver found that the rifle by his side had been overlooked. He could not resist the temptation to raise it and take a parting shot at the fleeing figures. In the growing dusk he thought he saw one of the bandits fall. When he ran up to investigate, he found two dead men, not one — but he had fired but a single shot!

When the stage reached Carrizo, the two remaining bandits had already passed through there and were obviously headed for Vallecito. After a short rest, the driver herded his passengers into the coach and started on the 17-mile trail that would bring him to Vallecito and the last stop on his run.

Excitement was high at the Vallecito station when the stage arrived. The stationkeeper told this story. Two horsemen had stopped at the station, one riding a large white horse. They seemed to be in a heated argument, although they in no way annoyed the keeper or his wife. One produced a bottle and they drank heavily. One of the men accused the other of having killed a companion so that the loot would not have to be divided into four parts. He charged, too, that the leader, O'Hara, would kill again if he got the chance. At this point, O'Hara broke off the argument, saying that he had to care for his horse. He left the room, but suddenly returned and shot his partner in cold blood. But as the wounded man fell, he managed to draw his gun and in turn kill O'Hara. The wounded man soon died.

It was only hours after the holdup, but all four bandits were dead. Where was the stolen $65,000? It was not on their bodies, nor in their saddlebags. There could only be one conclusion — they had buried it along the trail someplace between the site of the robbery and the Vallecito station.

Vallecito is a place of palling desert stillness. It is a place with stories to be told, and stories that will never be told.

Near the station for many years were two unmarked graves, now completely lost. These were long pointed out as the graves of the two bandits.

The second version of the story concerns a lone bandit who reportedly robbed the stage of $65,000 near Vallecito. He was pursued by the station agent, and seeing that he had only minutes to get rid of the gold, hid it. He then hid, intending to ambush the agent, but he was observed. They both drew at the same time, fired and killed each other.

Vallecito may have its ghosts, and they may guard the treasure — if it was ever there.

Reading Sources

Reading Sources:

TREASURE OF LA ESMERELDA

Mitchell, John D., "Lost Treasure of Del Bac," *Desert Magazine*, July, 1948, pp. 15-16

——————— *Lost Mines and Buried Treasures Along the Old Frontier*, Desert Magazine Press, Palm Desert, Calif., 1953, pp. 61-64

TREASURE OF TUMACACORI

Abbott, Clifton, "Father Kino, Empire Builder of the Southwest," *Travel Magazine*, May, 1942, pp. 5-9

Arnold, Oren, "Enchanting Treasure of the Padres," *Westways Magazine*, October, 1956, pp. 30-31

——————, "I Hunt Ghost Gold," *Saturday Evening Post*, December 28, 1946, pp. 10-11, 34

Beaubein, Paul, "Excavations at Tumacacori, 1934," *Southwestern Monuments Association Special Report No. 15*, Santa Fe, N. M., 1937

Bolton, Herbert Eugene, *Rim of Christendom*, Macmillan, N. Y., 1936

Caywood, Louis R., "The Spanish Missions of Northwestern New Spain, Jesuit Period — 1687-1767," *The Kiva*, Vol. V, No. 2

——————, "Tumacacori — A Portrayal of Spanish History in Arizona and Sonora," *Arizona Highways Magazine*, Feb., 1943, pp. 20-27

Farish, Thomas Edwin, *History of Arizona*, Filmer Bros., Phoenix, 1915

Heald, Phyllis W., "Lost Bells of Tumacacori," *Desert Magazine*, Aug., 1958, pp. 5-6

Hinton, Richard J., *Handbook of Arizona*, Payot, Upham & Co., San Francisco, 1878

Hollenbeck, Cleve and Williams, *Legends of the Spanish Southwest*, Arthur H. Clark Co., Glendale, Calif., 1938

Huntington, Mary Margaret, "In the Path of Father Kino," *Westways Magazine*, May, 1949, pp. 2-3

Jackson, Earl, "Tumacacori's Yesterday," *Southwestern Monuments Association, Popular Series No. 6*, Santa Fe, N. M., 1951

_____, "Tumacacori," *Arizona Highways Magazine*, July, 1946, pp. 4-5

Lockwood, Frank C., *Pioneer Days in Arizona*, Macmillan, N. Y., 1951

Lovelace, Leland, *Lost Mines and Hidden Treasure*, Naylor, San Antonio, 1956

Miller, Joseph, *The Arizona Story*, Hastings House, N. Y., 1952, pp. 178-179

Mitchell, John D., *Lost Mines of the Great Southwest*, The Journal Co., Phoenix, 1933, pp. 67-72, 74-78

National Park Service, *Tumacacori National Monument*, U. S. Government Printing Office, Washington, D. C.

Newhall, Nancy, "The Shell of Tumacacori," *Arizona Highways Magazine*, Nov., 1952, pp. 5-13

Pinkley, Frank, "Repair and Restoration of Tumacacori," *Southwestern Monuments Association, Special Report No. 10*, National Park Service, Casa Grande National Monument, Ariz., 1946

Proctor, Gil, "Tucson — Tubac — Tumacacori — Tohell," *Arizona Silhouettes*, Tucson, 1956

_____, *People of the Moonlight*, The Publications Press of Pasadena, 1958, pp. 93-107

Robinson, Will H., *Under Turquoise Skies*, Macmillan, N. Y., 1928, p. 440

Rose, Milton F., "I Found a Lost Mine," *True West Magazine*, March-April, 1959, pp. 32-33, 49-52

Santschi, R. J., *Treasure Trails*, Century Press, Glen Ellyn, Ill., Vol. I, pp. 63-64

Stoner, Rev. Victor R., "Original Sites of the Spanish Missions of Santa Cruz Valley," *The Kiva*, Vol. II, Nos. 7 and 8

————, "The Spanish Missions of Santa Cruz Valley," *The Kiva*, Vol. I, No. 9

Storm, Barry, *Thunder Gods Gold*, Southwest Publishing Co., Phoenix, 1946, p. 161

Work Projects Administration, *Arizona — A State Guide*, Hastings House, N. Y., 1940

Wyllys, Rufus Kay, *Arizona — The History of a Frontier State*, Hobson & Kerr, Phoenix, 1950, p. 249

LOST MINE OF THE TONTO APACHES

Mitchell, John D., "Lost Quartz Vein of the Tonto Apache Indians," *Desert Magazine*, Feb., 1942

————, *Lost Mines and Buried Treasure Along the Old Frontier*, Desert Magazine Press, Palm Desert, Calif., 1953, pp. 207-210

LA PURISIMA CONCEPCION MINE

Hebner, William F., "The Lost Pimeria Alta Mine," *True West* Magazine, May-June, 1960, pp. 32-33

Mitchell, John D., *Lost Mines of the Great Southwest*, The Journal Co., Phoenix, 1933, pp. 74-78

————, *Lost Mines and Buried Treasure Along the Old Frontier*, Desert Magazine Press, Palm Desert, Calif., 1953, pp. 163-168

————, "Lost Silver Mine of the Jesuits," *Desert Magazine*, November, 1950

Proctor, Gil, "Tucson — Tubac — Tumacacori — Tohell," *Arizona Silhouettes*, Tucson, 1956

PANCHO'S LOST MINE

Weight, Harold O., "Lost Apache Gold in the Little Horn Mountains," *Desert Magazine*, Jan., 1957, pp. 13-17

————, *Lost Mines of Old Arizona*, Calico Press, Twenty-nine Palms, Calif., 1959, pp. 54-61

TREASURE OF GUADALUPE MINE

Bolton, Herbert Eugene, *The Padre on Horseback,* Sonora Press, San Francisco, 1932

Cosulich, Bernice, "Tucson," *Arizona Silhouettes,* Tucson, 1953

McAllister, R. W., *Lost Mines of California and the Southwest,* Thomas Bros., Los Angeles, 1953, pp. 21-22

Miller, Joseph, *The Arizona Story,* Hastings House, N. Y., 1952

Mitchell, John D., "Lost Silver Mine of the Jesuits," *Desert Magazine,* November, 1950, pp. 25-26

_____, *Lost Mines and Buried Treasure Along the Old Frontier,* Desert Magazine Press, Palm Desert, Calif., 1953, pp. 145-147

_____, *Lost Mines of the Great Southwest,* The Journal Co., Phoenix, 1933, pp. 67-69, 74-78, 108

Proctor, Gil, "Tucson — Tubac — Tumacacori — Tohell," *Arizona Silhouettes,* Phoenix, 1956

TREASURE OF CARRETA CANYON

Coffman, F. L., *1001 Lost, Buried or Sunken Treasures,* Thomas Nelson & Sons, N. Y., 1958, pp. 73-74

Mitchell, John D., *Lost Mines and Buried Treasure Along the Old Frontier,* Desert Magazine Press, Palm Desert, Calif., 1953, pp. 115-120

_____, "Lost Treasure of Carreta Canyon," *Desert Magazine,* Jan., 1953, pp. 27-28

TREASURE OF SAN JOSE DEL TUCSON MISSION

Cosulich, Bernice, "Tucson," *Arizona Silhouettes,* Tucson, 1953, p. 55

Ramsdell, H. L., "Little Known Missions of the Southwest," *Golden Bear* Magazine, April, 1906, pp. 32-33

LOST DUTCHMAN MINE

Ackerman, R. C., "Madman of the Superstitions," *True West* Magazine, Jan.-Feb., 1956, pp. 22 et seq.

Arnold, Oren, "I Hunt Ghost Gold," *Saturday Evening Post*, Dec., 28, 1944.

————, "The Golden Ghost That Killed Ten Men," Los Angeles *Times Sunday Magazine,* Feb., 4, 1934

————, "Gold in the Mountains," *Arizona Highways Magazine,* Feb., 1932

————, *Ghost Gold,* Naylor, San Antonio, 1954

Austin, Mary, "Treasures in the Southwest," *Frontier Times* Magazine, Feb., 1944

Bagwell, Mary L., "The Lost Dutchman Mine," *Desert Magazine,* Jan., 1954, pp. 18-19

Barnard, Barney, "The Truth About the Dutchman's Lost Mine," *True West* Magazine, July-Aug., 1955

————, "The Story of Jacob Walzer and His Famous Hidden Mine," Mesa *Tribune,* 1954

Bernhard, M. A., "Lost Dutchman Mine," (a letter) *True West* Magazine, Jan.-Feb., 1956, pp. 54-55

Botkin, B. A. (Ed.), *A Treasury of Western Folklore,* Crown, N. Y., 1951

Chambliss, Catherine, "The Lure of Superstition," *Arizona Highways Magazine,* Nov., 1944, pp. 31-34

Clark, Howard D., *Lost Mines of the Old West,* Ghost Town Rock & Book Shop, Buena Park, Calif., 1946

Coniston, Ralph, "60 Billion Dollars in Lost Gold," *True West* Magazine, May-June, 1955 (Reprinted from *Mechanix Illustrated* Magazine, April, 1950)

Coolidge, Dane, *Arizona Cowboys,* Dutton, N. Y., 1938

Corle, Edwin, *The Gila,* Rinehart, N. Y., 1951

Edmiston, Ray L., "La Sombrera and the Mountain of Gold," *Prospector-Outdoorsman,* July, 1960

Garman, Robert L., "Quest For the Peralta Gold," *Desert Magazine,* Feb., 1953

Higham, D. F., *True Story of Jacob Walzer,* McMath Co., El Paso, 1946

Howe, Carl, "Did The Dutchman Find Montezuma's Treasure," *True West* Magazine, Jan.-Feb., 1957

Krippene, Ken, *Buried Treasure,* Permabooks, N. Y., 1950

Lesure, Thomas B., "Trek For Lost Gold," *Desert Magazine,* March, 1954

Lively, W. Irven, *The Mystic Mountains: A History of the*

Superstition Mountains, Copyright by the author, 1955
Los Angeles *Times,* April 10, 1950, "Lost Mystery Mine Legend Revived," Part 1, page 26
Lovelace, Leland, *Lost Mines and Hidden Treasure,* Naylor, San Antonio, 1956
McAllister, R. W., *Lost Mines of California and the Southwest,* Thomas Bros., Los Angeles, 1953
McClintock, James H., *Arizona — The Youngest State,* J. H. Clarke Co., Chicago, 1916, Vol. II
Marranzino, Pasquale, (title unknown); Rocky Mountain *News,* Jan. 25, 1947
_____, in *Western Folklore Quarterly,* April, 1947, Vol. VI, No. 2, pp. 185-186
Maxor, E. J., "Killer Mine," *Western Tales* Magazine, April, 1960
Miller, Joseph, *Arizona: The Last Frontier,* Hastings House, N. Y., 1956
Mitchell, John D., *Lost Mines of the Great Southwest,* The Journal Co., Phoenix, 1933, pp. 125-130
_____, *Lost Mines and Buried Treasure Along the Old Frontier,* Desert Magazine Press, Palm Desert, Calif., 1953
Monagan, George R., "Dutchman's Lost Mine Found?", *True West* Magazine, Mar.-Apr., 1956
New York Times (no title available), July 17, 1949
Oakland (Calif.) *Tribune* (no title available), April 17, 1949
Oliver, Harry, *Desert Rat Scrap Book,* June, 1950
Peck, Anne Merriam, *Southwest Roundup,* Dodd, Mead, N. Y., 1950
Penfield, Thomas, *Lost Treasure Trails,* Grosset & Dunlap, N. Y., 1954
Prospector-Outdoorsman (no author), "Hoax or Hogwash? — Search For the Lost Dutchman Still Kills," March, 1960
Rascoe, Jesse Ed., *Western Treasures Lost and Found,* Frontier Book Co., Toyahvale, Texas, 1961
Reed, Allen C., "Trek For Gold," *Arizona Highways Magazine,* March, 1951
Rogers, Don, "Stay Away From Up There," *Family Circle Magazine,* Feb. 18, 1938
Rosecrans, Ludwig G., *Spanish Gold and the Lost Dutchman,*

Printed by Lofgren Prtg. & Office Supply Co., Mesa, Ariz.

Santschi, R. J., *Treasure Trails,* Century Press, Glen Ellyn, Ill., 1949, Vol. II

Scudder, Martin, "Superstition Mine," *Overland Monthly,* April, 1923

Sims, Ely, *The Lost Dutchman Mine,* Morrow, N. Y., 1953

Stewart, A. J., "The $500,000,000 Treasure That's Up For Grabs," *Western Action* Magazine, Sept., 1960

Storm, Barry, *Thunder Gods Gold,* Southwest Publishing Co., Phoenix, 1946

——————, "Bonanza of the Lost Dutchman," *Desert Magazine,* May, 1945

——————, "Curse of the Thunder Gods," *Desert Magazine,* April, 1945

——————, "Walz and The Lost Dutchman Mine," *Desert Magazine,* May, 1945

——————, *Gold of the Superstitions,* Sims Prtg. Co., Phoenix, 1940

——————. *Trial of the Lost Dutchman,* Goldwaters, Phoenix, 1939

——————, "Lost Mines of the Peraltas," *Desert Magazine,* March, 1945

Taylor, John A., "How the Dutchman Got His Gold," *True West* Magazine, Nov.-Dec., 1956

Time Magazine, "Search For Lost Dutchman's," June 22, 1959

True West Magazine, "Mystery of the Dutchman's Lost Mine," (letters from readers), Nov.-Dec., 1955

Tucson *Citizen,* "Superstition's Gold," March 4, 1941 (This story was mimeographed and distributed by the Arizona Bureau of Mines, Tucson, in answer to the many requests received for information about the Lost Dutchman Mine)

Walker, C. Lester, "Where to Find Buried Treasure," *Harper's* Magazine, Nov., 1947

Western Folklore Quarterly (untitled), Vol. IX, 1950, pp. 78-79 (the article deals with the sale of "authentic" Lost Dutchman maps)

213

Western Folklore Quarterly (untitled), Vol. IX, No. 4, Oct., 1950

Work Projects Administration, *Arizona — A State Guide*, Hastings House, N. Y., 1940

WAGONER'S LOST LEDGE

McAllister, R. W., *Lost Mines of California and the Southwest*, Thomas Bros., Los Angeles, 1953

Storm, Barry, *Thunder Gods Gold*, Southwest Pub. Co., Phoenix, 1946

GONZALES' LOST MINE

Rosecrans, Ludwig C., *Spanish Gold and the Lost Dutchman*, Lofgren Prtg. & Office Supply Co., Mesa, Ariz., 1953

Storm, Barry, *Thunder Gods Gold*, Southwest Pub. Co., Phoenix, 1946

LOST MINE OF SQUAW HOLLOW

McAllister, R. W., *Lost Mines of California and the Southwest*, Thomas Bros., Los Angeles, 1953

Mitchell, John D., "The Lost Squaw Hollow Gold Ledge," *Desert Magazine*, Jan., 1949

_____, *Lost Mines and Buried Treasure Along the Old Frontier*, Desert Magazine Press, Palm Desert, Calif., 1953

_____, *Lost Mines of the Great Southwest*, The Journal Co., Phoenix

TREASURE OF THE CURSED CERRO COLORADO

Coffman, F. L., *1001 Lost, Buried and Sunken Treasures*, Thomas Nelson & Sons, N. Y., 1958 (Ed: this is a listing only and the reader is advised that if he seeks any real information in this book, he is in for a disappointing experience.)

Valkenburg, Richard Van, "Haunted Silver," *Desert Magazine*, Sept., 1948

214

Work Projects Administration, *Arizona — A State Guide,* Hastings House, N. Y., 1940

LOST MINE OF THE ORPHANS

Childs, Thomas: letter on file in the reference library of the Arizona Pioneers' Historical Society, Tucson, Ariz.

Pelon, Don, "A Girl — A Boy — A Murder: Gold on the Desert," *Prospector-Outdoorsman,* Sept., 1960

TREASURE OF RANCHO DE LOS YUMAS

Weight, Harold and Lucile, "William B. Rood and the Story of Rancho de los Yumas," *Calico Print,* Aug.-Sept., 1952

——————, *William B. Rood,* Calico Press, Twentynine Palms, Calif., 1959 (A 24-page booklet consisting largely of a reprint of the *Calico Print* article.)

Weight, Harold O, "The Phantom Horseman," *Westways Magazine,* Jan., 1957

JOHN D. LEE LOST MINE

Clark, John D., "The Lee Lost Lode," *Ghost Town News,* Buena Park, Calif., Vol. V, No. 30

DeRoss, Rose Marie, *Woman of the Rivers,* Desert Magazine Press, 1958, pp. 22-23

Kelly, Charles, "John D. Lee's Lost Gold Mine," *Desert Magazine,* Aug., 1946

——————, "Lee's Ferry on the Colorado," *Desert Magazine,* Nov., 1943

Wilson, Rufus Rockwell, *Out of the West,* Wilson-Erickson, 1936

Work Projects Administration, *Arizona — A State Guide,* Hastings House, 1940

NIGGER BEN'S LOST MINE

Coffman, F. L., *1001 Lost, Buried and Sunken Treasures,* Thomas Nelson & Sons, N. Y., 1957 (A listing only)

215

Farish, Thomas Edwin, *History of Arizona*, Filmer Bros., Phoenix, 1915

Lovelace, Leland, *Lost Mines and Hidden Treasure*, Naylor, San Antonio, 1956

McAllister, R. W., *Lost Mines of California and the Southwest*, Thomas Bros., Los Angeles, 1953

McClintock, James H., *Arizona — The Youngest State*, S. J. Clarke Co., Chicago, 1916, Vol. II, p. 392

Miller, Joseph, *The Arizona Story*, Hastings House, N. Y., 1952

Mitchell, John D., *Lost Mines of the Great Southwest*, The Journal Co., Phoenix

_____, *Lost Mines and Buried Treasure Along the Old Frontier*, Desert Magazine Press, 1953

_____, "Big Antelope Placer," *Desert Magazine*, May, 1942

Stickney, Mary E., "Legends of Lost Mines," *Lippincott's Magazine*, April, 1899

Wyllys, Rufus Kay, *Arizona — The History of a Frontier State*, Hobson & Kerr, Phoenix, 1950

BLACK PRINCESS LOST MINE

Mitchell, John D., "Lost Mine of the Blond Mayo," *Desert Magazine*, May, 1952

_____, *Lost Mines and Buried Treasure Along the Old Frontier*, Desert Magazine Press, 1953

LOST SOPORI MINE AND TREASURE

McAllister, R. W., *Lost Mines of California and the Southwest*, Thomas Bros., Los Angeles, 1953

Mitchell, John D., *Lost Mines of the Great Southwest*, The Journal Co., Phoenix

_____, *Lost Mines and Buried Treasure Along the Old Frontier*, Desert Magazine Press, 1953, pp. 73-77

_____, "Lost Mine of the Blond Mayo," *Desert Magazine*, May, 1953

Wyllys, Rufus Kay, *Arizona — The History of a Frontier State*, Hobson & Kerr, Phoenix, 1950

BLACK JACK KETCHUM'S TREASURE

Burns, Walter Noble, *Tombstone: An Iliad of the South-west*, Doubleday, Garden City, 1927

Livingston, Carl B., "Hunting Down the Black Jack Gang," *The Wide World Magazine*, March, 1955

Walters, Lorenzo D., *Tombstone's Yesterdays*, Acme Prtg. Co., Phoenix, 1928

Work Projects Administration, *New Mexico — A Guide to the Colorful State*, Hastings House, 1940

LOST MINE OF SIERRA AZUL

Colton, Harold S., "Tracing the Lost Mines of the Padres," *Plateau*, Vol. XIII, No. 1 (Publication of the Northern Arizona Society of Science and Art; Museum of Northern Arizona, Flagstaff)

Espinosa, Jose Manuel, "The Legend of Sierra Azul," *New Mexico Historical Review*, Vol. IX, No. 2

ANTLERS GOLD OF DANIEL'S CANYON

Dobie, J. Frank, "Fever For Gold," *True West* Magazine, Nov.-Dec., 1958

LOST TREASURE OF MONTEZUMA'S HEAD

Lovelace, Leland, *Lost Mines and Hidden Treasure*, Naylor, San Antonio, 1956

Mitchell, John D., "Don Joaquin and His Gold Mine," *Desert Magazine*, May, 1943

—————, *Lost Mines and Buried Treasure Along the Old Frontier*, Desert Magazine Press, 1953

AZTEC MONTEZUMA'S TREASURE

Bailey, Philip A., *Golden Mirages*, Macmillan, N. Y., 1949

Hinton, Richard J., *The Handbook of Arizona*, Payot, Upham & Co., San Francisco, 1878

McAllister, R. W., *Lost Mines of California and the Southwest*, Thomas Bros., Los Angeles, 1953

Mitchell, John D., *Lost Mines and Buried Treasure Along the Old Frontier*, Desert Magazine Press, 1953
_____, *Lost Mines of the Great Southwest*, The Journal Co., Phoenix, 1933

TREASURE OF MONTEZUMA WELL

Arizona Highways Magazine, "Montezuma Well," July, 1954
Dobie, J. Frank, *Coronado's Children*, The Southwest Press, Dallas, 1930

MONTEZUMA TREASURE IN THE AJO MOUNTAINS

Bailey, Philip A., *Golden Mirages*, Macmillan, N. Y., 1949
Mitchell, John D., "Baboquivari and the Golden Owls," *Mining World Magazine*, Dec., 1951

LOST PADRE MINE

Ellinger, Ed., "Deep in the Heart of Sycamore Canyon," *Arizona Highways Magazine*, July, 1958
Richardson, Gladwell, "Lost Mine of Coconino," *Desert Magazine*, July, 1950

TREASURE OF HACIENDA DE SAN YSIDRO

Prospector-Outdoorsman, "Is It Still There?: Don Redondo's Gold," Sept., 1959
Weight, Harold O., "Lost Rancho On the Gila," *Westways Magazine*, March, 1956
Work Projects Administration, *Arizona — A State Guide*, Hastings House, N. Y., 1940

MONTEZUMA'S TREASURE AT CASA GRANDE

Mitchell, John D., *Lost Mines of the Great Southwest*, The Journal Co., Phoenix, 1933

LOST ADAMS DIGGINGS

Childs, Thomas, "Clue to Lost Adams Diggings," *Desert Magazine*, May, 1944 (a letter)

Dillon, George, "Apache Gold," *True West* Magazine, May-June, 1956. (Note: this supposedly "true" story is a confused mixture of both the Arizona and the New Mexico stories, and "true" of neither)

McAllister, R. W., *Lost Mines of California and the Southwest*, Thomas Bros., Los Angeles, 1953

McClintock, James H., *Arizona — The Youngest State*, J. H. Clarke Co., Chicago, 1916, Vol. II, p. 394

Mitchell, John D., *Lost Mines of the Great Southwest*, The Journal Co., Phoenix, 1933

LOST COWBOY MINE

Mitchell, John D., *Lost Mines of the Great Southwest*, The Journal Co., Phoenix, 1933

Santschi, R. J., *Treasure Trails*, Century Press, Glen Ellyn, Ill., 1942, Vol. I. (a listing only)

OUTLAW BROTHERS' TREASURE

Ferguson, Robert G., *The Search For Hidden Gold*, Vantage Press, N. Y., 1957

LOST SHEPHERD GIRL MINE

Dobie, J. Frank, "The Treasure is Always There," *True West* Magazine, Aug.-Sept., 1954

————, *Coronado's Children*, The Southwest Press, Dallas, 1930

Santschi, R. J., *Treasure Trails*, Century Press, Glen Ellyn, Ill., 1947, Vol. I

LOST TREASURE OF REDROCK

Lovelace, Leland, *Lost Mines and Hidden Treasure*, Naylor, San Antonio, 1956

219

McAllister, R. W., *Lost Mines of California and the Southwest*, Thomas Bros., Los Angeles, 1953
Mitchell, John D., *Lost Mines of the Great Southwest*, The Journal Co., Phoenix, 1933

BANDIT TREASURE OF STONEMAN LAKE

Forrest, Earl R., *Arizona's Dark and Bloody Ground*, Caxton, Caldwell, Idaho, 1950

BURT ALVORD TREASURE

Block, Eugene B., *Great Train Robberies of the West*, Coward – McCann, N. Y., 1959

RINCON CAVE TREASURE

Lovelace, Leland, *Lost Mines and Hidden Treasure*, Naylor, San Antonio, 1956

LOST COYOTERO MINE

Barnes, Will C., *Arizona Place Names*, University of Arizona Bulletin No. 2., Vol. VI, No. 1
Bieber, Ralph H. (editor), *Exploring Southwestern Trails – 1846-1854, by Philip St. George Cooke, William Henry Chase Whiting and Francois Xavier Aubrey*, The Southwest Historical Series VII, Arthur H. Clark Co., Glendale, Calif., 1938
Cozzens, Samuel Woodworth, *The Marvelous Country*, Henry L. Shepard & Co., Boston, 1874
Farish, Thomas Edwin, *History of Arizona*, Filmer Bros., Phoenix, 1915, Vol. I
Lockwood, Frank C., *Pioneer Days in Arizona*, Macmillan, N. Y., 1932
Lovelace, Leland, *Lost Mines and Hidden Treasure*, Naylor, San Antonio, 1956
Work Projects Administration, *Arizona – A State Guide*, Hastings House, N. Y., 1940

JOHN NUMMEL'S LOST MINE

Weight, Harold O., "The Ledge of Gold John Nummel Lost," *Desert Magazine*, March, 1956

————, "Lost Gold in the Trigos," *Desert Magazine*, April, 1959

————, *Lost Mines of Old Arizona*, Calico Press, Twenty-nine Palms, Calif., 1959

CASTLE DOME LOST MINE

Ferguson, Robert G., *Lost Treasure: The Search For Hidden Gold*, Vantage Press, N. Y., 1957

BURIED TREASURE OF BICUNER

Weight, Harold O., "Hidden Gold of Bicuner," *Desert Magazine*, June, 1955

————, *Lost Mines of Old Arizona*, Calico Press, Twenty-nine Palms, Calif., 1959

————, "Gold and Roses on Garces' Trail," *Desert Magazine*, Dec., 1950

CIENEGA BENDERS' TREASURE

Beebe, Lucius M. and Clegg, Charles, *The American West*, Dutton, N. Y., 1952

Conkling, Roscoe P. and Margaret B., *The Butterfield Overland Mail*, Arthur H. Clark Co., Glendale, Calif., 1947, Vol. II

Miller, Joseph, *The Arizona Story*, Hastings House, N. Y., 1952

LOST MINE OF THE TWO SKELETONS

Mitchell, John D., "Lost Pima Gold," *Desert Magazine*, Oct., 1952

————, *Lost Mines and Buried Treasure Along the Old Frontier*, Desert Magazine Press, Palm Desert, Calif., 1953

221

_____, "Lost Jack Rabbit Mine," *Mining World Magazine*, Feb., 1951

LOST SIX-SHOOTER MINE

Emrich, Duncan, *It's An Old Wild West Custom*, Vanguard, N. Y., 1948

McAllister, R. W., *Lost Mines of California and the Southwest*, Thomas Bros., Los Angeles, 1953

Mitchell, John D., *Lost Mines of the Great Southwest*, The Journal Co., Phoenix, 1933

Rose, Milton F., "The Lost Six-Shooter Mine," *True West Magazine*, July-Aug., 1960 and Sept.-Oct., 1960

Weight, Harold O., "Lost Gold in the Sands of La Posa," *Desert Magazine*, Feb., 1961

Wyllys, Rufus Kay, *Arizona — The History of a Frontier State*, Hobson & Kerr, Phoenix, 1950

SANDERS' LOST MINE

Miller, Joseph, *The Arizona Story*, Hastings House, N. Y., 1952

TREASURE OF SKELETON CANYON

Barnes, Will C., *Arizona Place Names*, University of Arizona General Bulletin No. 2, Vol. VI, No. 1

Bailey, Tom, "Arizona's Buried Treasure Mystery," *True Magazine*, Nov., 1944

Brimmer, Lenora, "Boothill Graveyard," *Arizona Highways Magazine*, Jan., 1948

Croy, Homer, "The Jovial Killer," *Saga Magazine*, May, 1954

Franke, Paul, *They Plowed Up Hell in Old Cochise*, Douglas Climate Club, Douglas, Ariz., 1950

Ferguson, Robert G., *Lost Treasure: The Search for Hidden Gold*, Vantage Press, N. Y., 1957

Heald, Weldon, "Buried Treasure of the Chiricahuas," *Desert Magazine*, Nov., 1951

James, Al, "The Treasure of Davis Mountain," *Real Men Magazine*, Aug., 1959

222

Lockwood, Frank C., *Pioneer Days in Arizona*, Macmillan, N. Y., 1932

McAllister, R. W., *Lost Mines of California and the Southwest*, Thomas Bros., Los Angeles, 1953

Mitchell, John D., "Loot of Monterey," *Desert Magazine*, July, 1940

—————, *Lost Mines and Buried Treasure Along the Old Frontier*, Desert Magazine Press, Palm Desert, Calif., 1953

Penfield, Thomas, *Lost Treasure Trails*, Grosset & Dunlap, N. Y., 1954

Santschi, R. J., *Treasure Trails*, Century Press, Glen Ellyn, Ill., 1949, Vol. II

Walters, Lorenzo D., *Tombstone's Yesterday*, Acme Prtg. Co., Tucson, 1928

Woods, Betty, "We Camped in the Devil's Kitchen," *Desert Magazine*, Aug., 1941

Wyllys, Rufus Kay, *Arizona — The History of a Frontier State*, Hobson & Kerr, Phoenix, 1950

FRENCHMEN'S LOST MINE

Clark, Howard D., *Lost Mines of the Old West*, Ghost Town Press, Buena Park, Calif., 1951

Coffman, F. L., *1001 Lost, Buried or Sunken Treasures*, Thomas Nelson & Sons, N. Y., 1957 (a listing only)

Frazier, S. M., *Secrets of the Rocks*, Hall & Williams, Denver, 1905

McAllister, R. W., *Lost Mines of California and the Southwest*, Thomas Bros., Los Angeles, 1953

Miller, Joseph, *The Arizona Story*, Hastings House, N. Y., 1952

Mitchell, John D., "The Frenchmen's Lost Gold Mine," *Desert Magazine*, Oct., 1942

—————, *Lost Mines and Buried Treasure Along the Old Frontier*, Desert Magazine Press, Palm Desert, Calif., 1953

—————, *Lost Mines of the Great Southwest*, The Journal Co., Phoenix, 1933

Weight, Harold O., "Lost Gold of the Arizona Frenchmen,"

223

Calico Print, Twentynine Palms, Calif., Vol. VII, No. 6
_____, *Lost Mines of Old Arizona*, Calico Press, Twenty-nine Palms, Calif., 1959

LOST MINE OF THE SILVER STAIRWAY

Mitchell, John D., *Lost Mines and Buried Treasure Along the Old Frontier*, Desert Magazine Press, Palm Desert, Calif., 1953

GERONIMO'S LOST GOLD MINE

Clark, Howard D., *Lost Mines of the Old West*, Ghost Town Press, Buena Park, Calif., 1951
Lovelace, Leland, *Lost Mines and Hidden Treasure*, Naylor, San Antonio, 1956
McAllister, R. W., *Lost Mines of California and the Southwest*, Thomas Bros., Los Angeles
Mitchell, John D., *Lost Mines of the Great Southwest*, The Journal Co., Phoenix, 1933
Storm, Barry, *Thunder Gods Gold*, Southwest Pub. Co., Phoenix, 1946

TREASURE OF THE MOUNTAIN OF NOISE

Mitchell, John D., "Lost Silver Mine of the Jesuits," *Desert Magazine*, Nov., 1950
_____, *Lost Mines and Buried Treasure Along the Old Frontier*, Desert Magazine Press, Palm Desert, Calif., 1953
Rose, Milton F., "I Found a Lost Mine," *True West* Magazine, March-April, 1959
Wallace, Norman G., "The Mystery of Cerro Ruido," *Arizona Highways Magazine*, Oct., 1945

LOST MINE OF COCONINO

Bailey, Philip A., *Golden Mirages*, Macmillan, N. Y., 1949
Bancroft, Hubert Howe, *History of Arizona and New Mexico*, History Co., San Francisco, 1889, Vol. XVI

Ferguson, Robert G., *Lost Treasure: The Search For Hidden Gold*, Vantage Press, N. Y., 1957

Hammond, George P. and Rey, Agapito (trans and ed), *Expedition Into New Mexico by Antonio de Espejo, 1582-1583*, Los Angeles, 1929

Lovelace, Leland, *Lost Mines and Hidden Treasure*, Naylor, San Antonio, 1956

Richardson, Gladwell, "Lost Mine of Coconino," *Desert Magazine*, July, 1950

Work Projects Administration, *Arizona — A State Guide*, Hastings House, N. Y., 1940

————, *New Mexico — A Guide to the Colorful State*, Hastings House, N. Y., 1940

LOST SILVER MINE OF MONUMENT VALLEY

Henderson, Randall, "Navajo Gods Guard the Silver of Pish-la-ki," *Desert Magazine*, Dec., 1950

Kelly, Charles, "Lost Silver of Pish-la-ki," *Desert Magazine*, Dec., 1940, pp. 5-8

Klinck, Richard E., *Land of Room Enough and Time Enough*, University of New Mexico Press, Sante Fe, 1953

————, "Desert Treasure," *Western Folklore Quarterly*, Vol. XII, 1953

Work Projects Administration, *Arizona — A State Guide*, Hastings House, N. Y., 1940

BLACK BURRO LOST MINE

Michaelson, Charles, "Lost Gold Mines," *Munsey's Magazine*, Dec., 1901

————, *Lost Gold Mines*, The Frontier Press, Houston, Texas, 1958

Williamson, J. G., *On Western Plains*, (A manuscript, apparently written about 1900, and now in the Munk Collection, Southwest Museum, Los Angeles)

APACHE GIRL LOST MINE

Haken, Frank D., *Tales Under the Stars*, Lippincott, Philadelphia, 1861

Moore, Lyle M., "Lost Mine of the Apache Heroine," *Land of Sunshine Magazine*, Los Angeles, 1902

SUBLETT'S LOST GOLD MINE

Barrett, Velma and Oliver, Hazel, *Odessa: City of Dreams,* Naylor, San Antonio, 1952

Clark, Howard D., *Lost Mines of the Old West,* Ghost Town Press, Los Angeles, 1951

_____, "The Crazy Prospector of the Guadalupes," *Ghost Town News,* May, 1946

Coffman, F. L., *1001 Lost, Buried or Sunken Treasures,* Thomas Nelson & Sons, N. Y., 1958

Coniston, Ralph, "60 Billion Dollars in Lost Gold," *True West* Magazine, May-June, 1955 (Reprinted from *Mechanix Illustrated* Magazine, April, 1950)

Davis, L. H., "The Lost Gold Mine of the Guadalupe Mountains," *Frontier Times* Magazine, April, 1924, (Originally published in the El Paso *Times,* 1912)

Dobie, J. Frank, *Tales of Old Time Texas,* Little, Brown, Boston, 1928

_____, *Coronado's Children,* Literary Guild, N. Y., 1931

_____, "The Southwest's Eldorado," New York *Herald-Tribune,* Jan. 11, 1931

_____, "Sublett Mine," Dallas *News,* March, 1931

Ferguson, Robert G., *Lost Treasure: The Search For Hidden Gold,* Vantage Press, N. Y., 1957

Gopcevic, V. Petrov, *El Dorado — A Description of the World's Great Treasures,* Parker Bros., Salem, Mass., 1941

Hunter, Jr., John Marvin, "The Lost Gold Mine," *Frontier Times* Magazine, Aug., 1950

Kay, Eleanor, "Lost Mines and Buried Gold," *New Mexico Magazine,* Sept., 1953

Lamb, Jim, "You, Too, Can be a Week-end Prospector," *New Mexico Magazine,* Oct., 1959

Lovelace, Leland, *Lost Mines and Hidden Treasure,* Naylor, San Antonio, 1956

_____, "Sublett's Lost Gold," *Ghost Town News,* Aug., 1943

McAllister, R. W., *Lost Mines of California and the Southwest*, Thomas Bros., Los Angeles, 1953

Mitchell, John D., *Lost Mines and Buried Treasure Along the Old Frontier*, Desert Magazine Press, Palm Desert, Calif., 1953

——————, "Lost Gold of the Guadalupes," *Desert Magazine*, March, 1948

Work Projects Administration, *New Mexico — A Guide to the Colorful State*, Hastings House, N. Y., 1940

——————, *Texas — A Guide to the Lone Star State*, Hastings House, N. Y., 1940

BELLE McKEEVER LOST MINE

Denver *Post*, Jan., 15, 1897

Denver *Post*, Dec. 26, 1899

Frazier, S. M., *Secrets of the Rocks*, Hall & Williams, Denver, 1905

Garrell, Stafford, "Arizona's Canyon of Gold Still Being Sought," *Frontier Times* Magazine, Feb., 1924

Lovelace, Leland, *Lost Mines and Hidden Treasure*, Naylor, San Antonio, 1956

McClintock, James H., *Arizona — The Youngest State*, J. H. Clarke Co., Chicago, 1916, Vol. II

——————, *Arizona: Prehistoric — Aboriginal — Pioneer*, J. H. Clarke Co., Chicago, 1916

Quiett, Glenn Chesney, *Pay Dirt*, Appleton-Century, N. Y., 1936

Weight, Harold O., *Lost Mines of the Old West*, Calico Press, Twentynine Palms, Calif., 1959

LOST NIGGER BILL MINE

Casey, Robert J., *The Texas Border*, Bobbs-Merrill, Indianapolis, 1950

Chandley, Mrs. Eugenia H., "Old 'Lost Nigger mine' in the Big Bend Area," *Sul Ross Skyline*, Alpine, Texas, March 22, 1939

Clark, Howard H., *Lost Mines of the Old West*, Ghost

Town Press, Buena Park, Calif., 1951
Dobie, J. Frank, *Coronado's Children*, Literary Guild, N. Y., 1931
_____, "The Lost Nigger Gold Mine," *Country Gentleman* Magazine, March, 1926
_____, "The Lost Apache Mine," *True West* Magazine, March-April, 1958
Gopcevic, V. Petrov, *El Dorado*, Parker Bros., Salem, Mass., 1941, p. 19
Haldeen, Braddy, "A Legend of the Lost Nigger Gold Mine," *California Folklore Quarterly*, Vol. 4, No. 4 (An excellent account)
Krippene, Ken, *Buried Treasure*, Permabooks, N. Y., 1950
McAllister, R. W., *Lost Mines and Treasures of California and the Southwest*, Thomas Bros., Los Angeles, 1953 (Very condensed)
Porter, Kenneth W., "Willie Kelley of the Lost Nigger Mine," *Western Folklore Quarterly*, Vol. 13, No. 1
Raht, Carl, *The Romance of Davis Mountains*, Raht Book Co., El Paso, 1919
Rascoe, Jesse Ed, *Western Treasures Lost and Found*, Frontier Book Co., Toyahvale, Texas, 1961
San Angelo (Texas) *Standard Times*, "Lost Nigger Mine Still Sought For Its Gold Riches in the Big Bend Country of West Texas," Aug. 17, 1939
Wally, George, "Secret of the Lost Nigger Mine," *True West* Magazine, Sept.-Oct., 1959
Work Projects Administration, *Texas — A Guide to the Lone Star State*, Hastings House, N. Y., 1940

THE MYSTERIOUS TREASURE OF KARL STEINHEIMER

Bancroft, Hubert Howe, *History of the North Mexican States and Texas*, History Pub. Co., San Francisco, 1883, Vol. II
Bertillion, L. D., "Steinheimer's Millions," *Legends of Texas*, Texas Folk-Lore Society, Austin, Texas, 1924
Coffman, F. L., *1001 Lost, Buried and Sunken Treasures*, Thos. Nelson and Sons, N. Y., 1957

228

Dobie, J. Frank, *Coronado's Children*, Literary Guild, N. Y., 1931

McAllister, R. W., *Lost Mines and Treasures of California and the Southwest*, Thomas Bros., Los Angeles, 1953

BANDIT TREASURE OF COLOSSAL CAVE

Arizona Highways, "Colossal Cave," Jan., 1947

Arnold, Oren, "I Hunt Ghost Gold," *Saturday Evening Post*, Dec. 28, 1946

Barnes, Will C., *Arizona Place Names*, University of Arizona General Bulletin No. 2, Vol. VI, No. 1

Carson, Raymond, "Colossal Cave," *Arizona Highway Magazine*, April, 1941

Folsom, Franklin, *Exploring American Caves*, Crown, N. Y., 1956

Freese, Ralph, "The Cave That Crime Built," *Westways Magazine*, March, 1957

Parcher, Frank M., *Colossal Cave*, Mountain States Press, Boise, Idaho, 1945 (A guide booklet)

Penfield, Thomas, *Lost Treasure Trails*, Grosset & Dunlap, N. Y., 1954

Work Projects Administration, *Arizona — A State Guide*, Hastings House, N. Y., 1940

YUMA'S LOST MINE

Coffman, F. L., *1001 Lost, Buried or Sunken Treasures*, Thomas Nelson & Sons, N. Y., 1957 (A listing only)

Dobie, J. Frank, *Coronado's Children*, Southwest Press, Dallas, 1930

_____, "Coronado's Children Tell More Tales," New York *Herald Tribune Magazine*, June 21, 1931

Heald, Weldon, "The Waters of the Aravaipa," *Arizona Highways Magazine*, May, 1950

Lovelace, Leland, *Lost Mines and Hidden Treasure*, Naylor, San Antonio, 1956

McAllister, R. W., *Lost Mines of California and the Southwest*, Thomas Bros., Los Angeles, 1953

Miller, Joseph, *The Arizona Story*, Hastings House, N. Y., 1952

Mitchell, John D., *Lost Mines and Buried Treasure Along the Old Frontier*, Desert Magazine Press, Palm Desert, Calif., 1953

_____, *Lost Mines of the Great Southwest*, The Journal Co., Phoenix, 1933

Santschi, R. J., *Treasure Trails*, Century Press, Glen Ellyn, Ill., 1949, Vol. II

MAJOR PEEPLES' LOST MINE

Mitchell, John D., "Big Antelope Placer," *Desert Magazine*, May, 1942

_____, *Lost Mines and Buried Treasure Along the Old Frontier*, Desert Magazine Press, Palm Desert, Calif., 1953

Wells, Edmund, *Argonaut Tales*, Grafton Press, N. Y., 1927

LOST SQUAW MINE

Lovelace, Leland, *Lost Mines and Hidden Treasure*, Naylor, San Antonio, 1956, pp. 127-129

McAllister, R. W., *Lost Mines of California and the Southwest*, Thomas Bros., Los Angeles, 1953, p. 16

Mitchell, John D., *Lost Mines of the Great Southwest*, The Journal Co., Phoenix. Copyright by M. F. Rose, Mesa, Ariz., 1933, pp. 99-100

WALNUT GROVE DAM TREASURE

Arizona Development Board, *Historical Markers in Arizona*, Phoenix, no date

Arnold, Oren, "I Hunt Ghost Gold," *Saturday Evening Post*, Dec. 28, 1946

McClintock, James H., *Arizona — The Youngest State*, J. H. Clarke Co., Chicago, 1916, Vol. V

Murbarger, Nell, "Henry Wickenburg's Town," *Westways Magazine*, March, 1950

Parkman, I. H., "Hassayampa Dam Disaster — 1890," *Desert Magazine*, Nov., 1955

Stein, E. A., "The Hassayampa," *Arizona Highways Magazine*, Sept., 1946

Work Projects Administration, *Arizona — A State Guide*, Hastings House, N. Y., 1940

LINCOLN — GLANTON TREASURE

Martin, Douglas D., *Yuma Crossing*, University of New Mexico Press, Albuquerque, 1954

Peplow, Edward H., Jr., *History of Arizona*, Lewis Historical Pub. Co., N. Y., 1958, Vol. I

Publications of the Historical Society of California, *The Glanton War*, Vol. VI, 1903 (This work contains the signed statements made before Don Abel Stearns, first Alcalde of the District of Los Angeles, by William Carr and Jeremiah Hill on April 23, 1850)

LOST GOLD OF CAMEL'S TANK

Lovelace, Leland, *Lost Mines and Hidden Treasure*, Naylor, San Antonio, 1956

————, "Lost Gold of the Camel's Tinaja," *Ghost Town Vews*, Aug., 1945

THE TREASURE OF DOUBTFUL CANYON

Claussen, W. Edmunds, "The Ghosts of Doubtful Canyon," *New Mexico Magazine*, May, 1949. pp. 22-23, 39-41

Conkling, Roscoe P. and Margaret B., *The Butterfield Overland Mail — 1857-1859*, Arthur H. Clark, Glendale, Calif., 1947. Vol. 2, pp. 127-129

Dobie, J. Frank, "Coronado's Children Tell More Tales," *New York Herald Tribune*, Jan. 21, 1931. pp. 4-6

Winsor, Roanna H. "Tubac — Arizona's First State Park," *Arizona Highways*, Sept. 1958. p. 28

FATHER LA RUE'S LOST MINE

James, Henry, *The Curse of the San Andres*, Pageant Press, New York, 1953

Newman, Larry, "Treasure," *American Weekly*, Oct. 23, 1949. p. 23

Trumbo, Theron Marcos, "Go Where the Gold Lies Buried," *Desert Magazine*, March, 1944. pp. 14-16

Wolle, Muriel Sibell, *The Bonanza Trail*, University of Indiana Press, Bloomington, 1953. p. 41

SIMEON TURLEY'S LOST MINE

Because the Turley story has not previously appeared in print there are no known sources of reference material. The following references, however, contain background material on Simeon Turley's activities in New Mexico:

Inman, Col. Henry, *The Old Santa Fe Trail*, Crane & Co., Topeka, Kans., 1916. pp. 118-126

New Mexico — a Guide to the Colorful State, compiled by WPA, Hastings House, New York, 1940. pp. 286-287

Ruxton, George F., *Adventures in Mexico and the Rocky Mountains*, Harper, New York, 1848. pp. 227-229

Twitchell, Ralph E., *Leading Facts in New Mexico History*, The Torch Press, Cedar Rapids, Iowa, 1911-1916. Vol. 2, pp. 236-238

THE HIDDEN GOLD OF MADAME BARCELO

Bailey, Tom, "Three Rocks — Two Graves — and a Fortune in Gold," *True West Magazine*, Jan. 1961. pp. 14-16, 41-42, 44

Radzinski, P. V., "Gambler's Gold," *Golden West Magazine*, July, 1901. pp. 34-37

THE MANY TREASURES OF SAM BASS

Dobie, J. Frank, *Legends of Texas*, Texas Folklore Society, Austin, 1924. pp. 226-230

Dobie, J. Frank, *Tales of Old Time Texas*, Little, Brown, & Co., Boston, 1955. pp. 89-90

Gard, Wayne, *Sam Bass,* Houghton Mifflin, Boston, 1936. pp. 245-247
Huffaker, Clair, "The Saga of Sam Bass," *Saga Magazine,* July, 1955. pp. 23-25, 71-74
Martin, Charles L., *A Sketch of Sam Bass the Bandit,* University of Oklahoma Press, Norman, 1965
Texas Folk and Folklore, Southern Methodist University Press, Dallas, 1954. pp. 115
Webber, Malcolm, "Sam Bass' Gold," *Frontier Times,* May, 1965. pp. 45, 58

TREASURE OF EL MUERTO SPRINGS

Casey, Robert J., *The Texas Border,* Bobbs-Merrill, Indianapolis, 1950
Dobie, J. Frank, *Coronado's Children,* Literary Guild, New York, 1931
Qualey, Jake, "The Gunslinger's $1,000,000 Gamble," *Male Magazine,* May, 1958. pp. 39, 56, 59, 60
Qualey, Jake, "Red Curly, Bloody Brigand of the Southwest," *Real West Magazine,* Sept., 1961. pp. 23-24, 59-63
Rascoe, Jesse Ed, *Western Treasures Lost and Found,* Frontier Book Co., Toyahvale, Texas, 1961. pp. 116-119

THE LOST TREASURE OF PALO DURO

Haley, J. Evetts, "Pastores del Palo Duro," *Southwest Review,* Vol. 19, No. 3, April, 1934. pp. 279-294
McAllister, R. W., *Lost Mines and Treasures of the Southwest,* Thomas Bros., Los Angeles, 1953. pp. 39
McCarty, John L., *Maverick Town: The Story of Old Tascosa,* University of Oklahoma Press, Norman, 1946. pp. 19-34

PIRATE TREASURE OF HENDRICKS LAKE

Bylinsky, Gene, "There's Money in Treasure Hunting," *Science Digest Magazine,* Dec. 1958. pp. 38-43
Rascoe, Jesse Ed, *Western Treasures Lost and Found,* Frontier Book Co., Toyahvale, Texas, 1961. pp. 104

233

Rieseberg, Lt. Harry E., "Lafitte's Pirate Gold," *Real West Magazine*, Sept., 1961. pp. 26-28, 52-54
Rieseberg, Lt. Harry E., "Sunkeon Galleon Silver!," *True West Magazine*, March, 1957. pp. 16, 42-43
Rieseberg, Lt. Harry E., "You Could Find Jean Lafitte's $2,000,000 Texas Treasure!," *Cavalcade Magazine*, July, 1959. pp. 34-37, 85
Waldrop, Barney, "Sunken Silver Stampede!," *Frontier Times*, Fall, 1958. pp. 29-30
Wall Street Journal, Sept. 18, 1958. p. 1

EMPIRE STAGECOACH TREASURE

Atwater, Jane, "Lost Wells-Fargo Gold," *Desert Magazine*, April, 1954. pp. 12-13
Lovelace, Leland, *Lost Mines and Hidden Treasure*, Naylor, San Antonio, 1956. pp. 86-88
Oliver, Harry, "Prison Window Cache of Gold," *Ghost Town News*, Aug. 1944. p. 25

DUCKETT LOST MINE

Ashbaugh, Don, "Anybody Want a Lost Mine?," *True West Magazine*, July 1959. pp. 27, 52
Rascoe, Jesse Ed, *Western Treasures Lost and Found*, Frontier Book Co., Toyahvale, Texas, 1961. pp. 70-72
Read, Effie O., "Memory Lane," Ely (Nev.) *Daily Times*, Oct. 29, 1956

LOST BREYFOGLE MINE

Chalfant, W. A., *Death Valley — The Facts*, Stanford University Press, Palo Alto, Calif., 1930. pp. 47-50, 115-116
Clark, Howard D., *Lost Mines of the Old West*, Ghost Town Press, Buena Park, Calif., 1951. pp. 38-40
Glassock, C. B., *Here's Death Valley*, Bobbs-Merrill, Indianapolis, 1940. pp. 78-81
Hamlin, H., "History of Gold Discoveries," *Pony Express Courier*, Jan. 1948. p. 3

Wilson, Neill C., *Silver Stampede*, Macmillan, N. Y., 1937.
pp. 17-18, 220
Wilson, Rufus Rockwell, *Out of the West*, Wilson-Erickson,
New York, 1936. pp. 356-358

OLD MAN LEE'S LOST MINE

Clark, Howard D., "The Lee Lost Lode," *Ghost Town
News*, Apr. 1946. p. 9
——————————— *Lost Mines of the Old West*, Ghost
Town Press, Buena Park, Calif., 1951. pp. 66-67
Michelson, Charles, *Lost Gold Mines*, The Frontier Press,
Houston, 1958. pp. 25-27
Pierce, R. A., *Lost Mines and Treasures of California*, published by author, Berkeley, Calif. p. 21
Wilson, Rufus Rockwell, *Out of the West*, Wilson-Erickson,
New York, 1936. pp. 328-329, 358

Index

Index

239

240

MYSTIC TRAVELLER SERIES

DIG HERE!

Lost Mines & Buried Treasure of the Southwest
by Thomas Penfield, introduction by David Hatcher Childress

The most amazing book on lost treasure ever written, giving the locations of well over 100 fabulous fortunes waiting to be found in the ore-rich Southwest! For the first time lost treasure stories of the Southwest are stripped bare of their legends and lies! Each treasure account is preceded by the approximate location, estimated total value and authentication. Reading sources for each a count are also included so you can do additional research on the intriguing facts and lore of these treasures. *Dig Here!* is a veritable gold mine itself, overflowing with fascinating lore, spellbinding backgrounds, driving Western drama—and exciting, reliable facts! Chapters include: Treasure of Tumacacori; Lost Mine of the Tonto Apaches; Lost Dutchman Mine; Treasure of the Cursed Cerro Colorado; Black Princess Lost Mine; Lost Treasure of Montezuma's Head; Aztec Montezuma's Treasure; Treasure of Montezuma's Well; Montezuma's Treasure at Casa Grande; Lost Adams Diggings; Treasure of Skeleton Canyon; Lost Mine of the Silver Stairway; Geronimo's Lost Gold Mine; The Mysterious Treasure of Karl Steinheimer; more.

228 PAGES. 6x9 PAPERBACK. ILLUSTRATED. BIBLIOGRAPHY. INDEX. $14.95. CODE: DIGH

GUARDIANS OF THE HOLY GRAIL

by Mark Amaru Pinkham

While in the Holy Land the Knights Templar succeeded in their quest of finding a "missing link" that unites the spiritual traditions of the east and west. They discovered it in the form of a very ancient manifestation of the Holy Grail from Asia. Although the Templar Knights had been schooled in the legend of Jesus Christ and his famous chalice while in their homeland of France, during their one hundred years in the Holy Land they discovered that Jesus's Holy Grail was but one of a long line of Holy Grail manifestations, and that a lineage of Guardians of the Holy Grail had existed in Asia for thousands of years prior to the birth of the Messiah. This book presents this extremely ancient Holy Grail lineage from Asia and how the Knights Templar were initiated into it. It also reveals how the ancient Asian wisdom regarding the Holy Grail became the foundation for the Holy Grail legends of the west while also serving as the bedrock of the European Secret Societies, which included the Freemasons, Rosicrucians, and the Illuminati. Also: The Fisher Kings; The Middle Eastern mystery schools, such as the Assassins and Yezidhi; The ancient Holy Grail lineage from Sri Lanka and the Templar Knights' initiation into it; The head of John the Baptist and its importance to the Templars; The secret Templar initiation with grotesque Baphomet, the infamous Head of Wisdom; more.

248 PAGES. 6x9 PAPERBACK. ILLUSTRATED. BIBLIOGRAPHY. $16.95. CODE: GOHG

PIRATES & THE LOST TEMPLAR FLEET

The Secret Naval War Between the Templars & the Vatican
by David Hatcher Childress

Childress takes us into the fascinating world of maverick sea captains who were Knights Templar (and later Scottish Rite Free Masons) who battled the Vatican, and the Spanish and Italian ships that sailed for the Pope. The lost Templar fleet was originally based at La Rochelle in southern France, but fled to the deep fiords of Scotland upon the dissolution of the Order by King Phillip. This banned fleet of ships was later commanded by the St. Clair family of Rosslyn Chapel (birthplace of Free Masonry). St. Clair and his Templars made a voyage to Canada in the year 1298 AD, nearly 100 years before Columbus! Later, this fleet of ships and new ones to come, flew the Skull and Crossbones, the symbol of the Knights Templar. They preyed on the ships of the Vatican coming from the rich ports of the Americas and were ultimately known as the Pirates of the Caribbean. Chapters include: 10,000 Years of Seafaring; The Knights Templar & the Crusades; The Templars and the Assassins; The Lost Templar Fleet and the Jolly Roger; Maps of the Ancient Sea Kings; Pirates, Templars and the New World; Christopher Columbus—Secret Templar Pirate?; Later Day Pirates and the War with the Vatican; Pirate Utopias and the New Jerusalem; more.

320 PAGES. 6x9 PAPERBACK. ILLUSTRATED. BIBLIOGRAPHY. $16.95. CODE: PLTF

CLOAK OF THE ILLUMINATI

Secrets, Transformations, Crossing the Star Gate
by William Henry

Thousands of years ago the stargate technology of the gods was lost. Mayan Prophecy says it will return by 2012, along with our alignment with the center of our galaxy. In this book: Find examples of stargates and wormholes in the ancient world; Examine myths and scripture with hidden references to a stargate cloak worn by the Illuminati, including Mari, Nimrod, Elijah, and Jesus; See rare images of gods and goddesses wearing the Cloak of the illuminati; Learn about Saddam Hussein and the secret missing library of Jesus; Uncover the secret Roman-era eugenics experiments at the Temple of Hathor in Denderah, Egypt; Explore the duplicate of the Stargate Pillar of the Gods in the Illuminists' secret garden in Nashville, TN; Discover the secrets of manna, the food of the angels; Share the lost Peace Prayer posture of Osiris, Jesus and the Illuminati; more. Chapters include: Seven Stars Under Three Stars; The Long Walk; Squaring the Circle; The Mill of the Host; The Miracle Garment; The Fig; Nimrod: The Mighty Man; Nebuchadnezzar's Gate; The New Mighty Man; more.

238 PAGES. 6x9 PAPERBACK. ILLUSTRATED. BIBLIOGRAPHY. INDEX. $16.95. CODE: COIL

THE CHILDREN OF THE SUN

A Study of the Egyptian Settlement of the Pacific
by W.J. Perry

A reprint of the groundbreaking work of Professor W.J. Perry, an early diffusionist who believed that civilization spread throughout the world via transoceanic voyaging—an idea that most historians still fail to accept, even in the face of mounting evidence. First published in 1923, this classic presents the fascinating evidence that envoys of the ancient Sun Kingdoms of Egypt and India travelled into Indonesia and the Pacific circa 1500 BC, spreading their sophisticated culture. Perry traces the expansion of megalithic building from its origin in Egypt through Indonesia and across the Pacific all the way to the Americas. These early mariners searched for gold, obsidian, and pearls in their incredible explorations from island to island—they were the Children of the Sun! Includes: The Coming of the Warriors; Rulers and Commoners: The Sky World; The Indo-Egyptian Alliance of Builders; The Oceania-Indonesian Alliance of Explorers; more.

554 PAGES. 6x9 PAPERBACK. ILLUSTRATED. BIBLIOGRAPHY. INDEX. $18.95. CODE: CSUN

24 hour credit card orders—call: 815-253-6390 fax: 815-253-6300

email: auphq@frontiernet.net   www.adventuresunlimitedpress.com   www.wexclub.com

ATLANTIS REPRINT SERIES

ATLANTIS: MOTHER OF EMPIRES
Atlantis Reprint Series
by Robert Stacy-Judd

Robert Stacy-Judd's classic 1939 book on Atlantis is back in print in this large-format paperback edition. Stacy-Judd was a California architect and an expert on the Mayas and their relationship to Atlantis. He was an excellent artist and his work is lavishly illustrated. The eighteen comprehensive chapters in the book are: The Mayas and the Lost Atlantis; Conjectures and Opinions; The Atlantean Theory; Cro-Magnon Man; East is West; And West is East; The Mormons and the Mayas; Astrology in Two Hemispheres; The Language of Architecture; The American Indian; Pre-Panamanians and Pre-Incas; Columns and City Planning; Comparisons and Mayan Art; The Iberian Link; The Maya Tongue; Quetzalcoatl; Summing Up the Evidence; The Mayas in Yucatan.
340 PAGES. 8x11 PAPERBACK. ILLUSTRATED. INDEX. $19.95. CODE: AMOE

MYSTERIES OF ANCIENT SOUTH AMERICA
Atlantis Reprint Series
by Harold T. Wilkins

The reprint of Wilkins' classic book on the megaliths and mysteries of South America. This book predates Wilkin's book *Secret Cities of Old South America* published in 1952. *Mysteries of Ancient South America* was first published in 1947 and is considered a classic book of its kind. With diagrams, photos and maps, Wilkins digs into old manuscripts and books to bring us some truly amazing stories of South America: a bizarre subterranean tunnel system; lost cities in the remote border jungles of Brazil; legends of Atlantis in South America; cataclysmic changes that shaped South America; and other strange stories from one of the world's great researchers. Chapters include: Our Earth's Greatest Disaster, Dead Cities of Ancient Brazil, The Jungle Light that Shines by Itself, The Missionary Men in Black: Forerunners of the Great Catastrophe, The Sign of the Sun: The World's Oldest Alphabet, Sign-Posts to the Shadow of Atlantis, The Atlanean "Subterraneans" of the Incas, Tiahuanacu and the Giants, more.
236 PAGES. 6x9 PAPERBACK. ILLUSTRATED. INDEX. $14.95. CODE: MASA

SECRET CITIES OF OLD SOUTH AMERICA
Atlantis Reprint Series
by Harold T. Wilkins

The reprint of Wilkins' classic book, first published in 1952, claiming that South America was Atlantis. Chapters include Mysteries of a Lost World; Atlantis Unveiled; Red Riddles on the Rocks; South America's Amazons Existed!; The Mystery of El Dorado and Gran Payatiti—the Final Refuge of the Incas; Monstrous Beasts of the Unexplored Swamps & Wilds; Weird Denizens of Antediluvian Forests; New Light on Atlantis from the World's Oldest Book; The Mystery of Old Man Noah and the Arks; and more.
438 PAGES. 6x9 PAPERBACK. ILLUSTRATED. BIBLIOGRAPHY & INDEX. $16.95. CODE: SCOS

THE SHADOW OF ATLANTIS
The Echoes of Atlantean Civilization Tracked through Space & Time
by Colonel Alexander Braghine

First published in 1940, *The Shadow of Atlantis* is one of the great classics of Atlantis research. The book amasses a great deal of archaeological, anthropological, historical and scientific evidence in support of a lost continent in the Atlantic Ocean. Braghine covers such diverse topics as Egyptians in Central America, the myth of Quetzalcoatl, the Basque language and its connection with Atlantis, the connections with the ancient pyramids of Mexico, Egypt and Atlantis, the sudden demise of mammoths, legends of giants and much more. Braghine was a linguist and spends part of the book tracing ancient languages to Atlantis and studying little-known inscriptions in Brazil, deluge myths and the connections between ancient languages. Braghine takes us on a fascinating journey through space and time in search of the lost continent.
288 PAGES. 6x9 PAPERBACK. ILLUSTRATED. $16.95. CODE: SOA

THE HISTORY OF ATLANTIS
by Lewis Spence

Lewis Spence's classic book on Atlantis is now back in print! Spence was a Scottish historian (1874-1955) who is best known for his volumes on world mythology and his five Atlantis books. *The History of Atlantis* (1926) is considered his finest. Spence does his scholarly best in chapters on the Sources of Atlantean History, the Geography of Atlantis, the Races of Atlantis, the Kings of Atlantis, the Religion of Atlantis, the Colonies of Atlantis, more. Sixteen chapters in all.
240 PAGES. 6x9 PAPERBACK. ILLUSTRATED WITH MAPS, PHOTOS & DIAGRAMS. $16.95. CODE: HOA

ATLANTIS IN SPAIN
A Study of the Ancient Sun Kingdoms of Spain
by E.M. Whishaw

First published by Rider & Co. of London in 1928, this classic book is a study of the megaliths of Spain, ancient writing, cyclopean walls, sun worshipping empires, hydraulic engineering, and sunken cities. An extremely rare book, it was out of print for 60 years. Learn about the Biblical Tartessos; an Atlantean city at Niebla; the Temple of Hercules and the Sun Temple of Seville; Libyans and the Copper Age; more. Profusely illustrated with photos, maps and drawings.
284 PAGES. 6x9 PAPERBACK. ILLUSTRATED. $15.95. CODE: AIS

24 hour credit card orders—call: 815-253-6390 fax: 815-253-6300
email: auphq@frontiernet.net   www.adventuresunlimitedpress.com   www.wexclub.com

ATLANTIS STUDIES

MAPS OF THE ANCIENT SEA KINGS
Evidence of Advanced Civilization in the Ice Age
by Charles H. Hapgood

Charles Hapgood's classic 1966 book on ancient maps produces concrete evidence of an advanced world-wide civilization existing many thousands of years before ancient Egypt. He has found the evidence in the Piri Reis Map that shows Antarctica, the Hadji Ahmed map, the Oronteus Finaeus and other amazing maps. Hapgood concluded that these maps were made from more ancient maps from the various ancient archives around the world, now lost. Not only were these unknown people more advanced in mapmaking than any people prior to the 18th century, it appears they mapped all the continents. The Americas were mapped thousands of years before Columbus. Antarctica was mapped when its coasts were free of ice.
316 PAGES. 7X10 PAPERBACK. ILLUSTRATED. BIB. & INDEX. $19.95. CODE: MASK

PATH OF THE POLE
Cataclysmic Pole Shift Geology
by Charles Hapgood

Maps of the Ancient Sea Kings author Hapgood's classic book *Path of the Pole* is back in print! Hapgood researched Antarctica, ancient maps and the geological record to conclude that the Earth's crust has slipped in the inner core many times in the past, changing the position of the pole. *Path of the Pole* discusses the various "pole shifts" in Earth's past, giving evidence for each one, and moves on to possible future pole shifts. Packed with illustrations, this is the sourcebook for many other books on cataclysms and pole shifts.
356 PAGES. 6X9 PAPERBACK. ILLUSTRATED. $16.95. CODE: POP.

RIDDLE OF THE PACIFIC
by John Macmillan Brown

Oxford scholar Brown's classic work on lost civilizations of the Pacific is now back in print! John Macmillan Brown was an historian and New Zealand's premier scientist when he wrote about the origins of the Maoris. After many years of travel thoughout the Pacific studying the people and customs of the south seas islands, he wrote *Riddle of the Pacific* in 1924. The book is packed with rare turn-of-the-century illustrations. Don't miss Brown's classic study of Easter Island, ancient scripts, megalithic roads and cities, more. Brown was an early believer in a lost continent in the Pacific.
460 PAGES. 6X9 PAPERBACK. ILLUSTRATED. $16.95. CODE: ROP

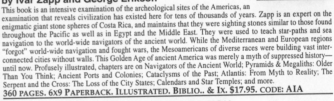

ATLANTIS IN AMERICA
Navigators of the Ancient World
by Ivar Zapp and George Erikson

This book is an intensive examination of the archeological sites of the Americas, an examination that reveals civilization has existed here for tens of thousands of years. Zapp is an expert on the enigmatic giant stone spheres of Costa Rica, and maintains that they were sighting stones similar to those found throughout the Pacific as well as in Egypt and the Middle East. They were used to teach star-paths and sea navigation to the world-wide navigators of the ancient world. While the Mediterranean and European regions "forgot" world-wide navigation and fought wars, the Mesoamericans of diverse races were building vast interconnected cities without walls. This Golden Age of ancient America was merely a myth of suppressed history—until now. Profusely illustrated, chapters are on Navigators of the Ancient World; Pyramids & Megaliths: Older Than You Think; Ancient Ports and Colonies; Cataclysms of the Past; Atlantis: From Myth to Reality; The Serpent and the Cross: The Loss of the City States; Calendars and Star Temples; and more.
360 PAGES. 6X9 PAPERBACK. ILLUSTRATED. BIBLIO.. & IX. $17.95. CODE: AIA

FAR-OUT ADVENTURES *REVISED EDITION*
The Best of World Explorer Magazine

This is a compilation of the first nine issues of *World Explorer* in a large-format paperback. Authors include: David Hatcher Childress, Joseph Jochmans, John Major Jenkins, Deanna Emerson, Katherine Routledge, Alexander Horvat, Greg Deyermenjian, Dr. Marc Miller, and others. Articles in this book include Smithsonian Gate, Dinosaur Hunting in the Congo, Secret Writings of the Incas, On the Trail of the Yeti, Secrets of the Sphinx, Living Pterodactyls, Quest for Atlantis, What Happened to the Great Library of Alexandria?, In Search of Seamonsters, Egyptians in the Pacific, Lost Megaliths of Guatemala, the Mystery of Easter Island, Comacalco: Mayan City of Mystery, Professor Wexler and plenty more.
580 PAGES. 8X11 PAPERBACK. ILLUSTRATED. REVISED EDITION. $25.00. CODE: FOA

RETURN OF THE SERPENTS OF WISDOM
by Mark Amaru Pinkham

According to ancient records, the patriarchs and founders of the early civilizations in Egypt, India, China, Peru, Mesopotamia, Britain, and the Americas were the Serpents of Wisdom—spiritual masters associated with the serpent—who arrived in these lands after abandoning their beloved homelands and crossing great seas. While bearing names denoting snake or dragon (such as Naga, Lung, Djedhi, Amaru, Quetzalcoatl, Adder, etc.), these Serpents of Wisdom oversaw the construction of magnificent civilizations within which they and their descendants served as the priest kings and as the enlightened heads of mystery school traditions. *The Return of the Serpents of Wisdom* recounts the history of these "Serpents"—where they came from, why they came, the secret wisdom they disseminated, and why they are returning now.
400 PAGES. 6X9 PAPERBACK. ILLUSTRATED. REFERENCES. $16.95. CODE: RSW

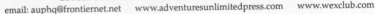

24 hour credit card orders—call: 815-253-6390 fax: 815-253-6300
email: auphq@frontiernet.net   www.adventuresunlimitedpress.com   www.wexclub.com

LOST CITIES

ANTI-GRAVITY

ANTI-GRAVITY

COSMIC MATRIX
Piece for a Jig-Saw, Part Two
by Leonard G. Cramp

Leonard G. Cramp, a British aerospace engineer, wrote his first book *Space Gravity and the Flying Saucer* in 1954. Cosmic Matrix is the long-awaited sequel to his 1966 book *UFOs & Anti-Gravity: Piece for a Jig-Saw.* Cramp has had a long history of examining UFO phenomena and has concluded that UFOs use the highest possible aeronautic science to move in the way they do. Cramp examines anti-gravity effects and theorizes that this super-science used by the craft—described in detail in the book—can lift mankind into a new level of technology, transportation and understanding of the universe. The book takes a close look at gravity control, time travel, and the interlocking web of energy between all planets in our solar system with Leonard's unique technical diagrams. A fantastic voyage into the present and future!
364 PAGES. 6X9 PAPERBACK. ILLUSTRATED. BIBLIOGRAPHY. $16.00. CODE: CMX

UFOS AND ANTI-GRAVITY
Piece For A Jig-Saw
by Leonard G. Cramp

Leonard G. Cramp's 1966 classic book on flying saucer propulsion and suppressed technology is a highly technical look at the UFO phenomena by a trained scientist. Cramp first introduces the idea of 'anti-gravity' and introduces us to the various theories of gravitation. He then examines the technology necessary to build a flying saucer and examines in great detail the technical aspects of such a craft. Cramp's book is a wealth of material and diagrams on flying saucers, anti-gravity, suppressed technology, G-fields and UFOs. Chapters include Crossroads of Aerodynamics, Aerodynamic Saucers, Limitations of Rocketry, Gravitation and the Ether, Gravitational Spaceships, G-Field Lift Effects, The Bi-Field Theory, VTOL and Hovercraft, Analysis of UFO photos, more.
388 PAGES. 6X9 PAPERBACK. ILLUSTRATED. $16.95. CODE: UAG

THE HARMONIC CONQUEST OF SPACE
by Captain Bruce Cathie

Chapters include: Mathematics of the World Grid; the Harmonics of Hiroshima and Nagasaki; Harmonic Transmission and Receiving; the Link Between Human Brain Waves; the Cavity Resonance between the Earth; the Ionosphere and Gravity; Edgar Cayce—the Harmonics of the Subconscious; Stonehenge; the Harmonics of the Moon; the Pyramids of Mars; Nikola Tesla's Electric Car; the Robert Adams Pulsed Electric Motor Generator; Harmonic Clues to the Unified Field; and more. Also included are tables showing the harmonic relations between the earth's magnetic field, the speed of light, and anti-gravity/gravity acceleration at different points on the earth's surface. New chapters in this edition on the giant stone spheres of Costa Rica, Atomic Tests and Volcanic Activity, and a chapter on Ayers Rock analysed with Stone Mountain, Georgia.
248 PAGES. 6X9. PAPERBACK. ILLUSTRATED. BIBLIOGRAPHY. $16.95. CODE: HCS

THE ENERGY GRID
Harmonic 695, The Pulse of the Universe
by Captain Bruce Cathie.

This is the breakthrough book that explores the incredible potential of the Energy Grid and the Earth's Unified Field all around us. Cathie's first book, *Harmonic 33*, was published in 1968 when he was a commercial pilot in New Zealand. Since then, Captain Bruce Cathie has been the premier investigator into the amazing potential of the infinite energy that surrounds our planet every microsecond. Cathie investigates the Harmonics of Light and how the Energy Grid is created. In this amazing book are chapters on UFO Propulsion, Nikola Tesla, Unified Equations, the Mysterious Aerials, Pythagoras & the Grid, Nuclear Detonation and the Grid, Maps of the Ancients, an Australian Stonehenge examined, more.
255 PAGES. 6X9 TRADEPAPER. ILLUSTRATED. $15.95. CODE: TEG

THE BRIDGE TO INFINITY
Harmonic 371244
by Captain Bruce Cathie

Cathie has popularized the concept that the earth is crisscrossed by an electromagnetic grid system that can be used for anti-gravity, free energy, levitation and more. The book includes a new analysis of the harmonic nature of reality, acoustic levitation, pyramid power, harmonic receiver towers and UFO propulsion. It concludes that today's scientists have at their command a fantastic store of knowledge with which to advance the welfare of the human race.
204 PAGES. 6X9 TRADEPAPER. ILLUSTRATED. $14.95. CODE: BTF

MAN-MADE UFOS 1944—1994
Fifty Years of Suppression
by Renato Vesco & David Hatcher Childress

A comprehensive look at the early "flying saucer" technology of Nazi Germany and the genesis of man-made UFOs. This book takes us from the work of captured German scientists to escaped battalions of Germans, secret communities in South America and Antarctica to todays state-of-the-art "Dreamland" flying machines. Heavily illustrated, this astonishing book blows the lid off the "government UFO conspiracy" and explains with technical diagrams the technology involved. Examined in detail are secret underground airfields and factories; German secret weapons; "suction" aircraft; the origin of NASA; gyroscopic stabilizers and engines; the secret Marconi aircraft factory in South America; and more. Introduction by W.A. Harbinson, author of the Dell novels *GENESIS* and *REVELATION*.
318 PAGES. 6X9 PAPERBACK. ILLUSTRATED. INDEX & FOOTNOTES. $18.95. CODE: MMU

24 hour credit card orders—call: 815-253-6390 fax: 815-253-6300
email: auphq@frontiernet.net   www.adventuresunlimitedpress.com   www.wexclub.com

FREE ENERGY SYSTEMS

LOST SCIENCE
by Gerry Vassilatos

Rediscover the legendary names of suppressed scientific revolution—remarkable lives, astounding discoveries, and incredible inventions which would have produced a world of wonder. How did the aura research of Baron Karl von Reichenbach prove the vitalistic theory and frighten the greatest minds of Germany? How did the physiophone and wireless of Antonio Meucci predate both Bell and Marconi by decades? How does the earth battery technology of Nathan Stubblefield portend an unsuspected energy revolution? How did the geoaetheric engines of Nikola Tesla threaten the establishment of a fuel-dependent America? The microscopes and virus-destroying ray machines of Dr. Royal Rife provided the solution for every world-threatening disease. Why did the FDA and AMA together condemn this great man to Federal Prison? The static crashes on telephone lines enabled Dr. T. Henry Moray to discover the reality of radiant space energy. Was the mysterious "Swedish stone," the powerful mineral which Dr. Moray discovered, the very first historical instance in which stellar power was recognized and secured on earth? Why did the Air Force initially fund the gravitational warp research and warp-cloaking devices of T. Townsend Brown and then reject it? When the controlled fusion devices of Philo Farnsworth achieved the "break-even" point in 1967 the FUSOR project was abruptly cancelled by ITT.

304 PAGES. 6x9 PAPERBACK. ILLUSTRATED. BIBLIOGRAPHY. $16.95. CODE: LOS

SECRETS OF COLD WAR TECHNOLOGY
Project HAARP and Beyond
by Gerry Vassilatos

Vassilatos reveals that "Death Ray" technology has been secretly researched and developed since the turn of the century. Included are chapters on such inventors and their devices as H.C. Vion, the developer of auroral energy receivers; Dr. Selim Lemstrom's pre-Tesla experiments; the early beam weapons of Grindell-Mathews, Ulivi, Turpain and others; John Hettenger and his early beam power systems. Learn about Project Argus, Project Teak and Project Orange; EMP experiments in the 60s; why the Air Force directed the construction of a huge Ionospheric "backscatter" telemetry system across the Pacific just after WWII; why Raytheon has collected every patent relevant to HAARP over the past few years; more.

250 PAGES. 6x9 PAPERBACK. ILLUSTRATED. $15.95. CODE: SCWT

THE TIME TRAVEL HANDBOOK
A Manual of Practical Teleportation & Time Travel
edited by David Hatcher Childress

In the tradition of The Anti-Gravity Handbook and The Free-Energy Device Handbook, science and UFO author David Hatcher Childress takes us into the weird world of time travel and teleportation. Not just a whacked-out look at science fiction, this book is an authoritative chronicling of real-life time travel experiments, teleportation devices and more. The Time Travel Handbook takes the reader beyond the government experiments and deep into the uncharted territory of early time travellers such as Nikola Tesla and Guglielmo Marconi and their alleged time travel experiments, as well as the Wilson Brothers of EMI and their connection to the Philadelphia Experiment—the U.S. Navy's forays into invisibility, time travel, and teleportation. Childress looks into the claims of time travelling individuals, and investigates the unusual claim that the pyramids on Mars were built in the future and sent back in time. A highly visual, large format book, with patents, photos and schematics. Be the first on your block to build your own time travel device!

316 PAGES. 7x10 PAPERBACK. ILLUSTRATED. $16.95. CODE: TTH

THE TESLA PAPERS
Nikola Tesla on Free Energy & Wireless Transmission of Power
by Nikola Tesla, edited by David Hatcher Childress

David Hatcher Childress takes us into the incredible world of Nikola Tesla and his amazing inventions. Tesla's rare article "The Problem of Increasing Human Energy with Special Reference to the Harnessing of the Sun's Energy" is included. This lengthy article was originally published in the June 1900 issue of The Century Illustrated Monthly Magazine and it was the outline for Tesla's master blueprint for the world. Tesla's fantastic vision of the future, including wireless power, anti-gravity, free energy and highly advanced solar power. Also included are some of the papers, patents and material collected on Tesla at the Colorado Springs Tesla Symposiums, including papers on: •The Secret History of Wireless Transmission •Tesla and the Magnifying Transmitter •Design and Construction of a Half-Wave Tesla Coil •Electrostatics: A Key to Free Energy •Progress in Zero-Point Energy Research •Electromagnetic Energy from Antennas to Atoms •Tesla's Particle Beam Technology •Fundamental Excitatory Modes of the Earth-Ionosphere Cavity

325 PAGES. 8x10 PAPERBACK. ILLUSTRATED. $16.95. CODE: TTP

THE FANTASTIC INVENTIONS OF NIKOLA TESLA
by Nikola Tesla with additional material by David Hatcher Childress

This book is a readable compendium of patents, diagrams, photos and explanations of the many incredible inventions of the originator of the modern era of electrification. In Tesla's own words are such topics as wireless transmission of power, death rays, and radio-controlled airships. In addition, rare material on German bases in Antarctica and South America, and a secret city built at a remote jungle site in South America by one of Tesla's students, Guglielmo Marconi. Marconi's secret group claims to have built flying saucers in the 1940s and to have gone to Mars in the early 1950s! Incredible photos of these Tesla craft are included. The Ancient Atlantean system of broadcasting energy through a grid system of obelisks and pyramids is discussed, and a fascinating concept comes out of one chapter: that Egyptian engineers had to wear protective metal head-shields while in these power plants, hence the Egyptian Pharoah's head covering as well as the Face on Mars! •His plan to transmit free electricity into the atmosphere. •How electrical devices would work using only small antennas. •Why unlimited power could be utilized anywhere on earth. •How radio and radar technology can be used as death-ray weapons in Star Wars.

342 PAGES. 6x9 PAPERBACK. ILLUSTRATED. $16.95. CODE: FINT

One Adventure Place
P.O. Box 74
Kempton, Illinois 60946
United States of America
•Tel.: 1-800-718-4514 or 815-253-6390
•Fax: 815-253-6300
Email: auphq@frontiernet.net
http://www.adventuresunlimitedpress.com
or www.adventuresunlimited.nl

10% Discount when you order 3 or more items!

ORDERING INSTRUCTIONS

➤➤ Remit by USD$ Check, Money Order or Credit Card

➤➤ Visa, Master Card, Discover & AmEx Accepted

➤➤ Prices May Change Without Notice

➤➤ 10% Discount for 3 or more Items

SHIPPING CHARGES

United States

➤➤ Postal Book Rate { $3.00 First Item
50¢ Each Additional Item

➤➤ Priority Mail { $4.50 First Item
$2.00 Each Additional Item

➤➤ UPS { $5.00 First Item
$1.50 Each Additional Item

NOTE: UPS Delivery Available to Mainland USA Only

Canada

➤➤ Postal Book Rate { $6.00 First Item
$2.00 Each Additional Item

➤➤ Postal Air Mail { $8.00 First Item
$2.50 Each Additional Item

➤➤ Personal Checks or Bank Drafts MUST BE

USD$ and Drawn on a US Bank
➤➤ Canadian Postal Money Orders in US$ OK

➤➤ Payment MUST BE US$

All Other Countries

➤➤ Surface Delivery { $10.00 First Item
$4.00 Each Additional Item

➤➤ Postal Air Mail { $14.00 First Item
$5.00 Each Additional Item

➤➤ Checks and Money Orders MUST BE US $
and Drawn on a US Bank or branch.

➤➤ Payment by credit card preferred!

SPECIAL NOTES

➤➤ RETAILERS: Standard Discounts Available

➤➤ BACKORDERS: We Backorder all Out-of-

Stock Items Unless Otherwise Requested

➤➤ PRO FORMA INVOICES: Available on Request

➤➤ VIDEOS: NTSC Mode Only. Replacement only.

➤➤ For PAL mode videos contact our other offices:

European Office:
Adventures Unlimited, Pannewal 22,
Enkhuizen, 1602 KS, The Netherlands
http: www.adventuresunlimited.nl
Check Us Out Online at:
www.adventuresunlimitedpress.com

Please check: ☑

☐ This is my first order   ☐ I have ordered before   ☐ This is a new address

Name

Address

City

State/Province   Postal Code

Country

Phone day   Evening

Fax   Email

Item Code	Item Description	Price	Qty	Total

Please check: ☑

☐ Postal-Surface

☐ Postal-Air Mail
(Priority in USA)

☐ UPS
(Mainland USA only)

Subtotal ➡	
Less Discount-10% for 3 or more items ➡	
Balance ➡	
Illinois Residents 6.25% Sales Tax ➡	
Previous Credit ➡	
Shipping ➡	
Total (check/MO in USD$ only) ➡	

☐ Visa/MasterCard/Discover/Amex

Card Number

Expiration Date

10% Discount When You Order 3 or More Items!

Comments & Suggestions	Share Our Catalog with a Friend